Organizations

ORGANIZATIONS

Second Edition

James G. March and Herbert A. Simon

with the collaboration of Harold Guetzkow

Copyright © James G. March and Herbert A. Simon, 1993

First published in 1958 by Wiley (USA)

Second Edition published 1993
Reprinted 1994, (twice)

Blackwell Publishers
238 Main Street
Cambridge, Massachusetts 02142
USA

108 Cowley Road
Oxford OX4 1JF
UK

Library of Congress Cataloging-in-Publication Data

March, James G.
  Organizations / James March and Herbert Simon. — 2nd ed.
    p.   cm.
  Includes bibliographical references (p.   ) and index.
  ISBN 0–631–18631–X (alk. paper)
  1. Organization.   I. Simon, Herbert Alexander, 1916–
II. Title.
HD31.M298   1993
658–dc20   92–42143
                                                          CIP

British Library Cataloguing in Publication Data

A CIP catalogue record for this book is available from the British Library.

Typeset in 11 on 13 pt Plantin by Times Graphics, Singapore
Printed in Great Britain by Athenaeum Press Ltd, Newcastle upon Tyne.

This book is printed on acid-free paper

Contents

List of Figures

Acknowledgments

The work represented by this book was undertaken initially by the triumvirate whose names appear on the title page. All of us shared in its planning and contributed to the broth of ideas in which the book took form. As a result of our local division of labor in the latter stages, and Harold Guetzkow's absence at the Center for Advanced Study in the Behavioral Sciences during the academic year 1956-7, the remaining two of us wrote the manuscript and made the decisions about its final content. We think it only fitting, however, that, by placing his name on the title page as a collaborator, we make Harold Guetzkow take a share of the praise and blame for the final product.

Anyone familiar with research in the Graduate School of Industrial Administration at Carnegie Tech will know that there are other persons who, though they have not been formal participants in the project, should be coopted into partnership with the authors. In particular, we owe a more than ordinary debt to Richard M. Cyert and to Allen Newell. The former's ideas and influence will be clearly discernible where the book touches on the theory of the firm, and the latter's in the treatment of human problem-solving. Other members of the Carnegie organization research group to whom the authors have turned frequently for suggestion and criticism include William Dill, Chadwick Haberstroh, and Donald B. Trow.

Outside the Carnegie group, we should like to acknowledge especially our many hours of fruitful work and discussion with Robert A. Dahl on the subject of influence measurement, and the help and guidance that John C. Harsanyi provided for our treatment of the relation between game theory and other theories of conflict. James S. Coleman, in the course of a seminar, contributed more than he probably now recalls to the book's organization. A first draft of the manuscript was submitted to the scrutiny of the members of the Research Training Institute on Organization Theory and Research sponsored at Carnegie Tech by the Social Science Research Council during the summer of 1957. This group included (in addition to Harsanyi and Newell) Robert F. Bales, Warren G. Bennis, Robert L. Chapman, Robert L. Hamblin, Stanley Hollander, Norman Kaplan, John T. Lanzetta, Harold J. Leavitt, Edith M. Lentz, Solomon B. Levine, Donald C. Pelz, John C. Pock, Daniel Shimshoni, and Charles K. Warriner. The revised draft has been much improved by their suggestions.

Leonard Cottrell, III, Julian Feldman, Peter S. Houts, Giandom-enico Majone, and Sylvia Sebulsky provided both thoughtful comments on the text and substantial assistance in preparing the bibliography. We have received help from a number of other students and research assistants, in particular Edward A. Feigenbaum, Henry J. Hart, Richard A. Hendricks, Carlton B. Hensley, Douglas K. Mims, Jr., William H. Starbuck, Frederick Stern, and Frederic M. Tonge, Jr.

Mrs. Evelyn L. Adams typed the manuscript and performed a variety of other tasks connected with the book that are both too diverse and too numerous to be enumerated here.

That scarcest of academic commodities — time to think — has been supplied by the generous support of the Ford Foundation for our program of theoretical and empirical studies of human behavior in organizations and by fellowship grants from the Center for Advanced Study in the Behavioral Sciences and the Ford Foundation. We are grateful to the Foundation and the Center for providing that support — and for providing it in a broad frame of reference that has permitted us to explore the directions that have seemed most fruitful for extending fundamental knowledge of organizational behavior and for making that knowledge useful to the conduct of human affairs. We are also grateful to the Graduate School of Industrial Administration for providing the kind of intellectual and organizational environment in which theory and research can thrive.

Introduction to the Second Edition

More than a third of a century ago, we undertook, together with Harold Guetzkow, a "propositional inventory" of theory about organizations. The intent was to list generalizations (preferably true ones) and to assess the empirical evidence supporting them. Of course, to inventory propositions one has to organize them, and so the book that evolved from this exercise also proposed a structure of organization theory.

Our book has continued to attract attention and interest over the intervening years. For some, it has provided a guide to the research on organizations published prior to 1958. For others, it has been a useful source of propositions about organizations, to be cited, emended, enlarged upon, and criticized. For still others, it has become an icon of a prehistoric age.

Sufficient interest continues in the book to suggest the usefulness of a new edition, retaining the original text, but adding some comments, stimulated by the text, about events in the world of organizations and organization theories during the 35 years since the first edition appeared. We are happy to add those comments, along with the warning that we are today probably not much wiser than we were then. It is perhaps an unfortunate symptom of authorship that we still enjoy reading the book from time to time and are surprised more often by the things we knew then, but have forgotten, than by the things we know now but did not know then.

If there were any general pronouncement we would want to utter today, it would be that no events during this long period have shaken the foundations of organizations or organization theory so roughly as to make them unrecognizable, or even greatly distorted. The years since 1958 have witnessed considerable change in the social context of organizations, particularly in the rhetoric, ideology, and reality of relations among ethnic and gender groups. They have witnessed considerable change in the technological context of organizations, particularly in information technology and robotics. The years since 1958 have also produced an impressive array of research findings on organizations; we are much better off with respect to both the amount of research being done on organizations and its quality than we were in the 1950s. Nevertheless, the new phenomena we have observed, and perhaps most of the new concepts as well, fit without too much Procrustean squeezing or folding into the earlier framework that was designed to hold them. That is one reason (among many) why we limit ourselves to these comments instead of rewriting the book.

What the Book is About

This book is about the theory of formal organizations. Organizations are systems of coordinated action among individuals and groups whose preferences, information, interests, or knowledge differ. Organization theories describe the delicate conversion of conflict into cooperation, the mobilization of resources, and the coordination of effort that facilitate the joint survival of an organization and its members.

These contributions to survival are accomplished primarily through control over information, identities, stories, and incentives. Organizations process and channel information. They shape the goals and loyalties of their participants. They create shared stories – an organization ethos that includes common beliefs and standard practices. They offer incentives for appropriate behaviors.

Effective control over organizational processes is limited, however, by the uncertainties and ambiguities of life, by the limited cognitive and affective capabilities of human actors, by the complexities of balancing trade-offs across time and space, and by threats of competition.

As organizational actors deal with each other, seeking cooperative and competitive advantage, they cope with these limitations by calculation, planning, and analysis, by learning from their experience and the experience and knowledge of others, and by creating and using systems of rules, procedures, and interpretations that store understandings in easily retrievable form. They weave supportive cultures, agreements, structures, and beliefs around their activities. This melange of organizational behaviors is the focus of this book. We try to understand how collections of individuals and groups coordinate themselves in relatively systematic ways.

Most of the organizations with which we deal are conventionally seen as hierarchies. Hierarchical descriptions of organization are common, partly because hierarchy is often efficient, partly because hierarchical orderings fit more general cultural norms for describing social relations in terms of domination and subordination. Hierarchy has two, nearly independent, aspects. First, it refers to the boxes-within-boxes structure that characterizes most organizations, with generally more intensive communication within boxes at any level than between different boxes at that level. Second, hierarchy refers to the common pyramidal arrangement of formal authority relations, stepwise from the "top" to the "bottom" of an organization.

The boxes-within-boxes character of hierarchy permits specialization of sub-units, keeping within bounds the amount of interaction and coordination among sub-units that is needed. At the same time, hierarchy facilitates the use of formal authority as a directing and coordinating mechanism.

Organizational processes are, however, not consistently hierarchical. They also involve networks of other types. They include flows of influence and control that go up and sideways as well as down. They reflect ecologies of interconnecting activities within which simple ideas of linear causal order and power are hard to sustain. They defy sharp definitions of organizational boundaries. There are some senses in which there are "principals" and "agents", or "insiders" and "outsiders", but such conceptions make an organization appear neater than it is.

The central unifying construct of the present book is not hierarchy but decision making, and the flow of information within organizations that instructs, informs, and supports decision making processes. The idea of "decision" can also be elusive, of course. Defining what a decision is, when it is made, and who makes it have all, at times, turned out to be problematic. Nevertheless, the concept seems to have served us reasonably well.

Several kinds of decisions are important for organizations. First there are decisions of individuals to participate in organizations (as employees, members, supporters, managers, customers, owners) or to leave them, and decisions as to what degree of effort and enthusiasm they will invest in their participation. Second, there are decisions that direct the organization's business, determine how to organize, what goals to proclaim, how to coordinate tasks to reach those goals, when to change directions or structure.

Chapters 3 and 4 of this book deal mainly with the first class of decisions; chapter 5 with the same decisions when the goals and strivings of organization members or of subunits within the organization come into conflict. Chapters 6 and 7 deal with the second class of decisions, chapter 6 focusing on the "steady state" activities, chapter 7 on activities directed toward organizational innovation and change – statics and dynamics, so to speak.

Although the central construct is decision making, much of the theory developed in the book is less a theory of choice than a theory of attention. Decision makers do not attend to all of their goals at once, nor all of their alternatives, nor all of the consequences of the alternatives. Particular goals are high on the agenda at particular times, and off the agenda at other times. Attention may be restricted to alternatives known from past experience, or to a few specific alternatives generated by a product development or a design process. Attention may focus on one set of consequences (e.g., liquidity) under one set of circumstances, and another set of consequences (e.g., share of market) under another.

Since, to indulge in understatement, not everything is attended to, understanding the ways in which attention is allocated is critical to understanding decisions. As a result, much of our own attention in the book is devoted to theories of search: to examining when, where, and how organizations search for information about urgent problems, alternatives, and their consequences.

The theories of organizational attention reflected in this book are built on two little ideas that have proven to have considerable power and appeal. The first is satisficing: the idea that organizations focus on targets and distinguish more sharply between success (meeting the target) and failure (not meeting the target) than among gradations in either. The second idea is that organizations devote more attention to activities that are currently operating below their own targets than they do to activities that are achieving their targets. In the years since 1958, these two ideas (along with their close correlates) have yielded a fairly rich harvest of implications for decision-making.

Conceiving organizations and decision-making as reflecting limits on rationality and an orderly pattern of attention-constrained action and search does not, of course, capture all of the things the book says, but it encompasses perhaps the central core.

What the Book Said Softly

Readers of the book have generally seemed to find our ideas on organizations useful, and we have the standard authors' conceit that most of the truths we did not write down explicitly can be seen as implicit in those we did. However, there are at least four broad features of our treatment that would be a little different if we were writing the book for the first time now:

1 We would give more attention to empirical observations as opposed to theoretical speculations;
2 We would place relatively less emphasis on analytically rational, as opposed to rule-based, action;
3 We would less often take the premises of decisions as given exogenously;
4 We would accord a greater role to the historical, social, and interpretive contexts of organizations.

Although we think the book anticipates much of what we say here about these points, it did not deal with any of them in as much detail as would be required if we were undertaking a comparable project today.

Speculations and Data

In our present view of the matter, the greatest deficiency in the book is its treatment of empirical evidence. Matters are not so bad in the first five chapters where we were able to draw upon a large body of literature. Of course there are many more such studies today, which could be used to buttress our case further or to amend it where our claims appeared to be speculative. The development of multi-variate statistical techniques, improved training in research design and analysis, and the diligence of researchers in generating useful data have combined to provide a reasonably solid empirical base for the topics considered in those chapters.

The difficulties are greater for the topics discussed in chapters 6 and 7. Here we were dealing somewhat less with individuals, and somewhat more with systems. Most of the relevant evidence we found took the form of monographic studies of particular organizations – case studies – and there was nothing in the extant literature on scientific methodology that told us how to make case studies into the sort of objective, reproducible, representative evidence that we were taught science is founded on. Even identifying the potentially relevant cases and collecting them turned out to be a virtually impossible job.

We were quite aware that to find and test hypotheses about organizational decision making processes, someone would have to examine such processes in real organizational contexts. Almost the only scholars who had done so had studied particular organizations over shorter or longer periods of time, operating largely in the mode of social historians or ethnographers. Their samples were samples of opportunity, representing no definable universe. Their data consisted largely of historical narratives, the causal connections induced by a liberal application of common sense and organizational shrewdness. There were few quantitative data.

Someone trying to repeat our undertaking today (if there were anyone so foolish) would be much better off in certain respects. There has been a considerable proliferation of studies of decision behavior, both in laboratory settings and in the field. Some of these studies have used archival data on decisions; others have placed experienced organizational participants in quasi-laboratory situations for observation; others have observed actual decision processes in organizations. Our empirical understanding of such things as risk-taking behavior in organizations, for example, is substantially more precise than it was in 1958.

There has been a considerable development, in sociology and psychology, of methods for dealing with nonquantitative verbal data in systematic ways. For example, in research on problem-solving in cognitive science, we now have methods for using as data the verbal thinking-aloud protocols of subjects performing problem-solving tasks. In sociology, there have been parallel developments in methods for analyzing the content of verbal texts of many kinds. We know a good deal today about how to encode and process such data, and how to use them to test hypotheses, including hypotheses in the form of computer programs that simulate the phenomena being studied.

There has perhaps been less progress in solving the problems of sampling populations of organizations or of organization members, and the problems of aggregating individual data or data from small units in ways that cast light on the behavior of the larger systems to which the individuals or units belong. Almost surely, however, these problems would at least bend and possibly yield if addressed vigorously enough and often enough. The increasing attention being paid by social scientists today to the work of social historians and ethnographers is a good omen of greater willingness to take case studies and historical narratives seriously as data for discovering and testing theories of organization.

Finally, there has recently been an upsurge, especially in economics departments, business schools, and psychology departments, of laboratory studies of decision making, markets, and small organizations. This work still seems to us to be too much dominated by ideas drawn from the formal structures of neoclassical economics and the mathematical theory of games; but exposure to the data coming from these laboratory experiments will almost inevitably confront experimenters with surprises and new ideas, leading them in time to conceptual frameworks and explanations that will suit the phenomena better than those used at present.

Perhaps the most critically needed and least advanced methodological development is reconstructing statistical theory to deal with the kinds of data that are beginning to be gathered, and the kinds of models that are being tested. Statistics for data analysis are not adapted to theories of organizations, with the result that the more sophisticated analyses of data are informed only by the crudest of theoretical models (e.g., linear regression) and the empirical status of the more interesting theoretical ideas is left uncertain. That situation has improved to a modest degree since 1958, but not much.

Logics of Action

Analysis-based action   The basic idea that humans make choices and that these choices are informed by assessing alternatives in terms of their consequences underlies much of contemporary social science, not to mention "common sense." This idea, particularly as it is manifested in the dogmas of neoclassical economics, has often been criticized as providing neither an accurate nor an attractive portrayal of the human spirit. Many authors have suggested that human beings are not capable of achieving perfect rationality. Fewer, but with compensating fervor, have suggested that the pursuit of rationality leads systematically to less intelligent behavior than do other decision methods.

Although those who criticize obsession with rationality will find many more tempting targets than our book, it is probably fair to place it in the "rational" section of the library. For the most part, we portray behavior as resulting from, and organized around, choices. And we interpret choices as depending on an evaluation of their consequences in terms of preferences. In those senses at least, this book is about rationality.

Its rationality is, however, a considerably qualified rationality. The people who inhabit the book are imagined to have reasons for what they do. Those reasons inform both their choices and their justifications (whether explanations or rationalizations) for their choices. Thus, they provide a basis for predicting both behavior and explanations of behavior.

The reasons reflect two related logics of action. The first, an analytic rationality, is a logic of consequences. Actions are chosen by evaluating their probable consequences for the preferences of the actor. The logic of consequences is linked to conceptions of anticipations, analysis, and calculation. It operates principally through selective, heuristic search among alternatives, evaluating them for their satisfactoriness as they are found.

The second logic of action, a matching of rules to situations, rests on a logic of appropriateness. Actions are chosen by recognizing a situation as being of a familiar, frequently encountered, type, and matching the recognized situation to a set of rules (sometimes called a performance program in the present book). The logic of appropriateness is linked to conceptions of experience, roles, intuition, and expert knowledge. It deals with calculation mainly as a means of retrieving experience preserved in the organization's files or individual memories.

The book explores both kinds of reasoning behavior, but it devotes more attention to the first than to the second. It is built heavily on the assumption that there are consequential reasons for action: that we can predict behavior in and by organizations by assessing the expected subjective value of alternative courses of action. This general frame is used to examine a wide variety of decisions.

Rationality (in the consequential or analytic sense) does not assure intelligence. To assume that people often have consequential reasons for what they do is quite different from assuming that they reliably select actions that would be objectively optimal in the light of their goals. The organizations portrayed in the book are rational in intent and in the ways in which they justify their choices (they are procedurally rational), but their pursuit of rationality does not assure either coherent or intelligent action (often their actions are not substantively rational).

Ambiguity of goals and goal conflict, as well as human ignorance and error are significant parts of the picture of behavior in organizations. The actions of individuals in an organization may aim at the official organizational goals, or some quite different and wholly personal goals. Their actions may be well adapted to their goals, or poorly adapted, for people are often misinformed, or lack information, or are unable to predict or even compute the consequences of their actions. Their goals may sometimes be well-specified and stable, but often they are unclear, inconsistent, and changing.

Nor does the assumption of intended, limited rationality, in this realistic sense, ignore the important role of emotions in behavior.

Still less does it omit the wide range of human wants and desires – pushed sometimes by greed, sometimes by altruism, sometimes by egoism, sometimes by loyalty to groups – that motivate human action.

The idea of limited, consequential rationality found in the book has become more or less standard in modern theories of decision-making, at least outside the hard core of orthodox neoclassical economic theory. Economics today pays continually increasing attention to the incomplete knowledge of economic actors, their uncertainties about the future and the limits on their ability to discover optimal actions. Limited rationality underlies contemporary theories of the firm, behavioral decision theory, and many theories derivative of these. Except for some relatively minor deviants (e.g., rational expectations theory), it has become the received doctrine. No received doctrine is received forever, so it is natural to ask whether we still hold to this one. The answer is yes, we do.

We believe that limited rationality still provides a powerful basic framework for examining organizations despite the elaboration of information technology, as embodied in computers, operations research and management science. Modern information and decision technology, with its disciplines of management science, decision science, operations research, and information engineering, had just begun to make inroads into organizational consciousness when this book was published. Those disciplines undertook to apply a new technology to organizational decision-making, using the conceptual framework of optimization theory and empowering it with mathematical tools that, fed with appropriate numerical data and powerful new computational equipment, could carry out calculations previously beyond imagination. Using the new technologies, the new disciplines sought to reduce or eliminate the restrictions on rationality imposed by the cognitive and calculative limitations of individuals and organizations. Since human informational and computational limitations are the fundamental premises of bounded rationality, improvements in information technology might plausibly be viewed as providing a major challenge to the idea.

These new tools have had a substantial impact on many kinds of decisions: For example, inventory and manufacturing control, and record and information management. The total impact upon organizations has been limited, however, by the fact that the new tools apply mainly to situations that can be described without too much distortion in mathematical form, and for which numerical data appropriate to the formulation can be gathered.

These conditions have restricted applications largely to middle-management and lower-management decisions. In general, the work of managers at higher levels has not been much changed despite frequent proclamations of an information technology revolution. Efforts to use modern technology to develop new forms of management information systems for organizations have been pursued in many organizations, but they have commonly produced systems that seem to match rather poorly the actual decision processes and managerial needs in organizations.

Electronic communication has also undergone extremely rapid development since the first edition of the book was published. Telefaxing was unknown as a commercial product in 1958, as was electronic mail. Although the former is now generic and the latter is spreading slowly, they do not yet seem to have changed the fundamental nature of the processes discussed in this book.

The matter is a little different with artificial intelligence and so-called "expert systems," and this for three reasons. First, they are not as limited as are the operations research and management science models to quantitative methods. Second, they take more fully into account the "boundedness" of human rationality, and its requirements for radical approximation and satisficing. Third, they combine the logic of consequences (heuristic search) with the logic of appropriateness (recognition and rule-based action). Consequently, artificial intelligence and the expert systems it has begun to spawn may in time penetrate further into the central core of managerial tasks than operations research and management science have. As yet, however, that possibility is far from realization. None of these developments in decision engineering has yet required a major rethinking of the application of the principles of limited rationality to management.

Rule-based action   The book probably understates the role of rule-based, or recognition-based, forms of action. Although we discuss performance programs, roles, and other forms of rule-based action, such discussions are generally subordinated to ideas of analysis-based action (as they are for the most part in other modern treatments of organizations). Recent work reasserts the pervasiveness of logics of appropriateness and raises the possibility that consequential, calculative logics may not capture important human techniques for acting intelligently.

Modern understanding of the cognitive bases of expert behavior has considerably clarified the respective roles in the decision-making process of systematic (and sometimes quantitative) consequential analysis, on the one hand, and the matching of appropriate action to recognized situations, on the other. The latter appears to be an important component of phenomena such as "intuition" that are frequent in the behavior of experienced decision makers.

The distinctive earmarks of intuition are rapid response (a matter of seconds) and inability of the respondent to report a sequence of steps leading to the result – even denial of awareness of any such steps. The response is not always right, but what impresses observers about intuition is that responses, especially those of experts, are frequently correct even though they seem to have required almost no processing time or effort. When we are especially impressed by intuition, we sometimes apply other honorific terms to it: "insight" or "creativity." When we are less impressed, we are more likely to call it "blind spots" or "jumping to conclusions."

The role and nature of intuition are illustrated by studies of chess playing. It has often been demonstrated that a grandmaster can play simultaneous games against 50 or more opponents, going from board to board and taking only a few seconds for each move, and still win virtually all of the games – provided that the opponents are no stronger than experts (400 or more Elo rating points below the grandmaster). In contrast with tournament games, where players often look ahead to the consequences of moves, sometimes exploring as many as 100 branches of the game tree, there is almost no time for such analysis in simultaneous play. When asked how they select moves with such speed, the grandmasters are likely to reply that they do it "intuitively."

Research on this performance has shown that a grandmaster's intuition is achieved by noticing cues on the board, cues – very familiar from past experience with many thousands of chess positions – that signal weaknesses the opponent has created in his or her arrangement of pieces. Intuition is simply skill in recognizing those things that have become familiar through past experience. A typical grandmaster, it has been shown, carries in memory at least 50,000 such cues (usually called "chunks") – familiar patterns of pieces that occur often in games – and, together with these cues, has stored rules indicating how they should be exploited to gain an advantage.

What does this research say about the relation between analysis and intuition? It says that intuition is synonymous with the familiar phenomenon of recognition. It says that when there is substantial time available for making decisions, the skilled chess player does a great deal of analysis (assisted, to be sure, by intuition in choosing the lines of play to analyze and in evaluating them). In rapid play there is no time for analysis, and the grandmaster relies almost wholly on intuition (that is, upon recognition). When moving rapidly, he or she does not play as well as under tournament conditions, but plays formidably enough to demonstrate that a substantial fraction of chess skill is encapsulated in intuition, that is, in the capacity to recognize familiar significant cues, and to retrieve stored knowledge about how to use them.

This story of chess skill has been duplicated in many other domains where expert behavior has been studied and experts interrogated in the course of designing so-called expert systems for computers. There is no reason to suppose that managerial skill is different along these dimensions from the other skills that have been studied. Expert managers use both consequential analysis and rule-based intuition (recognition) to reach their decisions. The experience of expert managers will often lead them to correct decisions without explicit, conscious calculation. Intelligent managers manage not by analysis alone, but by analysis thoroughly interwoven with the rich intuitions (capabilities for recognition) and rules for action acquired through years of training and experience in the managerial domain.

This process of gaining individual expertise by coding experience into recognition/action pairs is paralleled by organizational processes for developing pairings between rules and situations. In the book, we talk of performance programs. Organizations are collections of roles and identities, assemblages of rules by which appropriate behavior is paired with recognized situations. Some of these assemblages are imported into an organization by employing professionals; accountants do what accountants are trained to do. Other assemblages are developed in an organization through collective experience and stored in the organizational memory as standard procedures.

The processes of identification and socialization, by which individuals associate themselves with an identity and learn a role, are mechanisms for routinizing responses to the recognition of a situation. Organizations turn their own experience, as well as the experience and knowledge of others, into rules that are maintained and implemented despite turnover in personnel and without necessary comprehension of their bases. As a result, the processes for generating, changing, evoking, and forgetting rules become essential in analyzing and understanding organizations.

Although organizational action is driven by matching appropriate behavior to situations, the action is not uniquely determined by such performance programs, professional codes, or expert intuitions. Participants follow rules, but it is not always clear precisely which rules are appropriate. Different identities with different rules intrude on a single situation. Situations are unclear; they cannot always be recognized unambiguously; appropriate rules are difficult to specify; executing a rule may require skill and will that are not always forthcoming.

Rule-based action founded on a logic of appropriateness is discussed in the book, but is probably not given as much attention as we would now give it. Intuition at the individual level and rules at the organizational level play a more important part than the book accords them. This is true in two senses: First, much of the behavior we observe in organizations is "intuitive" in the sense that it occurs immediately upon recognition of a situation. The relevant cognitive and organizational processes are recognition and categorization processes more than they are processes of evaluating consequences.

Second, much of the intelligence we observe in organizational action comes not from explicit analysis but from rules. Rule-based action can, of course, lead to foolishness. Coding experience into rules by no means guarantees optimal or even suitable behavior. But any account of the ability of an organization to act intelligently toward its own goals must attend to the role of logics of appropriateness as well as logics of consequence.

Autonomous Preferences

Theories of choice, including the theories outlined in this book, tend to treat preferences as autonomous and antecedent to decisions. Individual choices are seen as being made in the service of individual preferences, but the process by which those preferences are shaped is treated as exogenous to the choice. The resulting theories tend to describe decision-makers as autonomous individuals and decision-making as proceeding in two, strictly sequential stages – setting goals, then making choices.

The book is explicit in treating the social character of decision-makers and their preferences. People in organizations are not viewed as isolates whose wants, identities and ideas are formed in independence of the other people who surround them. Organization members are social persons, whose knowledge, beliefs, preferences, loyalties are all products of the social environments in which they grew up, and the environments in which they now live and work. Because of these complex loyalties to a variety of groups and subgroups – including the self and family, organizations and their subunits – intrapersonal and interpersonal conflicts are omnipresent features of organizational life.

These loyalties develop and shape the actions of organization members. In particular, the strong loyalties to organizational units, global or parochial, that people acquire constitute a basic mechanism for securing adherence to organizational goals. The book does not deny the important role of monetary and other incentives, but it suggests that these latter motives are not capable, by themselves, of securing the level of attachments to organizational goals that are actually observed.

Devotion to organization goals, rather than to personal selfish interests, can be viewed as a form of altruism. If we wish to account for organizational identification, we must make the case for the robustness of altruism in the face of the apparently imperious Darwinian demands for individual "fitness" as a condition for survival. That case is not made in the present book, but it has become a central concern for students of population biology, as well as for students of decision making. It has been examined by one of us in a paper published in December 1990 in *Science*.

The decision-makers we portrayed in 1958 were unabashedly social. On the other hand, they were somewhat more static than perhaps they should have been. The book might well have attended more explicitly to the significance of the changing character of organizational goals in response to social and environmental influences. Organizations are sometimes described as instruments of purpose, that is, it is imagined that they are created to accomplish some collective purpose. There may often be truth in such a description, but it is misleading if it leads to ignoring the tendency of organizations to endure long after their original "purposes" are accomplished or forgotten.

When polio vaccine destroys the *raison d'être* of The March of Dimes, that society finds a new goal in the prevention and treatment of birth defects. A company, IBM, that grew with the applications of punched-card tabulating systems, first to the Census, then to Social Security, and then to business accounting systems, sees electronic computers on the horizon and embraces them, with all the new and unforeseen applications that have come with them.

Universities are prime examples of organizations that survive long after their initial goals have vanished, transforming them almost beyond recognition: the University of Paris in the 12th century and today, Carnegie Institute of Technology which became Carnegie Mellon University, innumerable normal schools and teachers' colleges that became universities.

The book does not pay much attention to this fluidity of goals. Nor does it pay much attention to the fact that links between problems and solutions, or between goals and decisions, may be constructed by organizational processes rather than being embedded in objective reality. The linkages may be imposed by an organizational structure that associates goals and actions by virtue of their organizational proximity. (A law enforcement agency may regard criminalizing an activity as the obvious way of eliminating it.) They may be imposed by a temporal structure that associates goals and actions by their simultaneity: if home ownership has increased while incomes are rising, promote home ownership to increase incomes further.

The idea that opportunities for choice attract all sorts of unrelated (but simultaneously available) problems, solutions, goals, interests, concerns – just as garbage cans attract garbage – was labeled by one of the authors and his colleagues the "garbage-can theory of decision making." He apologizes for introducing this pungent phrase into the organizational literature, but the phenomenon is real enough and important (and it is probably too late to banish the label). So a meeting called to discuss parking lots may become a discussion of sexual harassment, compensation policies, and football.

But perhaps the most conspicuous way in which we would elaborate the conception of goals found in this book is to recognize more explicitly the fact that actions may produce goals as readily as goals produce actions. It is convenient to think of goals as existing prior to organizations, shaping and directing them. The prior existence of utilities is one of the most treasured axioms of traditional theories of choice. But the conception is misleading. The process runs in both directions.

If we ask someone learned in music how we can advance our musical tastes, we will probably be told to listen to more music. In the same way, we learn what we want from life (whether we be organizations and communities or individuals) by living. By living, that is by producing and selling goods and services, business firms encounter problems and opportunities that are transformed into preferences and desires. New products swallow up their markets (autos for carriages; hand calculators for slide rules); inflation hikes their costs; social changes produce new markets (women's liberation and restaurants, the automobile and suburban shopping marts); government regulations condition their goals (health and safety rules, environmental regulations); new legal rules permit or exclude organizational forms (anti-trust, geographical limits on banks). We create our wants, in part, by experiencing our choices.

Closely related to the idea that actions generate their goals is the fact that action is itself an important goal in the lives of many people. The goal of a cruise ship is not to reach port, but to cruise. So in understanding organizations we must take into account that activity is one of the goods that organization members, perhaps managers especially, wish to consume. Being part of a "live-wire" organization is exhilarating. The power game can be a fun game, especially for the winners. Being an executive who makes decisions is empowering not only in giving control over resource allocation but also in encouraging a strongly positive conception of self. The pleasures are often in the process rather than in the outcome.

Historical and Social Contexts

In many respects, this book was a response to a classical point of view denying the significance of decision processes for decision outcomes. Such a view, once dominant in economic theories of organization and very general elsewhere, argued that organizational actions were instantaneous and unique adaptations to an external environment. Decisions were seen as uniquely determined by the constraints, thus predictable without attention to any features of the process by which decisions happened.

The implicit response in the present book was that decision outcomes are not uniquely determined by the context but depend in important ways on organizational and decision processes. Limitations on rationality introduce massive unpredictability; there are multiple equilibria; in any event, the time to equilibrium is rather slow relative to the changes in the context; external environments are not really exogenous but are (partly) created by the organization and its decisions. These elements of indeterminacy in action make organizational decisions impossible to predict simply from a knowledge of "objective" constraints.

We think the position of the book was well taken, but it may have resulted in understating the significance of the historical and social context of action. If action depends on expectations and preferences, then we need to ask where the expectations and preferences come from. If action depends on matching rules to situations, then we need to ask how the matches are defined and interpreted. If the realized branches of history transform the distributions from which future histories are drawn, then we need to be conscious of aspects of timing in action.

To answer such questions we must recognize the ways in which any particular organization is tied into a history and a collection of organizations from which it draws aspirations, beliefs, technologies, and personnel. We must become conscious of how ecologies of action, including cooperation and competition, affect the premises of action. We must see how the organization fits into a pattern of resource exchanges and dependencies with other organizations. We must model the extent to which features of an organization may be invariant, selected by convention rather than subject to intentional choice. We must attend to the social context of meaning within which deliberate action takes place.

Implicitly, the book concedes that not everything can be studied at once by everyone. Students of organizations make distinctions among micro-, meso-, and macro-organizational studies, corresponding to the individual, organizational, and societal levels of analysis. This book has elements of all three, but there is no doubt that it lies more fully in the first two levels than in the third. The book is written mainly from the viewpoint of someone seeking to understand organizations and the behavior of people in them, rather than someone trying to characterize a social system containing organizations. Thus, it is, for the most part, written from the perspective of understanding how an organization responds to changes in its (exogenous) environment. Studies of the external environment are essential in that view, but they can be carried out without simultaneous attention to studies of decision-making, and vice versa. A proper division of labor.

Modern efforts to model adaptive systems suggest that life is not that simple. Processes within an organization shape the external world, even as it is being shaped by that world. Technology is not just adopted and adapted to, it is changed. Information received includes echoes of information sent. Preferences mold the world which molds preferences. The code word is co-evolution. Ours is a path-dependent world in which small steps are easily escalated into irreversible, or nearly irreversible, commitments. Contemporary results in evolutionary studies, organizational learning, and population biology all indicate that it is more difficult to separate the internal processes of organizational decision-making from their historical and social contexts than we might previously have believed.

Finally, studies of organizations since the publication of the book have placed considerable emphasis on the symbolic and interpretive context of organizational behavior. Meaning makes a difference, and meaning is socially constructed and communicated through an interpretive language that permeates organizational life. In a society in which rational ideology is dominant, decision-making is (in part) a sacred ritual by which that ideology is confirmed and communicated. Organizations gather information and conduct analyses because that is what proper organizations and proper decision-makers do. At a different time and in a different society, decision-makers consulted oracles and prayed for revelations. As ideologies and worldviews change, organizations change, and vice versa.

Organizations organize themselves within a context of socially recognized metaphors. When a society induces a museum to describe its holdings as "products" and its patrons as "customers," it imposes a collection of meanings associated with those metaphors. When a society labels an institution of higher education a "community college" instead of a "junior college," it encourages a transformation of identity and purpose, the details of which are hard to anticipate. When a society imagines a business firm to be an instrument of stockholders, the firm becomes something different from what it becomes when it is imagined to be a producer of goods and services, or a source of support for its workers.

Some contemporary students of meaning in organizations would go further to assert that it is interpretation, rather than choice, that is central to life. Within such a view, organizations are organized around the requirement to sustain, communicate, and elaborate interpretations of history and life – not around decisions. Decisions are primarily instruments to interpretation, rather than the other way around. Although we think an interpretive perspective yields important insights into organizations, we would not go that far, even in retrospect. But we suspect that a 1992 book on organizations, even while reaffirming that there is a real world out there to which organizations are adapting and which they are affecting, would need to pay somewhat more attention than a 1958 book did to the social context of meaning within which organizations operate.

The historical, social, and interpretive contexts of organizations are pervasive and important. At the same time, however, it is possible to exaggerate the difficulties they create for the construction of the theory of organizations. That everything is (more or less) connected to everything else does not make all research impossible. The world of organization studies is still partially decomposable. It is just not quite as decomposable for all purposes as we might have once thought.

Final Thoughts

We have tried to indicate a few things that we might say differently now than we do in the main body of the book. They are, we think, mostly things that are anticipated in the book and are consistent with it, rather than things that require a radically different perspecitve. On the whole – and without much qualification – we are content to let the original text speak for itself.

Yet, in contemplating the past 35 years, we note that the study of organizations has expanded its scope and improved its quality. In 1958 almost none of the current research journals specializing in research on organizations existed. Now there are several of high quality. In 1958 students of organizations in the United States were almost entirely cut off from students of organizations in other countries. Now the international ties are rich with considerable cross-fertilization. In 1958 the study of organizations represented an insignificant part of economics, psychology, and sociology. Now organizational economics, organizational psychology, and organizational sociology are major subfields of their respective disciplines. In 1958 the systematic study of organizations was a small part of management departments in business schools. Now it is a large part of those departments and an important part of departments of strategy, human resources, industrial organization, and labor relations.

The point is not that organization research and theory represent uniquely expanding domains, nor that this particular book was especially significant to that expansion. The growth of the study of organizations over the past 35 years has been part of a phenomenal growth of the behavioral and social sciences generally. Nevertheless, part of the growth has probably come from the vitality and salience of the ideas. And if this book has contributed to making those ideas accessible, we are pleased.

When we wrote the book we thought the kinds of questions that it addressed were important ones. We still do. We hoped that a foundation had been laid for significant future research. We think those hopes have been justified. We imagined that by now we could both retire. That imagination proved illusory. There are still a few things to be done, and despite our great enthusiasm and affection for our colleagues, we are not yet prepared to let them have all the fun.

James G. March and
Herbert A. Simon

1

Organizational Behavior

This book is about the theory of formal organizations. It is easier, and probably more useful, to give examples of formal organizations than to define the term. The United States Steel Corporation is a formal organization; so is the Red Cross, the corner grocery store, the New York State Highway Department. The latter organization is, of course, part of a larger one – the New York State government. But for present purposes we need not trouble ourselves about the precise boundaries to be drawn around an organization or the exact distinction between an "organization" and a "nonorganization." We are dealing with empirical phenomena, and the world has an uncomfortable way of not permitting itself to be fitted into clean classifications.

Authors are often convinced that the particular subjects with which they are dealing are more significant than the world has acknowledged. We cheerfully make this claim for organization theory. However much organizations occupy the thoughts of practicing executives and administrators, and however many books for these practitioners have been written about them, the theory of organizations occupies an insignificant place in modern social science. Most current psychology and sociology textbooks do not devote even a short chapter to the subject of formal organizations. The *Handbook of Social Psychology* (Lindzey, 1954) contains chapters on small groups, mass media, "industrial social psychology" (with only passing references to organizations), leadership, and voting behavior. There is no comparable chapter on formal organizations, and only scattered reference to them throughout the text.

One possible reason why formal organizations play such an unobtrusive part in the literature of modern social science is that they are not very important. We will indicate in the next paragraphs why we think this is not a good reason. A second possible reason is that there are few propositions about organizations that cannot be subsumed under other social science topics. This claim can be more accurately evaluated at the end of this book than at the beginning. A third possible reason is that very little has been written because very little is known. As we proceed with our examination of the literature we will see that this is not far from the truth.

1.1 The Significance of Organizations as Social Institutions

But why are organizations important? A superficial answer is that organizations are important because people spend so much of their time in them. The working force – that is to say, the bulk of the adult population – spends more than a third of its waking hours in the organizations by which it is employed. The life of the child takes place to almost an equal extent in the environment of the school organization; and an uncountable host of other organizations, mostly voluntary, account for a large chunk of the leisure time of child and adult alike. In our society, preschool children and nonworking housewives are the only large groups of persons whose behavior is not substantially "organizational."

The ubiquitousness of organizations is not their sole or principal claim for attention. As social scientists we are interested in explaining human behavior. Taking the viewpoint of the social psychologist, we are interested in what influences impinge upon the individual human being from his environment and how he responds to these influences. For most people, formal organizations represent a major part of the environment. Moreover, we would expect organizations to have an even more significant effect upon behavior than is suggested merely by looking at the time budget as we have done above. If we wished to sum up in a single quality the distinctive characteristics of influence processes in organizations, as contrasted with many other influence processes of our society, we would point to the *specificity* of the former as contrasted with the *diffuseness* of the latter.

A concrete example will help to point up the contrast we have in mind. Compare rumor transmission with the transmission of a customer order through a manufacturing company. Rumor transmission is truly a process of diffusion. Seldom does a rumor move outward along a single channel; indeed, in most cases it would soon die if it did not spread out broadly from its original source. The customer order, on the other hand, is transmitted along definite channels, and usually relatively few of them, to specific destinations. We do not wish to imply that there is *no* selectivity in the transmission of rumors, or *no* uncertainty in the destination of formal organizational communications. There certainly is a great deal of both. But the difference in degree in the specificity of channels between the two cases is striking.

Not only are organizational communications characteristically specific with respect to the channels they follow, but they also exhibit a high degree of specificity with respect to content. Here there is a strong contrast between organizational communications and communications through mass media. The audiences to whom newspapers and radio address themselves possess no common technical vocabulary; there is no subject about which they have any shared special knowledge; there is no good way of predicting what they will be thinking about when the mass communication reaches them. In principle at least, the recipient of an organizational communication is at the opposite pole. A great deal is known about his special abilities and characteristics. This knowledge is gained from considerable past experience with him and from a detailed knowledge of the work environment in which he operates.

When a mass medium exerts influence or attempts to give instruction, its messages are usually of the simplest variety – "go to your corner druggist now, and . . ." – and its appeals are to widely shared motivations. Organizational instructions, on the contrary, frequently contain great detail; often motivation can be assumed. Not only can organization communication be detailed, but it can be cryptic, relying on a highly developed and precise common technical language understood by both sender and recipient. Again we do not wish to imply any contrast of black and white, which would clearly be contrary to fact, but only to point to characteristic differences of degree that are large in magnitude and highly significant.

The great specificity that characterizes communications in organizations can be described in a slightly different way, using the sociological concept of *role*. Roles in organizations, as contrasted with many of the other roles that individuals fill, tend to be highly elaborated, relatively stable, and defined to a considerable extent in explicit and even written terms. Not only is the role defined for the individual who occupies it, but it is known in considerable detail to others in the organization who have occasion to deal with him. Hence, the environment of other persons that surrounds each member of an organization tends to become a highly stable and predictable one. It is this predictability, together with certain related structural features of organization to be discussed presently, that accounts for the ability of organizations to deal in a coordinated way with their environments.

The high degree of coordination of organization behavior can be illustrated by comparing coordination in organizations with the coordination that takes place in economic markets. To be sure, markets often exhibit considerable stability and predictability. A seller can bring his goods into the market with a fair notion of the total quantity that will be supplied and the prices at which goods wll be exchanged. But he does not know in advance who specifically will be the buyer of his wares or at what precise price. Transactions that take place within organizations, far more than in markets, are preplanned and precoordinated. The automobile engine division knows exactly how many engine blocks to put into production – not because it has made a forecast of the market, but because its production plan has been coordinated with the plans for producing completed automobiles in other departments of the company.

A biological analogy is apt here, if we do not take it literally or too seriously. Organizations are assemblages of interacting human beings and they are the largest assemblages in our society that have anything resembling a central coordinative system. Let us grant that these coordinative systems are not developed nearly to the extent of the central nervous system in higher biological organisms – that organizations are more earthworm than ape. Nevertheless, the high specificity of structure and coordination within organizations – as contrasted with the diffuse and variable relations *among* organizations and among unorganized individuals – marks off the individual organization as a sociological unit comparable in significance to the individual organism in biology.

1.2   The Literature of Organization Theory

In this book we shall review in a systematic way some of the important things that have been said about organization by those who have studied them and written about them. We have already observed that the effort devoted by social scientists to understanding organizations has not been large. Nevertheless, organizations impinge on so many aspects of our society that pieces, bits, and snatches of organization theory and empirical data can be assembled from a wide range of sources. (1) Many executives and administrators have recorded their organizational experiences in biographical or systematic form in books and articles. (2) The scientific management movement has been concerned with organization theory, and almost every standard text-book in management devotes a chapter or two to a statement of principles of good organization. (3) Some sociologists, most of them influenced by Max Weber's analysis of "bureaucracy," have theorized about organizations and carried out some systematic observations. (4) Social psychologists have shown particular interest in two aspects of organization behavior: in leadership and supervision on the one hand, and in morale and employee attitudes on the other. More recently, they have undertaken some studies of the effects of communication patterns upon organizational behavior. (5) Political scientists have been concerned with problems quite parallel to those of the scientific management group – the efficient operation of governmental organizations – and also with the problem of securing external (democratic) control over governmental administration. (6) Economists have theorized about the business firm as a building block for their broader concern with the operation of markets and the pricing and allocative mechanisms in the economy. Moreover, organizational considerations have played an important, if unsystematic, role in the debate over planning versus *laissez faire*.

Any attempt to bring together this scattered and diverse body of writing about organizations into a coherent whole must surmount two serious problems. The literature leaves one with the impression that after all not a great deal has been said about organizations, but it has been said over and over in a variety of languages. Consequently, we require a serious effort toward the construction of a common language.

The second problem is that there is in the literature a great disparity between hypotheses and evidence. Much of what we know or believe about organizations is distilled from common sense and from the practical experience of executives. The great bulk of this wisdom and lore has never been subjected to the rigorous scrutiny of scientific method. The literature contains many assertions, but little evidence to determine – by the usual scientific standards of public testability and reproducibility – whether these assertions really hold up in the world of fact.

In this book we will review and examine what evidence exists, but it is not our purpose to provide new evidence. In two ways, however, we will try to take steps toward the empirical testing of current theories of organizations: We will restate some existing hypotheses in a form that makes them amenable to testing, giving considerable attention to the operational definition of variables; and in a number of instances we will indicate what kinds of tests are relevant and practicable.

1.3 Organization of This Book

In organizing our material, we wished to impose order without imposing a parochial point of view stemming from a particular or special conception of organization theory. We have tried to steer a middle course between eclecticism and provincialism. We shall let the reader judge how far we have succeeded.

Propositions about organizations are statements about human behavior, and imbedded in every such proposition, explicitly or implicitly, is a set of assumptions as to what properties of human beings have to be taken into account to explain their behavior in organizations. Propositions about organizational behavior can be grouped in three broad classes, on the basis of their assumptions:

1 Propositions assuming that organization members, and particularly employees, are primarily *passive instruments*, capable of performing work and accepting directions, but not initiating action or exerting influence in any significant way.
2 Propositions assuming that members bring to their organizations *attitudes, values,* and *goals*; that they have to be motivated or induced to participate in the system of organization behavior; that there is incomplete parallelism between their personal goals and organization goals; and that actual or potential goal conflicts make power phenomena, attitudes, and morale centrally important in the explanation of organizational behavior.
3 Propositions assuming that organization members are *decision makers and problem solvers*, and that perception and thought processes are central to the explanation of behavior in organizations.

There is nothing contradictory among these three sets of assumptions. Human beings are all of these things, and perhaps more. An adequate theory of human behavior in organizations will have to take account of the instrumental aspects of human behavior, of the motivational and attitudinal, and of the rational. Nor has any considerable body of writing about organizations single-mindedly and consistently adopted one of these viewpoints. Nevertheless, as we review the literature, the differences in emphasis are quite evident. Because theorizing involves abstracting, the theorists of organization have focused their attention on the particular, partial aspects of the human organism that seem to them particularly significant for their purposes. Thus, the model of the employee as instrument is prominent in the writings of the scientific management movement. In the last several decades the second model, emphasizing attitudes and motivations, has gained the greater prominence in research on bureaucracy, human relations, leadership and supervision, and power phenomena. The third model, emphasizing the rational and intellective aspects of organizational behavior, has been less extensively used than the other two, but is represented particularly by the work of economists and others on the planning process, and by the work of psychologists on organizational communication and problem-solving.

We shall use these three models, then, as our primary basis for sorting out propositions and organizing existing knowledge. The next chapter, chapter 2, deals with the employee as instrument, as he appears in the scientific management literature. The three following chapters, 3, 4, and 5, deal with propositions that rest primarily on the second model; chapters 6 and 7 are concerned primarily with the decision-making and problem-solving aspects of organizational behavior.

1.4 Some Types of Propositions

The central core of this book is a series of propositions about organizations. We have tried, as far as possible, to use standard formats in stating these propositions – even at the expense, occasionally, of style. We could not use a single format, because the propositions are of several different kinds, which we can illustrate with a few examples:

1. Propositions stating the dependence of one variable on one or more other (independent) variables. These propositions are of the familiar "y is a function of x" form, where the term "function" is used in its mathematical sense. There are two species of this general kind of proposition:

(a) Propositions with variables capable of assuming a range of values. Example: "The lower the satisfaction of the organism, the greater the amount of search it will undertake." The dependent variable here is "amount of search," the independent variable "level of satisfaction."

(b) Propositions in which one or more of the variables are of a dichotomous, all-or-none kind or take on discrete values that are not ordered. Example: "In small organizations, purpose departmentalization, by interfering with process specialization, leads to serious inefficiencies." The dependent variable, "efficiency," is an ordinal or cardinal number, but the independent variable, "type of departmentalization," takes on one of several discrete values – in this case "specialization by purpose" or "specialization by process." In some propositions a variable that is basically dichotomous is transformed into a continuous variable by stating the relation in terms of frequencies. Example: "Increases in the balance of inducements over contributions decrease the propensity of an individual member to leave the organization." Remaining in an organization or leaving is an all-or-none choice, but the variable may be replaced by a turnover measure – the percentage of members who leave during some specified time.

2. Propositions embodying a qualitative descriptive generalization about organizations. Example: "One of the important activities that goes on in organizations is the development of programs for new activities that need to be routinized for day-to-day performance." This proposition could be "quantitized" by constructing a measure of the *amount* of the activity in question that goes on in organizations. Apart from the fact that no one has data with which to confront the quantitized proposition, the original proposition does not state a relation between two variables. It is perhaps best interpreted as a simple qualitative anatomical statement that holds for most organizations most of the time, comparable to: "A man has a heart that contracts periodically."

3. Propositions asserting that a particular organizational structure or process performs a particular function (using function, now, in its biological or sociological sense – "the function of the heart is to circulate the blood"). Example: "Rigidity of behavior increases the defensibility of individual action." If we introduce measures of rigidity of behavior and degree of defensibility of action, then this proposition contains a statement of functional relation in the mathematical sense. But it contains more. It implies also that rigidity of behavior performs the function of making action defensible. Functional analysis, in this sense, is a fruitful tool for the study of self-maintaining systems.

When we state propositions of the first type, we will number the variables and the propositions. Thus, if a proposition states that the value of dependent variable 3.7 varies with the values of independent variables 3.3, 3.4, and 3.6, we will number the proposition "[3.7:3.3, 3.4, 3.6]." The distinctions between dependent and independent variables are not arbitrary, but are assertions about the direction of the causal arrow. That is, each proposition asserts there is a mechanism through which the independent variables of that proposition influence the dependent variable.

A separate series of numbers prefixed by "A," will be used for the variables in propositions of the second, anatomical, type. Propositions about sociological functions, and the variables in them, will be numbered when they are stated in the same form as propositions of the first type. In this case, the function becomes the dependent variable; the mechanism that performs the function, the independent variable. Thus, in the example cited above, "amount of rigidity of behavior" is the independent variable; "degree of defensibility of action" is the dependent variable.

1.5   Some Psychological Postulates

Our final task in this introductory chapter is to state some postulates about the human organism, and particularly its central nervous system, that underlie the entire analysis. Psychologists will recognize these assumptions as generally compatible with the theories of Tolman (1932) and Tolman and Egon Brunswick (1935), with recent trends in the theory of cognition and perception – e.g., the work of Bruner and his associates (1956) – and with the viewpoint that the human organism can be regarded as a complex information-processing system (Simon, 1947, 1955, 1956; March, 1955a; Newell, 1955; Newell, Shaw, and Simon, 1958).

The behavior of an organism through a short interval of time is to be accounted for by (1) its internal state at the beginning of the interval, and (2) its environment at the beginning of the interval. The same two sets of factors, the initial state and the environment, determine not only the behavior but also what the internal state will be at the next moment of time. This is a familiar description of an organism, which provides for the simultaneous influence of nature and nurture and which is compatible with the ordinary mathematical descriptions of dynamic systems.

The internal state of the organism, by the terms of the description, is implicitly a function of its whole previous history. In the human organism most of the internal state is contained in what we call the memory. The memory includes (but is not limited to) all sorts of partial and modified records of past experiences and programs for responding to environmental stimuli. More specifically, the human memory content can usually be viewed as divided into two parts by any given time: a part that exerts a significant influence on the behavior at that time; and a part much larger than the first that exerts little or no influence on the behavior at that time. We will call the part of the memory that is influencing behavior at a particular time the *evoked set*, and any process that causes some memory content to be transferred from the second (unevoked) category to the first a process for *evoking* that content.

Empirically, it appears that changes in the total content of the memory take place relatively slowly through the processes we generally call *learning*. Changes in the content of the evoked set may take place very rapidly. On the basis of this and other differences between learning and evoking processes, it is important to maintain the distinction between the two processes in a theory of influence. Behavior can be influenced by bringing about changes in the memory content (learning), or by changing the active determiners of current behavior (evocation). There is no reason a priori to suppose that influence of these two kinds is subject to the same laws.

A parallel distinction can be made between those aspects of the environment, at any given time, that have a significant influence on behavior during the next time interval and those which do not. The former are often called *stimuli*. Stimuli are generally parts of the environment that are changing rapidly or suddenly (e.g., a rapidly moving object in the visual field). There is a strong mutual interaction between stimuli and the evoked set. The stimuli that are present at a given time are major determiners of what set will be evoked or maintained; conversely, the set at any given time will be a major determiner of what parts of the environment will be effective as stimuli. There is no circularity in this relation – just the usual kind of mutual interaction among variables of a dynamic system.

The division of the internal state of the organism into evoked and unevoked parts, and the parallel division of the environment into stimuli and "unnoticed" remainder, is a fundamental characteristic of organisms that distinguishes them from most of the dynamic systems encountered in physics and chemistry. We need not argue whether the division, either in state or environment, is quite as sharp as we have made it; it is sharp enough to incorporate it as a prominent feature in a theory of human behavior. Just how we draw the line between the active and passive parts of internal state or environment will depend, among other things, upon the interval of time we select for our observations. If we take a very short interval of time – a fraction of a second, say – then the active elements in set and stimulus will be very few indeed. If we take a long interval – a week, say – a large part of the memory content may be during some portion of that interval a part of the psychological set, and a correspondingly large number of environmental events a part of the stimuli that influence behavior. In the case of a long time-interval, we will often use phrases like "definition of the situation" or "frame of reference" in place of set.

This choice of terms does not seem to us to reflect any very fundamental distinctions, but conforms more closely to ordinary usage than would a strict adherence to the term "set" in all contexts.

The memory content, thus divided into "active" and "passive" elements, can also be classified in a different way. It includes: (a) values or goals: criteria that are applied to determine which courses of action are preferred among those considered; (b) relations between actions and their outcomes: i.e., beliefs, perceptions, and expectations as to the consequences that will follow from one course of action or another; and (c) alternatives: possible courses of action.

When one of these elements is evoked by a stimulus, it may also bring into the evoked set a number of other elements with which it has become associated through the learning processes. Thus, if a particular goal has been achieved on previous occasions by execution of a particular course of action, then evocation of that goal will be likely to evoke that course of action again. Habitual responses are extreme instances of this in which the connecting links between stimulus and response may be suppressed from consciousness. In the same way, the evocation of a course of action will lead, by association, to evocation of consequences that have been associated with the action.

This, then, is the general picture of the human organism that we will use to analyze organizational behavior. It is a picture of a choosing, decision-making, problem-solving organism that can do only one or a few things at a time, and that can attend to only a small part of the information recorded in its memory and presented by the environment. We shall see that these particular characteristics of the human organism are basic to some of the salient characteristics of human behavior in organizations.

2

"Classical" Organization Theory

We can distinguish two main lines of development in traditional organization theory. The first, deriving from the work of Taylor, focuses upon the basic physical activities involved in production and is typified by time study and methods study. The second, of which the works of Gulick and Urwick provide good examples, is more concerned with the grand organizational problems of departmental division of work and coordination. In this chapter we will describe the major distinctive features and problems of these two areas of theory.

2.1 Taylor's Scientific Management

When Frederick W. Taylor (1907, 1911, 1919, 1947) investigated the effective use of human beings in industrial organizations, he set himself substantially the general task of organization theory: to analyze the interaction between the characteristics of humans and the social and task environments created by organizations. The actual area of behavior that was considered by Taylor and his successors in the scientific management movement was much narrower, however. Because of the historical accidents of their positions and training, and the specific problems they faced in industry, Taylor and his associates studied primarily the use of men as adjuncts to machines in the performance of routine productive tasks.

In time and methods study, the scientific management group was concerned with describing the characteristics of the human organism as one might describe a relatively simple machine for performing a comparatively simple task. The goal was to use the rather inefficient human organism in the productive process in the best way possible. This was to be accomplished by specifying a detailed program of behavior (a "method," or set of methods) that would transform a general-purpose mechanism, such as a person, into a more efficient special-purpose mechanism.

The scientific management movement brought considerable precision of measurement into the organization of the individual employee's production activities (we shall examine the measurement procedures later). It raised and partially answered a number of fundamental questions in human engineering. It stimulated an impressive number of studies of the physiological constraints on simple physical operations (Wechsler, 1952). It showed that it was feasible to specify precisely the activities involved in routine production tasks. In this respect the work in scientific management is more relevant to mechanization and automation than to the broader psychological aspects of human behavior in organizations. Since the role of machines in organizations is not our central concern, we shall not discuss further the implications of the scientific management movement for the trend toward automation (Diebold, 1952, esp. pp. 31–53).

Let us turn to that portion of the work that relates to the utilization of human beings in organizations. Because the theories of human behavior implicit in this approach encompass primarily physiological variables, we may refer to the work as "physiological organization theory." The theory is limited to a narrow range of tasks, and emphasizes a limited number of physiological variables. We will consider each of these limits in turn.

Types of tasks in physiological organization theory

The scientific management group has been most concerned with the kinds of tasks that are performed on the production floor or in clerical departments. Several important attributes distinguish these tasks from other kinds of activities in industrial organizations. First, they are largely repetitive, so that the daily activity of an individual worker can be divided into a large number of cyclical repetitions of essentially the same, or closely related, activities. Second, these tasks do not require complex problem-solving activity by the worker who handles them. For the instructed or experienced worker, each task has its standard method of performance. Later in this volume we will contrast this situation with that in which a more elaborate procedure for decision-making is necessary.

Because they are relatively routine, the tasks with which the theory has been concerned can be described fairly completely in terms of overt behavior, without explicit reference to the mental processes of the worker. We can imagine, for example, describing in behavioral terms what is involved in tightening a bolt, for any reasonably experienced worker has a routine procedure for performing this task.

It would be quite another matter to describe the activities involved in determining a price, designing a machine, or scheduling production in terms of overt behavioral movements. Although recent developments in the theory of human higher mental-processes now make it possible to specify in some detail the steps involved in problem-solving, the specification is in very different terms from the usual description of a manual task (Dinneen, 1955; Newell and Simon, 1956; Bruner, Goodnow, and Austin, 1956). Traditional time and methods study has avoided problem-solving tasks, and thus has not dealt with the aspects of human behavior that will concern us throughout most of this volume.

We can illustrate the characteristics of time study and methods study with some examples of formulas in a standard work on the subject: Lowry, Maynard, and Stegemerten, *Time and Motion Study* (1940, pp. 357–426). These formulas cover the activities of (a) mounting panels in enclosing cabinets, (b) machining nonferrous metals on a lathe, and (c) bench-molding alloy castings in a brass foundry. Although the last two of these activities would normally be performed by a highly trained worker and do not represent the simplest activities to be found in manufacturing, nevertheless each can be and is highly programmed with respect to the specific steps needed to accomplish the task. The detailed description of the lathe operation, for example, consists of some 183 specific tasks of which the first 10 are: "pick up part and move to machine, place medium part in chuck, tighten independent chuck 18-inch lathe, tighten chuck with pipe on wrench, true up part on chuck, pick up aligning bar from floor, pick up surface gage, align part in halves (with surface gage), remove aligning bar to floor, lay aside surface gage" (p. 388).

Of course, even such close descriptions of behavior do not define the muscular activity explicitly, and certainly do not determine it in detail. The instruction "pick up part and move to machine" can be executed in many ways. However, one aim of the time-study man is so to define the task as to restrict considerably the behavioral alternatives with which the worker is faced. This is done, in the first place, by the detail of the job description. Neither the instruction "machine this object on the lathe" nor any of the 183 subinstructions uniquely determines a set of muscular movements, but there is a striking difference in the degree to which each fixes activities. Freedom to choose the method of performance is further restricted by the time standards. The 0.0049 hour allowed to "pick up part and move to machine" restricts severely the number of ways in which a worker can perform that activity.

Specifications of the human organism

The characteristics of the human organism that are considered in scientific management theory follow from the types of tasks with which the theory deals. When behavior is viewed as a sequence of highly regularized physical activities, the relevant dimensions relate primarily to the neurophysiology of the human organism. We can discuss these under the headings of capacity, speed, durability, and cost.

Capacity There is an upper limit to the production rate that a human organism can achieve. In part, the capacity measure merely summarizes the separate factors of speed and fatigue, but it also serves as an independent description of qualitative human properties. If a task requires 5 hands and 12 fingers, a human being is the wrong kind of machine to execute it. Capacity in this sense becomes an important consideration in the design of man-machine systems.

The notion of capacity also underlies some of the principles of motion economy to be found in the scientific management literature. Production can often be increased by making simultaneous use of hands and feet – by eliminating "unused" capacity in the form of members that are idle during part of the work cycle.

Speed Time study emphasizes the speed characteristics of the human organism – how fast individuals of varying degrees of skill, exerting varying degrees of "effort," can perform a particular task (e.g., "pick up part and move to machine"). Vast quantities of data about unit times have been assembled and analyzed in an effort to set time standards for complex tasks.

A goal for time study, never fully attained, has been to find a set of "basic" activities and unit times for each of them, so that standard times for more complex activities can be constructed by analyzing them into their basic components and adding up the unit times for the components. The Gilbreths' (1917) list of 18 classes of basic activities – therbligs – is the best-known effort in this direction.

Unfortunately, the therblig is not homogeneous, but is a highly variable unit whose performance time depends on a host of attendant conditions. Moreover, the interactions among the components of a complex task are often sufficiently important that the time required for the whole task is not equal to the sum of the times required for the components taken separately.

A number of "systems" for setting time standards by summing times for units tasks have been constructed in recent years. These have had a certain amount of industrial application, and appear to be workable at least for relatively simple hand-assembly tasks and the like. One such system is methods-time measurement, described by Maynard, Stegemerten, and Schwab (1948). Tables of time data have been compiled for the therbligs: reach, move, turn, grasp, position, disen- gage, and release. These tables give the standard time for each therblig as a function of three or four parameters. For example, the time required to "reach" depends on whether the hand was previously in motion, on the distance it is to be moved, on the accuracy with which the object to be reached must be located, etc.

At present, time standards for industrial jobs are still usually estimated directly, and only in a minority of cases are they synthesized from standard data on component units. The human organism, even when it is regarded as a neurophysiological "machine," has proved far more complex than pioneers like Gilbreth hoped and expected when they undertook to analyze human work into its elementary therbligs.

Time study has also met with difficulties in defining the levels of skill and effort that are implicit in the time standards. Often it is unclear whether standard times reflect "average time using average skill and average effort," "minimum time," or "average time over a series of trials by individuals randomly selected from a pool of industrial workers." At least part of the confusion stems from the methods commonly used for making the estimates. Very definite specifications are generally laid down for details of observation, but only vague specifications for data analysis.

For example, measures of "skill" and "effort" are presumably taken simultaneously with measures of speed, and the analysis depends to a critical extent upon these estimates. But techniques for normalizing the time readings to allow for differences in skill and effort are exceedingly rough. As a result, time standards tend to be simply averages based on readings taken over a sample of individuals and situations in which the same (or nearly the same) task is performed. Furthermore, the estimation procedures reflect only slightly recent developments in the theory of statistical sampling and estimation. Failure to incorporate such developments in the technique is a source of additional serious errors (Abruzzi, 1952).

Durability "Durability" in human beings is associated primarily with muscle fatigue. The discussion of fatigue is in some respects the most sophisticated part of the literature of physiological organization theory (Gilbreth and Gilbreth, 1919; Hill, 1926, 1927a, 1927b; Muscio, 1920; Vernon, 1921; Viteles, 1932). The model consists of a sequence of statements defining very general functional relations. With respect to activity within any single muscle group, the model specifies the following:

1 The current rate of activity (i.e., production rate) in a given muscle group is a decreasing function of fatigue in that group.
2 Fatigue in a given muscle group is an increasing function of total past activity in that group.

Hence,

3 Fatigue in a given muscle group is an increasing function of past work time in that group and a decreasing function of past rest time in that group.

In addition, it is usually specified that there is "fatigue generalization," so that:

4 Current fatigue in a given muscle group is an increasing function of total past activity in other muscle groups.

The model makes the production rate in a given muscle group a function of the work and rest time patterns in that and other muscle groups. It does not, however, provide very specific information, since the amount of fatigue is highly dependent on the exact characteristics of the several functions specified. For example, virtually all of the literature on time study suggests that it is efficient to allow rest time under some conditions. Suppose that either the function relating fatigue to activity or the function relating production rate to fatigue is discontinuous, so that production rate decreases only slowly as work time increases, up to some critical value at which there is a sharp decrement. If the functions have this discontinuous character (as part of the literature asserts), it would be efficient to provide rest just before exhaustion sets in. However, if the functions are continuous with varying slopes, rest may be optimal under conditions other than exhaustion (Gilbreth and Gilbreth, 1919, p. 40). The evidence on fatigue that would allow us to choose between these possibilities is relatively fragmentary and impressionistic (Ryan, 1947).

Two specific propositions in the literature should be mentioned. We can view the relation between work time and rest time in the following way. Starting from any given production rate, the rate decreases as work time increases. To restore the initial rate requires a certain amount of rest. We can specify "recovery time," therefore, as a function of work time. Recovery time for a given muscle group is a positively accelerating function of work time in that and other muscle groups. The proposition can be found in the Gilbreths' work (1919, p. 5). That it can be true over the whole range of work time seems unlikely, but it is a proposition of considerable importance to the theory.

The second specific proposition is derived from the proposition about fatigue generalization. Minimum recovery time for the whole organism can be achieved only by resting all of the muscle groups simultaneously. It is a standard observation in the literature that when only a single muscle group is "at rest", it does not recover rapidly enough to warrant its inactivity (Mayo, 1924; Hersey, 1925). In the course of activity by one muscle, all of the muscles are partially active and cannot be rested efficiently.

Cost   Time and methods study is concerned with two cost units: time and money. The theory deals basically with time measurements, and the relation between costs measured in time and costs measured in money is complex.

In the first place, the relation must be consistent with wage rates as determined by competitive markets for labor. The economic theory of wages undoubtedly exaggerates the importance of competition as a determinant of payments, and underestimates the importance of internal processes within the organization. On the other hand, the market ordinarily does set limits to which internal arrangements must conform (Bach, 1957, pp. 580–96).

Secondly, the wage payment is supposed to be set so as to motivate the worker to produce at the rate of which he is capable (to use the physiological "machine" to capacity). But the arrangements for incentive payments based on time study contain implicit motivational assumptions that are always oversimple, and frequently quite erroneous.

For a typical statement of motivational assumptions in time-study work, we can turn again to Lowry, Maynard, and Stegemerten: "The principal objectives of the employee are to secure maximum earnings commensurate with the effort expended, while working, in so far as conditions will permit, in a healthful and agreeable environment" (1940, p. 6). If we take the qualifying phrases seriously, the statement becomes hopelessly vague; if we do not, it places almost exclusive emphasis on the direct link of wage payments with production and efficiency as measured in terms of time standards.

Such an emphasis is misplaced for several reasons. First, it is a matter of record that time- and methods-study efforts have been far from uniformly successful in persuading workers that their long-run interests lie in maximizing their incentive pay (Viteles, 1953, pp. 18–61). Second, the effects of incentive plans are further complicated by the existence of collective bargaining, and the generally cool attitudes of unions toward them.

Quite apart from union attitudes, the available evidence on the motivation of workers casts serious questions on the automatic efficacy of wage incentives as a motivating device. Some of the evidence will be considered in more detail in chapter 3. The general conclusions it suggests are: (a) that wage payments represent only one (but perhaps the major single one) of a number of rewards in the system; (b) that the utilities associated with wages may be discontinuous – reflecting some notion of "satisfactory" wages – and hence may not be at all linearly (or even monotonically) related to wage payments; (c) that these utilities change through time with shifts in aspirations, so that the impact of wage incentives is not stable.

The propositions of physiological organization theory

We have now examined the range of tasks with which the scientific management theories have been primarily concerned and the neurophysiological variables that enter into the theory. In the last section, we gave some examples of propositions in the theory, particularly those relating to the topic of fatigue. In the present section, we shall survey more broadly the main kinds of propositions that are to be found in the scientific management literature.

The work of Taylor and his followers is, on the whole, more easily described in terms of techniques than of propositions. It takes the point of view of the engineer rather than the natural scientist, and prescribes procedures for the efficient organization and conduct of routine work. Taylor's principal prescriptions were three: (1) Use time and methods study to find the "one best way" of performing a job. By the best way is meant the way that permits the largest average rate of production over the day. (2) Provide the worker with an incentive to perform the job in the best way and at a good pace. In general, do this by giving him a specified bonus over day rates if he meets the standard of production. (3) Use specialized experts (functional foremen) to establish the various conditions surrounding the worker's task – methods, machine speeds, task priorities, etc.

It can be seen from these prescriptions that Taylor's contribution was not a set of general principles for organizing work efficiently, but a set of operating procedures that could be employed in each concrete situation to discover the methods that would be efficient in that situation and to secure their application. Taylor's invention of time study is more accurately compared to the invention of the microscope than, say, to the cell hypothesis. The second prescription – that relating to incentives – has already been considered briefly, and will be discussed further in chapter 3. The third, on functional foremanship, belongs more properly to our discussion of departmentalization later in the present chapter. We will conclude this section on Taylor's work by considering some of the generalizations about motion economy that were obtained through the further development of his first prescription.

Motion economy is mentioned here because, apart from the study of fatigue, it is the one area in which the work in physiological organization theory took a propositional form. The propositions stem largely from the research and writing of Frank and Lillian Gilbreth (1909, 1911, 1912, 1914, 1917).

The principles of motion economy fall into three groups: principles related to (a) the use of the human body, (b) the arrangement of the work place, (c) the design of tools and equipment. They have been summarized in a variety of forms, of which the following list of 22 principles is typical (Barnes, 1949, pp. 556–7):

1 The two hands should begin as well as complete their motions at the same time.
2 The two hands should not be idle at the same time except during rest periods.
3 Motions of the arms should be made in opposite and symmetrical directions and should be made simultaneously.
4 Hand motions should be confined to the lowest classification with which it is possible to perform the work satisfactorily.
5 Momentum should be employed to assist the worker whenever possible, and it should be reduced to a minimum if it must be overcome by muscular effort.
6 Smooth, continuous motions of the hands are preferable to zigzag motions or straight-line motions involving sudden and sharp changes in direction.
7 Ballistic movements are faster, easier, and more accurate than restricted (fixation) or "controlled" movements.
8 Rhythm is essential to the smooth and automatic performance of an

operation and the work should be arranged to permit easy and natural rhythm wherever possible.

9 There should be a definite and fixed place for all tools and materials.

10 Tools, materials, and controls should be located close in and directly in front of the operator.

11 Gravity feed bins and containers should be used to deliver the material close to the point of use.

12 "Drop deliveries" should be used wherever possible.

13 Materials and tools should be located to permit the best sequence of motions.

14 Provisions should be made for adequate conditions for seeing. Good illumination is the first requirement for satisfactory visual perception.

15 The height of the work place and the chair should preferably be arranged so that alternate sitting and standing at work are easily possible.

16 A chair of the type and height to permit good posture should be provided for every worker.

17 The hands should be relieved of all work that can be done more advantageously by a jig, fixture, or a foot-operated device.

18 Two or more tools should be combined wherever possible.

19 Tools and materials should be pre-positioned wherever possible.

20 Where each finger performs some specific movement, such as in typewriting, the load should be distributed in accordance with the inherent capacities of the fingers.

21 Handles such as those used on cranks and large screwdrivers should be designed to permit as much of the surface of the hand to come in contact with the handle as possible.

22 Levers, crossbars, and handwheels should be located in such positions that the operator can manipulate them with the least change in body position and with the greatest mechanical advantage.

Detailed comment is hardly necessary. The physiological character of the propositions is evident, as is their empirical basis and the lack of an explicit underlying theory of the human mechanism. Their whole flavor is that of engineering principles, rather than generalizations belonging to "pure" science. As such, they undoubtedly have importance within a domain bounded on the one hand by tasks in which motivation is a relevant consideration and on the other hand by tasks requiring more computation. An extension beyond that domain, however, cannot be made effectively without considerably expanding the framework.

2.2 Theories of Departmentalization

Although an explicit theory of departmentalization can be traced back to Aristotle (*Politics*, Book IV, Chap. 15), we will consider the theory here in its contemporary form in the well-known essay by Luther Gulick (Gulick and Urwick, 1937). To have a short name for this line of development, we label it the "administrative management theory." Among the prominent exponents of the theory, in addition to Gulick, have been Haldane (1918), Fayol (1930), Mooney and Reiley (1939), and Urwick (1943).

Although there was considerable communication and overlap between the students of organization we have assigned to "scientific management" or "physiological organization theory" and those we are now labeling "administrative management theorists," the two bodies of doctrine are conceptually rather distinct. They share, particularly in their more formal versions, a preoccupation with the simpler neuro-physiological properties of humans and the simpler kinds of tasks that are handled in organizations. As we shall see, however, the administrative management theorists tended to carry their analysis, at least at the level of wisdom and insight, beyond the boundaries set by their formal models.

Since the formal body of theory is somewhat more limited in scope than the area considered in a less formal way, we will begin our analysis with the formal structure, and later supplement it with comments on the broader ramifications.

The general problem to which the formal theory addresses itself is the following: Given a general purpose for an organization, we can identify the unit tasks necessary to achieve that purpose. These tasks will normally include basic productive activities, service activities, coordinative activities, supervisory activities, etc. The problem is to group these tasks into individual jobs, to group the jobs into administrative units, to group the units into larger units, and finally to establish the top level departments – and to make these groupings in such a way as to minimize the total cost of carrying out all the activities. In the organizing process each department is viewed as a definite collection of tasks to be allocated among, and performed by, the employees of the department. To understand the formal theory, it is important to recognize that the total set of tasks is regarded as given in advance.

Departmentalization as an assignment problem

The problem of allocating a given set of activities efficiently among a number of persons has received some attention from mathematicians and game theorists, who refer to it as the optimal assignment problem.

The form of the problem that has usually been considered is a little different from that treated here. The usual statement (Kuhn and Tucker, 1953, p. 5) is:

> Given n persons and n jobs, and a set of real numbers a_{ij}, each representing the value of the ith person on the jth job, what assignments of persons to jobs will yield the maximum total value?

A brute-force solution to the assignment problem involves testing all possible permutations of persons among jobs. Since the number of possible arrangements is $n!$, this becomes obviously infeasible if n is more than a very small number. Several efforts have been made to reduce the computational task to manageable dimensions, with some measure of success (Kuhn, 1955). What has emerged has not been general propositions about optimal assignment, but computational routines that, when combined with the power of modern digital computers, give promise of providing numerical solutions for the problem in individual cases.

The form of the assignment problem that is particularly relevant to the theory of departmentalization is somewhat different from that described above, and has received little attention in the literature. With any possible set, S, of activities, we associate a number, $t(S)$, that measures the time required for a person to perform this set of activities. By $(S_1 + S_2)$ we mean the set of activities obtained by adding the activities S_1 to the activities S_2. In general, the time required to perform the sum of the two sets of activities will not be equal to the sum of the times required for each set alone: $t(S_1 + S_2) \neq t(S_1) + t(S_2)$.

A set of activities, S, is a *task* if it can be performed by a person in a certain specified time, T (say 8 hours): $t(S) \geq T$. To determine the total number of persons required to perform the whole set of activities, we partition it into subsets, each of which is a task. There are many such partitionings, and the number of tasks will vary from one partitioning to another. We define an *efficient* partitioning as one that minimizes the number of tasks – and consequently, the number of persons and number of man-hours.

The complication in finding an efficient partitioning lies in the nonadditivity in times required to perform sets of activities. The rationale of this, as applied to first-level jobs, is that most activities involve initial "setup" costs of various kinds, and that these costs often can be economized by combining activities that have them in common: There are short-run costs of this kind associated with changeover from one activity to another; there are longer-run costs associated with various kinds of training and information-gathering. Because there are numerous and important complementarities of these kinds, there are great differences in the economy of performance of tasks with different groupings (Simon, Smithburg, and Thompson, 1950, pp. 137–45).

Some propositions can be deduced from the formalization of the assignment problem that are equivalent to standard propositions in the literature on departmentalization, but the formalization does not appear to give much that is new, except to contribute precision to the statements.

In an organization that has the usual pyramidal structure, a single task must include only activities related to a single department: the department to which the employee performing that task is assigned. Further, if for reasons of economy in the use of personnel, a single task must be limited to a range of activities requiring only a restricted number of skills and processes (e.g., clerical skills and processes), then the task partitioning must be subpartitioning of *both* the departmental and process partitionings. It may well happen that the most efficient task partitioning that satisfies these two constraints is not by any means the most efficient of all possible task partitionings. That is to say, it might be more efficient, if it were only feasible, to combine steno-graphic activities from one department with those from another into a single task; or it might be efficient to define a task requiring skill in both medicine and legal analysis. The constraints forbid combinations of these sorts.

The constraints on combining activities into tasks are likely to be most significant when the total number of activities is small relative to the range of different purposes and processes, for then it will be impossible to group activities into full-time tasks preserving similarity of both purpose and process. Hence, in small organizations, purpose departmentalization, by interfering with process specialization, can lead to serious inefficiencies; while in large organizations it may be possible to introduce process specializations as subdivisions of the purpose departmentalization, and hence to preserve the important complementarities.

These propositions have been made in common-sense terms by Gulick (Gulick & Urwick, 1937) and others:

> First [organization by major process] . . . by bringing together in a single office a large amount of each kind of work (technologically measured), makes it possible in each case to make use of the most effective divisions of work and specialization.

Second, it makes possible also the economies of the maximum use of labor saving machinery and mass production. These economies arise not from the total mass of the work to be performed, not from the fact that the work performed serves the same general purpose but from the fact that the work is performed with the same machine, with the same technique, with the same motions. (p. 23)

... there is danger that an organization erected on the basis of purpose will fail to make use of the most up-to-date technical devices and specialists because ... there may not be enough work of a given technical sort to permit efficient subdivision. (p. 22)

Is there any advantage in placing specialized services like private secretaries or filing in [process departments]? In a very small organization, yes; in a large organization, no. In a small organization, where there is not a full-time job on some days for each secretary, it is better to have a central secretarial pool than to have a private secretary for each man. In a large organization, the reverse is true. (p. 20)

A study of the mathematical structure of the assignment problem suggests that there is little to be hoped for in the way of global generalizations beyond the propositions, just stated, that are already to be found in the nonmathematical literature on the subject. Task allocations will be efficient to the extent that they are based upon similarities in activities that are recognized as yielding important complementarities in task performance. These are what we generally mean by "process" similarities.

A serious limitation of the theory is that there is apparently no way of recognizing process similarities in general, except through the complementarities associated with them. Hence, propositions like "with low work volume, organization by process is efficient" are largely tautological. At best, they instruct us to search for possible complementarities of activities as a basis for grouping.

Beyond this point, solution of the assignment problem requires specific empirical knowledge of the specific empirical complementarities that exist – e.g. the structure of human skills and machine capacities – an obvious point that is not always made clear in the discussion of recommendations for organizational structure.

Generalization: coordination problems

One peculiar characteristic of the assignment problem, and of all the formalizations of the departmentalization problem in classical organization theory, is that, if taken literally, problems of coordination are eliminated. Since the whole set of activities to be performed is specified in advance, once these are allocated to organization units and individuals the organization problem posed by these formal theories is solved.

Of course, writers on organization theory are aware that coordination is a highly significant problem. Our point is simply that this problem is absent from the formal models, and hence that the formal models depart widely from what is asserted in a common-sense way about organizations. As is often the case, common sense appears to be more relevant to the real-world phenomena than do the models. To fill this gap between formal theory and wisdom, we need a framework that recognizes that the set of activities to be performed is not given in advance, except in a most general way – that one of the very important processes in organizations is the elaboration of this set of activities, and the determination of which precise activities are to be performed at which precise times and places.

We will introduce this generalization in two stages: only the first of the two will be examined in any detail in this chapter. The first generalization is that the activities of the organization may belong to well-defined, highly routine types, but the occasion for the performance of any particular activity may depend on environmental stimuli – "instructions," "information," and what not. Thus, automobiles are produced on the assembly line in an exceptionally routine way, yet there are all sorts of contingencies to be settled in each case, such as body style, color, and motor type.

The second generalization, to be considered at length in chapters 6 and 7, recognizes that often not even the *contingent* program of activities is given in advance; that, in fact, one of the important activities that goes on in organizations is the development of programs for new activities that need to be routinized for day-to-day performance.

Let us return to the first stage of generalization. Behavior in the organization is not determined in advance and once for all by a detailed blueprint and schedule. Even if it is highly routinized, the routine has the character of a strategy rather than a fixed program. Specific activities are performed in response to signals and stimuli of one sort or another. Moreover, the appropriateness of particular activities is invariably dependent, frequently to a very important extent, upon the time of performance. There may be a standard job ticket giving detailed specifications for producing a particular product in a factory, but this job ticket becomes a program for human (and machine) behavior only when an order is received for that product and when the order has been scheduled for production.

We can describe such a routinized organization in a static way in terms of the kinds of activities that are performed from time to time, but this is very different from describing the actual set of activities, with the time subscripts attached. It is because activities are conditional, and not fixed in advance, that problems of organization, over and above the assignment problem, arise. For convenience, we may make the following specifications, without interpreting them too strictly:

(a) the times of occurrence of activities may be conditional on events external to the organization or events internal to the organization;
(b) the appropriateness of a particular activity may be conditional on what other activities are being performed in various parts of the organization;
(c) an activity elaborated in response to one particular function or goal may have consequences for other functions or goals.

As far as we are aware, no one has constructed a formal model of the departmentalization problem that takes account of the contingent character of activities. Let us sketch out briefly what such a model would look like, and then return to the common-sense propositions about organization that are related to this model.

In the revised model of departmentalization, the roster of kinds of activities (i.e., the whole set of job specifications, formulas, blueprints of standard products, standard operating procedures, etc.) is given in advance, together with a large number of conditional statements that specify the conditions under which each activity will be performed.

If all the conditions on which activity is contingent refer to the external environment, then we return to the assignment problem in a new form. In this case, specific activities are not assigned to departments, but conditional responsibilities for performance. Tasks are described either in terms of these conditional statements, or in terms of the probability distributions of activities that will in fact occur. The condition in the assignment problem that a task should represent not more than a day's work becomes a condition that the expected average amount of time required, or the time required *at most*, in any given period, should not exceed a day's work. These concepts of average load or maximum load again permit us to define a time function on each possible set of activities, and to go through with the solution of the assignment problem.

If some activities are conditional *on other activities*, the situation becomes more complicated. To handle this complication, we must introduce as variables determinants of the ease and accuracy of communication (e.g., communication is easy within a professional group, difficult across professional lines; communication is easy along lines of the formal hierarchy, difficult across such lines, etc.). Ease and accuracy of communication may depend upon both motivational and cognitive factors.

The problem of arranging the signalling system for interdependent conditional activities is the coordination problem. Here is a simple example: If hiring is done by the personnel department, then this department must be informed when there is a vacancy, and what kinds of skills are required for the position. Its hiring activities will vary accordingly. (Of course, if the roster of activities is sufficiently detailed, the "what kind" can always be turned into a "when.")

When two organizational plans – two allocations of tasks – are compared in terms of this model, one of the central variables is the degree of *self-containment* of the several organization units (Simon, Smithburg, and Thompson, 1950, pp. 266–7). A unit is self-contained to the extent and degree that the conditions for carrying out its activities are independent of what is done in the other organization units. If there are time costs associated with the coordination, then these costs must be balanced against the time costs associated with lack of complete process specialization. This proposition has often been made in the classical literature, as the following passages from Gulick (Gulick and Urwick, 1937) indicate:

The advantages of [organization by purpose] are three: first, it makes more certain the accomplishment of any given broad purpose or project by bringing the whole job under a single director with immediate control of all the experts, agencies and services which are required in the performance of the work. No one can interfere. The director does not have to wait for others, nor negotiate for their help and co-operation; nor appeal to the chief executive to untangle a conflict. He can devote all his energies to getting on with the job. (p. 22)

These are the major advantages of organization on the basis of process. There are, of course, offsetting difficulties . . . (p. 24)

And finally, the necessity of effective co-ordination is greatly increased. Purpose departments must be co-ordinated so that they will not conflict but will work shoulder to shoulder. But whether they do or do not, the individual major purposes will be accomplished to a considerable extent and a failure in any service is limited in its effect to that service. Process departments must be co-ordinated not only to prevent conflict, but also to guarantee positive co-operation. They work hand in hand. They must also time their work so that it will fit together, a factor of lesser significance in the purpose departments. A failure in one process affects the whole enterprise, and a failure to co-ordinate one process division, may destroy the effectiveness of all the work that is being done. (p. 24)

The significance of self-containment as an organizational variable has been examined by Ely Devons (1950) in the context of British wartime administration, and by Marschak and Radner (1954) and Marschak (1955) in a formal model of optimal decision-making in teams.

The problem of departmentalization that emerges out of this section and the previous one centers on two variables: self-containment (or, alternatively, coordination requirements), and skill specialization. Its central proposition is that the forms of departmentalization that are advantageous in terms of one of these outcomes are often costly in terms of the other: Process departmentalization generally takes greater advantage of the potentialities for economy through specialization than does purpose departmentalization; purpose departmentalization leads to greater self-containment and lower coordination costs than does process departmentalization. As size of organization increases, the marginal advantages accruing to process organization from the first source become smaller, while the coordination costs become larger. Hence, the balance of net efficiency shifts from process to purpose organization as the size of organization increases.

In conclusion, we repeat that the schemes we have described in this section and the previous one leave out of account the dynamics of program elaboration – the processes of developing new activities and programs of activities where these have not existed before. The more general model that encompasses these factors takes us pretty much beyond the limits of classical organization theory, at least insofar as that theory has been formalized.

How administrative management theory views organization members

Before we leave the classical theory, we wish to comment on the way in which organization members are viewed in that theory. First, in general there is a tendency to view the employee as an inert instrument performing the tasks assigned to him. Second, there is a tendency to view personnel as a given rather than as a variable in the system.

Although there are some exceptions in the literature, the grand theories of organizational structure have largely ignored factors associated with individual behavior and particularly its motivational bases. As a result, many of the observations made about the physiological organization theories apply here also.

The tendency to take the set of persons functioning in the organization as an initial condition rather than a variable also conceals some important aspects of behavior in organizations. This assumption of fixed personnel may be removed even in dealing with the assignment problem. We can treat the capacities of persons and machines to perform the specified activities [and hence the function $t(S)$] as variables that depend on what persons and machines are employed, and how the employees are trained. This will introduce such questions as the "investment" cost associated with the performance characteristics of the persons and machines.

2.3 Operational and Empirical Problems of Classical Administrative Science

Thus far, our primary focus has been on the mode of problem formulation in the classical school. Some comments are also necessary regarding the meaningfulness and validity of the major propositions that have been proposed. In an earlier work, Simon (1947, Chap. 2) has discussed in some detail a number of the problems connected with making the propositions in organization theory operational. Consequently, we will limit our present attention to a pair of examples that seem to us to illustrate the range of problems involved.

Principles of organization

We consider first the so-called "principles of organization" listed by James D. Mooney in his essay in the Gulick-Urwick volume of 1937. Mooney specifies five "principles": (1) perpendicular coordination, (2) horizontal coordination, (3) leadership, (4) delegation, and (5) authority. What is distinctly unclear from his presentation, however, is precisely what a "principle" is. Among other things, it is "fundamental," "essential," "inevitable," and "universal." Literally, in his exposition, each principle is essentially a word or at most a word with one qualifier, the distinctive feature of which is that it is italicized in print.

Mooney never makes clear whether his "principles" are action recommendations or definitions. Perhaps the most charitable interpretation is that a principle is a phenomenon or state of affairs that is (empirically) observed to be present whenever an organization is observed. From Mooney's point of view, however, it then becomes necessary to define some independent specifications of what is meant by an "organization" so that the principles do not become simply a part of the definition of an organization. Since this is not done with any consistency, the Mooney essay and other similar essays tend to become empirically vacuous.

Theory of departmentalization

Our second example is less transparent and, consequently, raises more interesting problems. In Gulick's theory of departmentalization, the independent variable is the mode of grouping work in the organization. Gulick (Gulick and Urwick, 1937) proposes the following values for this variable, i.e., the following alternative ways of grouping work: (a) by purpose, (b) by process, (c) by clientele, (d) by place, (e) by time. In most classifications in writings on business administration the same values are used, but with the substitution of (a) product for (a) purpose.

The observational problem posed by Gulick's theory is this: How do we determine which of these bases of departmentalization characterizes a particular organization? To consider the problem in its simplest form we take into account only the formal organizational hierarchy and we assume that there is formal unity of command, so that any one employee can belong to only one department.

Under one set of assumptions, the problem is not difficult. Suppose that we are given (a) a complete list of the tasks performed in the organization: and (b) a map of the means–ends relations of the individual tasks to the organizational purpose. Then, we will call the organization a "purpose" organization if the separate departments correspond to separate subgraphs of the means-ends graph. To distinguish among "process," "clientele," "place," and "time" departmentalization we must define what we mean by similarity with respect to these variables. Place and time are relatively simple; perhaps clientele is also. Similarity of process appears to mean similarity with respect to skills employed, knowledge employed, information employed, and equipment employed. Hence, to classify activities by process, we need a whole series of propositions with respect to what kinds of "similarities" are relevant.

The problem of determining what is in fact the basis of departmentalization becomes more difficult if we are not given in advance a map of the means–ends hierarchy. In this case, we first have to construct this map before we can distinguish purpose from process specialization. Moreover, unless the map thus constructed is unique, or substantially so, the form of departmentalization will be ambiguous. In what sense does a unique means-ends map of a set of tasks exist?

Logical sense   It might be possible to show that there is only one logically consistent way of analyzing the means-ends connections of a set of activities. Unfortunately, this is almost certainly not the case. In general, means are sufficient, but not necessary, sets of activities for achieving goals. Hence, a priori logical analysis is inadequate for discovering a unique means-ends map.

Physical sense   The world may be so constructed that there are in fact (not by logical necessity) only a few ways of reaching any particular objective. This seems to be true of some, but not all, objectives; but we have at least the small consolation that the world appears to be so constructed that the means-ends relations are not nearly as complicated and intertwined as they might be.

Psychosociological sense   Even if the objective task environment does not impose a unique means-ends ordering on activities, limits on human inventive abilities in a particular social environment may accomplish approximately that result. That is, members of a particular culture, faced with the task of skinning a cat, may think of only one of all the possible ways: the particular way that is current in that culture. If ready-made means exist in a culture – so that most tasks are accomplished simply by combining numbers of these – then those cultural givens could be discovered as a starting point for constructing the means-ends map. Discovering the cognitive means-ends maps would perhaps require nothing more sophisticated than questions like: "Why do you . . . ?" or "How do you . . . ?" or possibly observations of behavior.

Our point is not merely that it is no trivial matter to determine what the means-ends map is in a particular situation. What is more important is that none of the classical literature even raises this problem or regards its solution as essential to the empirical testing of its propositions. It is not surprising that, as a consequence, the propositions have received very little testing indeed.

Empirical tests of theory

Perhaps the most critical failure of classical administrative science is that it does not confront theory with evidence. In part, this is a consequence of the difficulties of operationalism mentioned above. The theories tend to dissolve when put into testable form. This, however, does not account completely for the neglect of empirical work. As workers in the same general area, we must share the onus of blame for the paucity of empirical evidence that we observe surrounding the "practical" recommendations of administrative theorists. The facts are clear and will, we fear, become somewhat clearer when we return to the "grand questions" in the later sections of the present volume.

2.4   Conclusion

These brief surveys of physiological organization theory and classical administrative science have been designed more to point out the important limitations and the broad empirical and formal needs of the theories than to indicate in any detail their applications. With respect to the empirical needs of the physiological group, a more useful statement of the constraints on simple muscular activity by humans will probably come from laboratory studies of fatigue, coordination, and speed of human subjects engaged in physical tasks. The greatest need of the same group appears to be to estimate the form of the crucial functions that underlie the hypotheses or rules of thumb found in the literature.

In the case of classical administrative science, the problems of making operational the definitions of key variables and of providing empirical verification for those propositions that can be made operational seem particularly pressing.

As for the limitations, we have mentioned five basic ones: (1) The motivational assumptions underlying the theories are incomplete and consequently inaccurate. (2) There is little appreciation of the role of intraorganizational conflict of interests in defining limits of organizational behavior. (3) The constraints placed on the human being by his limitations as a complex information-processing system are given little consideration. (4) Little attention is given to the role of cognition in task identification and classification as well as in decision. (5) The phenomenon of program elaboration receives little emphasis.

Paired with each of these limitations in the classical approach to scientific management is a body of research and theory that has developed in recent years. In the chapters that follow we propose to explore present knowledge about the motivational, conflict of interest, cognitive, and computational constraints that human beings place on organizations. In the course of that discussion we hope to make clear why we consider classical organization theory to represent only a quite small part of the total theory relevant to organizational behavior.

3

Motivational Constraints: Intraorganizational Decisions

In chapter 2 we saw that traditional organization theory views the human organism as a simple machine. In this model, leaders are limited in their achievement of organization goals only by the constraints imposed by the capacities, speeds, durabilities, and costs of these simple "machines." The problems the theory attacks and the solutions it proposes focus on these constraints.

The postulates of the traditional theory, explicit and implicit, amount to rather severe assumptions about the environment of an individual in an organization, the impact of that environment on him, and his response to it. The environment is viewed as a well-defined stimulus or system of stimuli. Each such stimulus (e.g., an administrative order) evokes in the individual to whom it is directed a well-defined and predictable psychological set. The set that is evoked by the stimulus includes a program for generating a specified behavioral response – the response that is "appropriate" to the stimulus in question. Hence, there exists in any organization a repertoire of response programs; there is a unique stimulus or cue for each such program; and when the stimulus occurs, it induces that response and only that response.

In the present chapter, we consider the unanticipated consequences of treating an organization as though it were composed of such machines. This does not mean that the "classical" theory is totally wrong or needs to be totally displaced. It means that under certain circumstances, which we will try to specify, dealing with an organization as a simple mechanism produces outcomes unanticipated by the classical theory.

3.1   Influence Processes

Basically, our predictions of these additional phenomena and departures from the classical theory will be derived from a simple model of influence processes in organizations. We begin by sketching briefly the influence theory we shall use (March, 1955a; Simon, 1955). As in chapter 1, we will speak of the "stimuli" that impinge on the individual, of the psychological "set" or "frame of reference" that is evoked by these stimuli, and of the "response" or "action" that results.

A stimulus may have unanticipated consequences because it evokes a *larger* set than was expected, or because the set evoked is *different* from that expected. At the extreme, the evoked set may not even include the reaction to the stimulus that was intended. This is perhaps rare. The more usual problem is that the organism has a rich network of associations with any given element that is evoked. A single cue evokes a large number of possible responses, a large number of expectations of their consequences, and a large number of attitudes, preferences, evaluations of those consequences.

A second difficulty is that the stimulus itself may include elements not intended by the organization hierarchy when providing it. The participant who is to respond to the stimulus situation may see cues that were not deliberately placed there. As a simple example, he may respond to the tone of voice in which an order is given as well as to its content. When this happens, the set evoked by the stimulus situation will again be larger than, and different from, that anticipated; and the response will be correspondingly unexpected.

A third difficulty arises because the individual who is supposed to respond to a stimulus mistakes it for another – because he discriminates inadequately between them – or simply does not respond at all because the stimulus does not define the situation for him completely. In these cases, through lack of experience or training, the set evoked by a stimulus is actually smaller than that desired.

These "pathological" processes – the evocation of unanticipated associations, the unanticipated provision of stimuli, and failures of stimuli to evoke the anticipated set – underlie the phenomena we shall discuss in this chapter. Hence, the problems discussed here partly stem from, and are aggravated by, the use of the "machine" model by the organizational hierarchy in governing its own behavior. We shall be interested particularly in how these unanticipated consequences restrict the adaptiveness of the organization to the goals of the top administrative hierarchy. This interest will lead us to consider the direction and control of large-scale bureaucratic organizations, problems of morale, and the relation between morale and productivity. We shall see that there exist in these areas at least some empirical data for testing hypotheses about the unanticipated consequences of treating employees in terms of the simple "machine" model.

3.2   Theories of Bureaucracy

Modern studies of "bureaucracies" date from Weber (1946, 1947) as to both time and acknowledged intellectual debt. But, in a sense, Weber belongs more to the preceding chapter than he does to the present one. His major interests in the study of organizations appear to have been four:

1 to identify the characteristics of an entity he labelled "bureaucracy";
2 to describe its growth and the reasons for its growth;
3 to isolate the concomitant social changes;
4 to discover the consequences of bureaucratic organization for the achievement of bureaucratic goals (primarily the goals of a political authority).

It is in the last-named interest that Weber most clearly differentiates himself from the other writers who will be considered here. Weber wishes to show to what extent bureaucratic organization is a rational solution to the complexities of modern problems. More specifically, he wishes to show in what ways bureaucratic organization overcomes the decision-making or "computational" limits of individuals or alternative forms of organization (i.e., through specialization, division of labor, etc.).

Consequently, Weber appears to have more in common with Urwick, Gulick, and others than he does with those who regard themselves as his successors. To be sure, Weber goes beyond the "machine" model in significant ways. In particular, he analyzes in some detail the relation between an official and his office. But, in general, Weber perceives bureaucracy as an adaptive device for using specialized skills, and he is not exceptionally attentive to the character of the human organism.

When we turn from Weber to the more recent students of bureaucracy, however, we find them paying increasing attention to the "unanticipated" responses of the organization members (Merton, 1936; Gouldner, 1957). Without denying Weber's essential proposition that bureaucracies are more efficient (with respect to the goals of the formal hierarchy) than are alternative forms of organization, the research and analyses of Merton (1940), Selznick (1949), and Gouldner (1954) have suggested important dysfunctional consequences of bureaucratic organization. In addition – explicitly in the case of Gouldner and implicitly in the other two authors – they have hypothesized that the unintended consequences of treating individuals as machines actually encourage a continued use of the "machine" model.

The general structure of the theoretical systems of all three writers is remarkably similar. They use as the basic independent variable some form of organization or organizational procedure designed to control the activities of the organization members. These procedures are based primarily on what we have called the "machine" model of human behavior. They are shown to have the consequences anticipated by the organizational leaders, but also to have other, unanticipated, consequences. In turn, these consequences reinforce the tendency to use the control device. Thus, the systems may be depicted as in figure 3.1.

The several systems examined here posit different sets of variables and theoretical relations. However, their structures are sufficiently similar to suggest that these studies in "bureaucracy" belong to a single class of theories.

The Merton model

Merton (1940) is concerned with dysfunctional organizational learning: organization members generalize a response from situations where the response is appropriate to similar situations where it results in consequences unanticipated and undesired by the organization. Merton asserts that changes in the personality of individual members of the organization stem from factors in the organizational structure. Here personality refers to any fairly reliable connection between certain stimuli and the characteristic responses to them. The label "person-

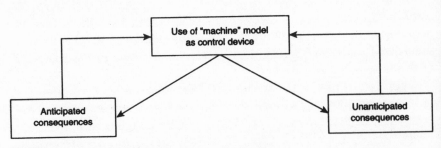

Figure 3.1 The general bureaucracy model.

ality" is attached to such a response pattern when the pattern does not change easily or rapidly.

Merton's system of propositions begins with a *demand for control* (3.1) made on the organization by the top hierarchy. This demand takes the form of an increased *emphasis on the reliability of behavior* (3.2) within the organization [3.2:3.1].* From the point of view of the top hierarchy, this represents a need for accountability and predictability of behavior. The techniques used to secure reliability draw upon what has been called here the "machine" model of human behavior. Standard operating procedures are instituted, and control consists largely in checking to ensure that these procedures are, in fact, followed.

Three consequences follow from this emphasis on reliability in behavior and the techniques used to install it:

1. There is a reduction in the *amount of personalized relationships* (3.3) [3.3:3.2]. The bureaucracy is a set of relationships between offices, or roles. The official reacts to other members of the organization not as more or less unique individuals but as representatives of positions that have specified rights and duties. Competition within the organization occurs within closely defined limits; evaluation and promotion are relatively independent of individual achievement (e.g., promotion by seniority).

2. *Internalization of the rules of the organization* (3.4) by the participants is increased [3.4:3.2]. Rules originally devised to achieve organizational goals assume a positive value that is independent of the organizational goals. However, it is important to distinguish two phenomena, both of which have been called the "displacement of goals." In one case, a given stimulus evokes an activity perceived as leading to a preferred state of affairs. In a series of such situations, the repeated choice of the acceptable alternative causes a gradual transfer of the preference from the final state of affairs to the instrumental activity. In the other case, the choice of a desired alternative reveals additional desirable consequences not originally anticpated. The instrumental activity has, therefore, positively valued consequences even when it does not have the originally anticipated outcomes. It is this latter phenomenon (secondary reinforcement) that is operating in the present situation: the organizational setting brings about new personal or subunit consequences through participation in organizationally motivated actions.

---

*See pp. 27–8 for an explanation of the numbering system used for the propositions.

3. There is increased *use of categorization as a decision-making technique* (3.5) [3.5:3.2]. To be sure, categorizing is a basic part of thinking in any situation. The special feature involved here is a tendency to restrict the categories used to a relatively small number and to enforce the first formally applicable category rather than search for the possible categories that might be applied and choose among them. An increase in the use of categorization for decision-making decreases the *amount of search for alternatives* (3.6) [3.6:3.5].

The reduction in personalized relationships, the increased internalization of rules, and the decreased search for alternatives combine to make the behavior of members of the organization highly predictable; i.e., they result in an increase in the *rigidity of behavior* (3.7) of participants [3.7:3.3, 3.4, 3.6]. At the same time, the reduction in personalized relationships (particularly with respect to internal competition) facilitates the development of an *esprit de corps*, i.e., increases the *extent to which goals are perceived as shared among members of the group* (3.8) [3.8:3.3]. Such a sense of commonness of purpose, interests, and character increases the *propensity of organization members to defend each other against outside pressures* (3.9) [3.9:3.8]. This, in turn, solidifies the tendency toward rigid behavior [3.7:3.9].

The rigidity of behavior has three major consequences. First, it substantially satisfies the original demands for reliability [3.2:3.7]. Thus, it meets an important maintenance need of the system. Further needs of this sort are met by strengthening in-group identification, as previously mentioned [3.2:3.8]. Second, it increases the *defensibility of individual action* (3.10) [3.10:3.7]. Simple categories rigorously applied to individual cases without regard for personal features can only be challenged at a higher level of the hierarchy. Third, the rigidity of behavior increases the *amount of difficulty with clients* (3.11) of the organization [3.11:3.7] and complicates the achievement of client satisfaction – a near-universal organizational goal. Difficulty with clients is further increased by an increase in the *extent of use of trappings of authority* (3.12) by subordinates in the organization [3.11:3.12], a procedure that is encouraged by the in-group's defensiveness [3.12:3.9].

The maintenance of part of the system by the techniques previously outlined produces a continuing pressure to maintain these techniques, as would be anticipated. It is somewhat more difficult to explain why the organization would continue to apply the same techniques in the face of client dissatisfaction. Why do organizational members fail to behave in each case in a manner appropriate to the situation? For the answer one must extend Merton's explicit statements by providing at least one, and perhaps two, additional feedback loops in the system. (It is not enough to say that such behavior becomes a part of the "personality." One must offer some explanation of why this apparently maladaptive learning takes place.)

The second major consequence of rigidity in behavior mentioned above (increased defensibility of individual action) is a deterrent to discrimination that reinforces the emphasis on reliability of behavior [3.2:3.10]. In addition, client dissatisfaction may in itself reinforce rigidity. On the one hand, client pressure at lower levels in the hierarchy tends to increase the *felt need for the defensibility of individual action* (3.13) [3.13:3.11]. On the other hand, remedial action demanded by clients from higher officials in the hierarchy may be misdirected. To the extent to which clients perceive themselves as being victims of discrimination (a perception that is facilitated in American culture by the importance attached to "equal treatment"), the proposals of clients or of the officials to whom they complain will probably strengthen the emphasis on reliability of behavior. This conflict between "service" and "impartiality" as goals for public organizations seems to lie behind a good deal of the literature on public bureaucracies.

We see that Merton's model is a rather complex set of relations among a relatively large number of variables. A simplified version of the model, designed to illustrate its major features, is provided in figure 3.2.

The Selznick model

Where Merton emphasizes rules as a response to the demand for control, Selznick (1949) emphasizes the delegation of authority. Like Merton, however, Selznick wishes to show how the use of a control technique (i.e., delegation) brings about a series of unanticipated consequences. Also, like Merton, Selznick shows how these consequences stem from the problems of maintaining highly interrelated systems of interpersonal relations.

Selznick's model starts with the demand for control made by the top hierarchy. As a result of this demand, an increased *delegation of authority* (3.14) is instituted [3.14:3.1].

Delegation, however, has several immediate consequences. As intended, it increases the *amount of training in specialized competences* (3.15) [3.15:3.14]. Restriction of attention to a relatively small number of problems increases experience within these limited areas and

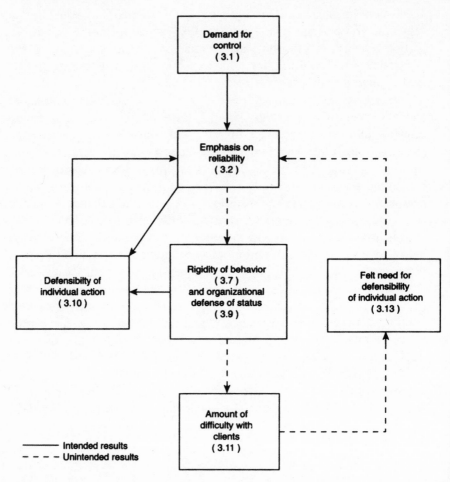

Figure 3.2 The simplified Merton model.

improves the employee's ability to deal with these problems. Operating through this mechanism, delegation tends to decrease the *difference between organizational goals and achievement* (3.16) [3.16:3.15], and thus to stimulate more delegation [3.14:3.16]. At the same time, however, delegation results in departmentalization and an increase in the *bifurcation of interests* (3.17) among the subunits in the organization [3.17:3.14]. The maintenance needs of the subunits dictate a commitment to the subunit goals over and above their contribution to the total organizational program. Many individual needs depend on the continued success and even expansion of the subunit. As in the previous example, the activities originally evaluated in terms of the organization goals are seen to have additional important ramifications for the subunits.

Bifurcation of interests is also stimulated by the specialized training that delegation (intendedly) produces. Training results in increased competence and, therefore, in increased *cost of changing personnel* (3.18) [3.18:3.15] and this results, in turn, in further differentiation of subunit goals [3.17:3.18].

The bifurcation within the organization leads to increased *conflict among organizational subunits* (3.19) [3.19:3.17]. As a consequence, the *content of decisions* (3.20) made within the organization depends increasingly upon considerations of internal strategy, particularly if there is little *internalization of organizational goals by participants* (3.21) [3.20:3.19, 3.21]. As a result there is an increase in the difference between organizational goals and achievement [3.16:3.20] and this results in an increase in delegation [3.14:3.16]. (The general subject of intraorganizational conflict is discussed in chapter 5.)

This effect on daily decisions is accentuated by two other mechanisms in Selznick's system. The struggle for internal control not only affects directly the content of decisions, but also causes greater *elaboration of subunit ideologies* (3.22) [3.22:3.19]. Each subunit seeks success by fitting its policy into the official doctrine of the large organization to legitimize its demands. Such a tactic increases the *internalization of subgoals by participants* (3.23) within subunits [3.23:3.22].

At the same time, the internalization of subgoals is reinforced by a feedback from the daily decisions it influences. The necessity for making daily decisions creates a system of precedents. Decisions depend primarily on the operational criteria provided by the organization, and, among these criteria, subunit goals are of considerable importance [3.20:3.23]. Precedents tend to become habitual responses to the situations for which they are defined as relevant and thus to reinforce the internalization of subunit goals [3.23:3.20]. Obviously, internalization of subgoals is partially dependent on the *operationality of organizational goals* (3.24). By operationality of goals, we mean the extent to which it is possible to observe and test how well goals are being achieved. Variations in the operationality of organizational goals affect the content of daily decisions [3.20:3.24] and thus the extent of subunit goal internalization.

From this it is clear that delegation has both functional and dysfunctional consequences for the achievement of organizational goals. It contributes both to their realization and to their deflection. Surprisingly, the theory postulates that both increases and decreases in goal achievement cause an increase in delegation. Why does not normal learning occur here? The answer seems to be that when goals are not achieved, delegation is – within the framework of the "machine" model – the correct response, and the model does not consider alternatives to simple delegation. On the other hand, the model offers explicity at least two "dampers" that limit the operation of the dysfunctional mechanisms. As is indicated in figure 3.3, where the skeleton of the Selznick model is outlined, there are two (not entirely independent) variables treated as independent but potentially amenable to organizational control, each of which restrains the runaway features of daily decision-making. By suitable changes in the extent to which organizational goals are operational or in the internalization of organizational goals by participants, some of the dysfunctional effects of delegation can be reduced. (To be sure, this ignores the possible effect of such procedures on the maintenance problems of the subunits and the consequent results for the larger organizations, but these are problems we are not prepared to attack at the moment.)

The Gouldner model

In terms of the number of variables and relations, Gouldner's model (1954) is the simplest of the three presented here; but it exhibits the major features of the two previous systems. Like Merton, Gouldner is concerned with the consequences of bureaucratic rules for the maintenance of organization structure. Like both Merton and Selznick, he attempts to show how a control technique designed to maintain the equilibrium of a subsystem disturbs the equilibrium of a larger system, with a subsequent feedback on the subsystem.

In Gouldner's system, the *use of general and impersonal rules* (3.25) regulating work procedures is part of the response to the demand for control from the top hierarchy [3.25:3.1]. One consequence of such rules is to decrease the *visibility of power relations* (3.26) within the group [3.26:3.25]. The visibility of authority differences within the work group interacts with the *extent to which equality norms are held* (3.27) to affect the *legitimacy of the supervisory role* (3.28) [3.28:3.26, 3.27]. This, in turn, affects the *levels of interpersonal tension* (3.29) in the work group [3.29:3.28]. In the American culture of egalitarian norms, decreases in power visibility increase the legitimacy of the supervisory position and therefore decrease tension within the group.

Gouldner argues that these anticipated consequences of rule-making do occur, that the survival of the work group as an operating unit is

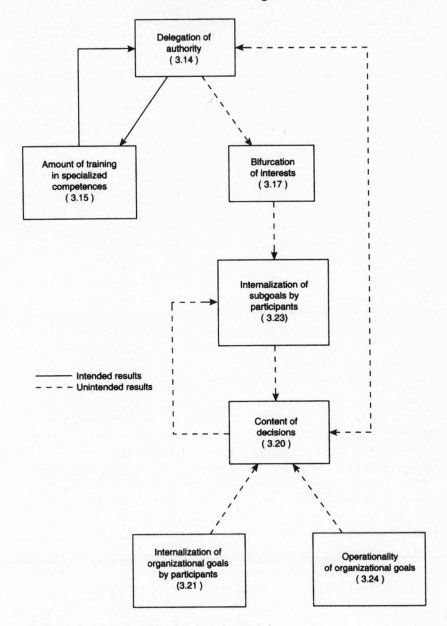

Figure 3.3 The simplified Selznick model.

substantially furthered by the creation of general rules, and that consequently the use of such rules is reinforced [3.25:3.29].

At the same time, however, work rules provide cues for organizational members beyond those intended by the authority figures in the organization. Specifically, by defining unacceptable behavior, they increase *knowledge about minimum acceptable behavior* (3.30) [3.30:3.25]. In conjunction with a low level of internalization of organizational goals, specifying a minimum level of permissible behavior increases the disparity between organization goals and achievement by depressing behavior to the minimum level [3.16:3.21, 3.30].

Performance at the minimum level is perceived by hierarchical superiors as a failure. In short, the internal stabilizing effects of the rules are matched by the unbalance they produce in the larger organization. The response to the unbalance is an increase in the *closeness of supervision* (3.31) over the work group [3.31:3.16]. This response is based on the "machine" model of human behavior: low performance indicates a need for more detailed inspection and control over the operation of the "machine".

In turn, however, close supervision increases the visibility of power relations within the organization [3.26:3.31], raises the tension level in the work group, and thereby upsets the equilibrium originally based on the institution of rules. The broad outline of the model is shown in figure 3.4.

Gouldner's model leaves some puzzles unexplained. In particular, why is increased supervision the supervisory response to low performance? It seems reasonable that the tendency to make such a response is affected both by role perceptions and by a third equilibrating process in the system – the individual needs of the supervisors. Thus, the intensity of supervision is a function of the *authoritarianism* of supervisors (3.32) and a function of the *punitivity of supervisory role perception* (3.33) [3.31:3.32, 3.33].

As in the Selznick model, the existence of "dampers" on the system poses the question of their treatment as external variables. Appropriate manipulation of equality norms, perceived commonality of interest, and the needs of supervisors will restrict the operation of the dysfunctional features of the system. The failure of top management to use such techniques of control suggests that the system may be incompletely defined.

Problems of verification

We have sketched three major "models" of bureaucratic behavior. To

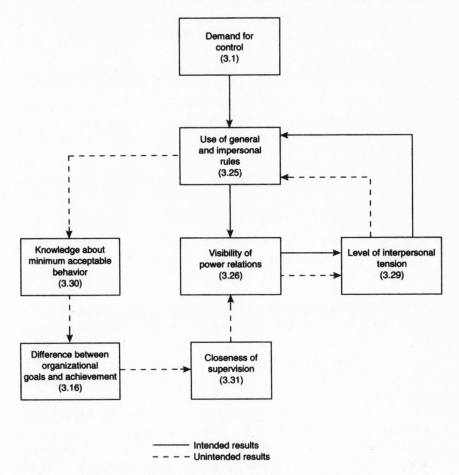

Figure 3.4 The simplified Gouldner model.

what extent are the hypotheses empirically verified? Both Selznick and Gouldner base their propositions on extended observations of single organizations in the field. The data on which Merton relies are somewhat less specific but appear to be distilled from a set of generally accepted characterizations of organizational behavior.

Such evidence raises two major problems. First, what is the role of field research in verifying hypotheses about organizational behavior? The field situation fails to meet many of the major assumptions underlying standard techniques of statistical inference. The second problem is distinctly related to the first. What is the standing of the single case as evidence? For example, one of the knottier complications in this area is deciding what the sample size really is.

At least some of the propositions advanced by these three writers will be re-examined below in different contexts. Some hypotheses relating the closeness of supervision to employee satisfaction are considered later in the present chapter, and some hypotheses concerning organizational conflict can be found in chapter 5. As we will suggest in those passages, there is evidence for some of the propositions over and above the single field studies discussed here. The evidence is scarcely conclusive and far from complete, but on the whole tends to be consistent with the general models used by Merton, Selznick, and Gouldner. What little we can say beyond that is indicated below.

Implications of the bureaucracy models

Other quite comparable models could be added to those examined here. Bendix (1947) has discussed limits on technical rationality within an organization and pointed out the intriguing complications involved in the use of spy systems as systems of control. Dubin (1949) has presented a model quite similar to that of Merton. Blau (1955) has examined the changes in operating procedures that occur at a relatively low level in the hierarchy under the pressure of work group needs.

In the sample of three cases from the "bureaucracy" literature we have presented (as well as in the others mentioned), complications arise in each of the three ways predicted from the influence model outlined previously. The elaboration of evoking connections, the presence of unintended cues, and organizationally dysfunctional learning appear to account for most of the unanticipated consequences with which these theories deal.

Many of the central problems for the analysis of human behavior in large-scale organizations stem from the operation of subsystems within the total organizational structure. The sociological studies of the work group analyzed here have focused on the ways in which the needs of individuals, the primary work group, and the large organization interact to affect each other. We now turn to the study of morale and productivity, where we also find that the study of the psychology of work has focused on the same interactions, with perhaps a greater emphasis on the relations between the needs of individual personalities and the needs of the organization.

3.3 Satisfaction and Productivity

Few aspects of organizational behavior have been subject to as much speculation as have morale, productivity, and turnover. They are obviously important to the operating executive's day-to-day operations. Indeed, if we accept the economist's characterization of the administrator, productivity is one of the fundamental secondary criteria (after profit) for his success. At the same time, propositions relating such achievement variables as productivity to the characteristics of the organization are basic to the student of organizations.

The model of individual behavior implicit in the "traditional" approach to productivity recognizes only those constraints on performance that have obvious machine analogues (Taylor, 1911). To organize efficiently is to define the physiological capacity of the human organism and to program activities to make full use of that capacity. More recently, students of individual behavior in an organizational setting have introduced into the model of organizational behavior a series of concepts like morale, satisfaction, and cohesiveness. Attempts to relate these variables directly to productivity have failed to reveal any consistent, simple relation (Viteles, 1953; Brayfield and Crockett, 1955). High morale is not a sufficient condition for high productivity, and does not necessarily lead to higher productivity than low morale. Somewhat reluctantly, theorists of industrial motivation have come to recognize that present satisfactions are often less important in influencing human behavior than perceived relations between present alternatives and future states.

Hence, it has become increasingly clear that important unanticipated consequences follow when the "machine" model of human organisms is used to stimulate production. It has also become clear that simple theories built on concepts of morale and satisfaction have had little or no success. In the remainder of this chapter we will try to explain why this state of affairs exists and to indicate how the available research data can be used to outline a more adequate theory. In the first part we outline the relation between individual satisfaction and individual productivity, and in the second part we explore the important factors determining individual motivations to produce.

It will be argued in this and the succeeding chapter that there are important differences between two types of decisions by employees. The first is the decision to participate in the organization – or to leave the organization. The second is the decision to produce or to refuse to produce at the rate demanded by the organization hierarchy. The production decision is substantially different from the participation decision in that it evokes a significantly different set [A-3.1]. At least some of the confusion in the literature of morale and satisfaction stems from a failure to distinguish between turnover and productivity.

Consider the following general model:

1 The lower the *satisfaction* (3.34) of the organism, the more *search* for alternative programs (3.35) it will undertake [3.35:3.34].
2 The more search, the higher the *expected value of reward* (3.36) [3.36:3.35].
3 The higher the expected value of reward, the higher the *satisfaction* [3.34:3.36].
4 The higher the expected value of reward, the higher the *level of aspiration* (3.37) of the organism [3.37:3.36].
5 The higher the level of aspiration, the lower the satisfaction [3.34:3.37].

The system is summarized in figure 3.5. With a few additional assumptions, we can translate the model into simple mathematical form. One possible translation goes as follows:

Let S = satisfaction, A = level of aspiration, L = search rate, and R = expected value of reward. The following equations correspond to the set of verbal propositions:

(1) $$\frac{dA}{dt} = \alpha(R - A + a), \qquad \text{where } a > 0, \alpha > 0.$$

This interprets proposition 4 and adds to it an assertion about the

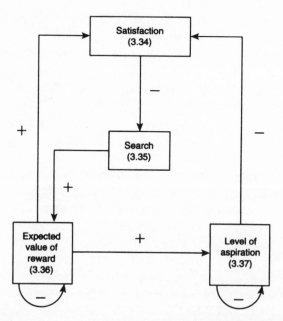

Figure 3.5 General model of adaptive motivated behavior.

dynamic process that leads to equilibrium. Since a is positive, at equilibrium the aspiration level will exceed the reward.

(2) $$S = R - A.$$

This interprets propositions 3 and 5.

(3) $$L = \beta(\bar{S} - S), \qquad \text{where } \bar{S} > 0, \beta > 0.$$

This interprets proposition 1. It also postulates a "desired" level of satisfaction, $\bar{S}$, at which search for increased satisfaction would cease.

(4) $$\frac{dR}{dt} = \gamma(L - b - cR), \qquad \text{where } \gamma > 0, b \geq 0, c > 0.$$

This interprets proposition 2. It postulates that a certain amount of search, $(b + cR)$, is required just to maintain the current level, R, of reward.

This system of equations determines completely the behavior of the dynamic system it describes. The system possesses a stable equilibrium.

Even without the mathematical statement, we can use the model to clarify the relations in which we are interested both in this chapter and in the remainder of the book. Before doing so, however, some qualification is in order.

It is clear that the search behavior specified depends on an underlying belief on the part of the organism that the environment is benign and on the fact that search is usually reasonably effective. By our verbal hypothesis 2, we are alleging that such requirements are, in fact, met. Hypothesis 1 will be true only of organisms that do perceive the world as benign. If the environment is preceived as malevolent and/or barren, search behavior will not necessarily follow from a decrease in satisfaction. Thus, aggression, withdrawal, and regression are certainly observable reactions to dissatisfaction that lead to frustration (Maier, 1949). These "neurotic" reactions are excluded from this model.

Similarly, hypothesis 2 will not be true if search is ineffectual. Ineffective search – cycling, stereotyping, etc. – is an important aspect of human problem-solving that is not included in the present model. Ultimately, we will require a set of hypotheses that deals with the switching from "normal" to "neurotic" reactions and from effective to ineffective search. For the present, we limit ourselves to the "normal" situation on both counts, although some special cases of "abnormalities" have already been considered in the bureaucratic models.

From this simple model of adaptive, motivated behavior we can see why the relation between satisfaction and individual productivity is complex. One would not predict that "satisfied" rats would perform best in a T-maze. Similarly, there is no reason for predicting that high satisfaction, per se, motivates a given individual to conform to the goals specified by the hierarchy.

Suppose a production employee is dissatisfied. We would predict that he would search for alternatives of action. What are the alternatives open to him? A rather large number of alternatives are likely to be evoked in such a situation, and a theory of motivation should specify the conditions under which these various alternatives are evoked. For simplicity, let us focus attention on just three key alternatives.

First, the employee can leave the organization. Some of the factors impinging on a decision to withdraw from the organization are discussed in chapter 4. At the moment, observe only that when satisfaction is low this alternative will frequently be evoked. The probability of accepting this alternative determines voluntary employee turnover.

Second, the employee can conform to the production norms of the organization. Given the system of control in any complex organization, together with the general cultural climate within which an organization operates (at least in the United States), it is hard to imagine a situation in which this alternative is not at least evoked.

Third, the employee can seek opportunities for satisfaction without high production. He may "play politics" in the organization, or he may turn to nonorganizational or suborganizational groups and conform to their norms. These norms may deviate widely from those specified by the organization and may specifically limit production.

We will explore these and other alternatives in greater detail below. We assert that these three general types of alternatives are virtually always evoked and that they provide at least a first approximation to the employee's decision problem. Let us say then that an employee chooses either (1) to leave the organization, or (2) to stay in the organization and produce, or (3) to stay in the organization and not produce [A-3.2]. Since the decision to leave the organization is considered in the next chapter, we will focus our attention at the moment on the decisions to stay inside the organization. Either decision (i.e., to produce or not to produce) can result in rewards that are perceived by the employee to be consequences of his behavior. That is, given either decision, under some conditions the employee will associate positive rewards with the behavior he has chosen; under other conditions the association will be much less strong or he will associate such behavior with outcomes he does not desire.

Individuals frequently perceive the rewards they receive as uncorrelated with their productivity, or as dependent on nonproduction variables and thus uncorrelated or negatively correlated with productive behavior. For example, if an employee operates to restrict productive effort in a manner dictated by subgroup norms and is subsequently rewarded by the subgroup (and without serious penalty from the organization), he will be motivated to restrict output.

From this we may conclude that high satisfaction, per se, is not a particularly good predictor of high production nor does it facilitate production in a causal sense. Motivation to produce stems from a present or anticipated state of discontent and a perception of a direct connection between individual production and a new state of satisfaction.

In this, we have not considered the extent to which high satisfaction facilitates high production, not by the satisfied individual himself but by others in the organization. Such a relation occasionally seems implicit in the literature of industrial relations. However, if there is no direct relation between individual high satisfaction and motivation to produce, it is not enough to show that high or low satisfaction is contagious in an organization. Rather, the theory must specify why and how the satisfaction level of one individual affects the productive habits of another.

Interpersonal factors in the relation between productivity and satisfaction have been too little studied to permit more than speculation. At the moment, psychological research is primarily directed toward "motivation to produce" rather than "productivity." As we shall see, there are important social factors impinging on the former, but current theory does not take account of interaction among persons in organized production except as it directly affects the goals of the individual participant.

3.4   Motivation to Produce

The general model we are proposing for the relation of satisfaction to productivity suggests some critical questions for investigation. Where the environmental reward is relatively constant over a series of "trials" (i.e., choices by the individual members of the organization), the crux of the problem is the choice situation. What alternatives are perceived by the individual? How does he evaluate those alternatives? What consequences does he anticipate as flowing from them? We will argue that the factors affecting motivation to produce – or conformity to the demands of the organizational hierarchy – fit naturally into a theory of influence like the one we have been developing.

The influence model asserts that an individual may be influenced by (1) changing the *values* associated with given states of affairs, (2) changing the *perceived consequences* of an alternative of action, and (3) changing the set of *states of affairs* that are *evoked* (either by changing cues or by changing connections between cues and evoked sets) [A-3.3]. Correspondingly, empirical studies of individual motivations to produce have tended to identify (a) factors relating to the goals of individuals, (b) factors relating to the expectations of consequences, and (c) factors relating to the set of alternatives perceived at the moment of decision.

We start with a basic proposition summarizing these three modes of influence.

• *Motivation to produce* (3.38) is a function of the *character of the evoked set* of alternatives (3.39), the *perceived consequences of evoked alternatives* (3.40), and the *individual goals* (3.41) in terms of which alternatives are evaluated [3.38:3.39, 3.40, 3.41].

If this proposition is accepted as basic to the theory, we must examine in turn each of these factors and see what propositions we can find relating to them.

3.4.1   The Evoked Set of Alternatives

The evocation of alternatives is an important topic in the next chapter, where the decision to participate in (or leave) the organization is discussed. Nevertheless, we must discuss this decision briefly at this point. In particular, we ask: Under what conditions is the alternative of leaving the organization evoked in the individual?

This question has not been examined in any detail in the literature. The most important single factor evoking the alternative of leaving appears to be the objective existence of serious work alternatives (Behrend, 1953). In general, the greater the *objective availability of external alternatives* (3.42), the more likely that such alternatives will be evoked [3.39:3.42]. The mechanisms involved in transforming objective availability into perceived availability are discussed more fully in chapter 4.

The environment, therefore, forms one important source of cues for the participant, but not the only one. He is subject to at least four other types of cues that help determine what set of behavior alternatives will be evoked. First, in a complex organization (particularly a business organization) he is peculiarly receptive to cues from the formal hierarchy. These include both the intended cues – falling under the rubric "control" – and the unintended ones. Second, cues emanate from the task itself. Third, a number of important cues stem from the officially prescribed work rewards. Systems of payment not only influence behavior on the job, but also evoke various behavior alternatives. This is particularly significant when the task is a simple one. Fourth, the individual receives cues from his associates in the organization. The work group itself provides information that often suggests alternatives of action. This may take the form of imitation, as when discontent of others serves as a cue.

Supervisory practices and evocation The effect of supervisory practices on the goals pursued by individual members of the organization is discussed below. A problem associated with this is the relation between supervisory practices and the evoked set of alternatives. Two dimensions of supervisory style that have been explored most fully in the literature will receive particular attention here: participation in decisions and closeness of supervision.

Supervisory styles may be ranged along a continuum: at one extreme, decisions are made by the supervisor and communicated to the workers without prior consultation; at another extreme, decisions are made on the basis of free and equal discussion. If individuals did, in fact, behave in the manner assumed in the "machine" model of human behavior, direct orders from supervisors would preclude the evocation of other alternatives, whereas participation would considerably increase evocation. The fact that the opposite result is observed can be explained in terms of two different mechanisms. On the one hand, there is a widely held cultural norm of independence in decision-making that makes at least *pro forma* participation in decisions a condition for their acceptance without further exploration of alternatives. On the other hand, where there is participation, alternatives are suggested in a setting that permits the organization hierarchy to control (at least in part) what is evoked. "Participative management" can be viewed as a device for permitting management to participate more fully in the making of decisions as well as a means for expanding the influence of lower echelons in the organization. In this respect, it resembles closely the phenomenon of co-optation discussed by Selznick (1949).

Probably both mechanisms are involved. Certainly most studies suggest that the more the *felt participation in decisions* (3.43), the less the visibility of power differences in the organization [3.26:3.43], and that the latter, in turn, lessens the evocation of organizationally disapproved alternatives [3.39:3.26]. This would suggest the reality of the independence norm as a factor. Moreover, most students of the subject argue that (provided the deception is successful) the perception of individual participation in goal-setting is equivalent in many respects to actual participation. Thus, actual influence over the specific decision being made is of less importance to the individual than acknowledgment of his influential position.

At the same time, the second mechanism is also plausible. The greater the amount of felt participation, the greater the *control of the organization* over the evocation of alternatives (3.44) [3.44:3.43]; and therefore, the less the evocation of alternatives undesired by the organization [3.39:3.44].

These results may well depend on the particular type of culture in which most of the studies have been executed, but they seem to have been verified in a number of western countries (Friedman, 1954; Krulee, 1955, Richmond, 1954).

Participation in decision-making is related empirically, although not strictly logically, to another important dimension of supervision that affects the evoked set of alternatives. We can distinguish close and highly specific supervision from supervision that is more general (Katz, Maccoby, Gurin, and Floor, 1951; Katz, Maccoby, and Morse, 1950). If the maintenance of ego and status position is important to individuals, the more detailed the supervision the greater will be the number of alternatives evoked of a nonorganizational character. At the same time, if the instructions given to an employee are so general relative to the *complexity of the task* (3.45) and the *computational ability of the individual* (3.46) that the means of achieving them are vague, serious misdirection can result. Consequently, the effect of the closeness of supervision will depend on the complexity of the task. Where the task to be performed is simple relative to the capabilities of the individual performing it, the more specific the supervisory instructions the greater the evocation of organizationally irrelevant or deleterious alternatives of action; where the task is highly complex relative to the capabilities of the individual, the more specific the supervision the less the evocation of such alternatives [3.39:3.31, 3.45, 3.46].

This proposition has at least some support in the empirical research conducted by the Michigan group. Katz, Maccoby, and Morse (1950) found that in an office situation supervisors of efficient units were more likely to give general rather than close supervision than were supervisors of less efficient units. On the other hand, Katz, Maccoby, Gurin, and Floor (1951) did not find this relation in railroad maintenance sections. The explanation they offer, which is quite consistent with the present hypothesis, has to do with the character of the two tasks and the ability of the railroad section chief to provide important assistance stemming from his technical knowledge (Torrance, 1953; Adams, 1954; Halpin, 1954).

These are the main ways in which supervisory practices have thus far been found to be related to the evoked set. Clearly, there may be other important dimensions of supervisory style as yet unconsidered.

Rewards and evocation   What is the effect, if any, of monetary rewards on the evocation of alternatives? Although the major effect of a change in rewards is to change the estimate of consequences, it is plausible to suppose that there is also some relation with the evoking phenomenon. We hypothesize: the probability that the evoked set of alternatives will include innovations is a function of the type of *incentive scheme* (3.47) used [3.39:3.47]. Innovation is most likely to occur where incentives are tied directly to innovation, next most likely under a system of company-wide incentives, least likely under a system linked to individual productivity.

Individual incentives induce greater individual effort since they are tied to individual activities, but unless they are linked directly to innovation, they do not evoke alternatives that require more than minor organizational or technological changes (Krulee, 1955). The reward system is an attention-centering cue that in the one case defines a broad organizational framework and in the other case a narrower individual one.

It goes without saying that even if this proposition is valid, some knowledge of the character of the task structure is necessary before a specific prediction can be made about the differential effect of the two types of rewards on productivity in a particular organization. Moreover, there is at present no persuasive empirical evidence for the proposition. Despite these reservations, this is both a reasonable and a potentially important hypothesis. Throughout this book it is argued that the factors influencing innovative behavior in an organizational context are among the most important factors for organization theory. In particular, we are concerned with the switching mechanisms by which organization members shift their attention from their more regular concerns to the search for new alternatives.

The work group and evocation Finally, we invoke a proposition relating to contagion within the work group itself. Individual members of the group provide cues (including standards) for each other. In part, however, they also evoke alternatives of action. Norms for production rates evoked in an individual worker tend to reflect the *behavior of adjacent individuals* (3.48) doing the same task [3.39:3.48].

Thus, it has been found (Wyatt, 1934) that workers in a candy-packaging operation changed their production rate according to the rate of their neighboring workers, and that in the case of at least one worker, her removal from the scene produced a substantial change in the total production of the group (Hewitt and Parfit, 1953). Such results lend credence to the evoking phenomenon. Pace-setting is difficult in the absence of external cues. Where several workers are doing essentially the same type of work, the speed of one's neighbor provides one of the best cues available.

These results, however, leave some unresolved problems. If A is B's "environment" as a neighbor, it is equally true that B is A's "environment." If, for example, the production of an individual worker moves toward the mean of his own rate and that of the workers adjacent to him, and if a number of workers are working in a circle, the total production of the group will be independent of their arrangement. Where some other spatial arrangement is used and the positions are not symmetrically disposed, total production will depend on the assignment of individuals to positions in the arrangement. In both cases, however, group members will converge toward equal production in the long run. Since the available empirical data do not clearly distinguish long- and short-run effects of manipulating the arrangement of workers, it is not certain that a model like this fits the actual relations. In particular, there are probably other factors that distinguish high and low producers – possibly including personality differences with respect to susceptibility to contagion.

The hypotheses about the evoked set of alternatives are diagrammed in figure 3.6. In general, they are both simple and not supported by such evidence as to be incontrovertible. However, there is some evidence to support virtually all of the propositions advanced here and they can be taken to represent at least the bare beginnings of a theory of worker motivation that includes evoking phenomena.

3.4.2 The Perceived Consequences of Evoked Alternatives

When a set of action alternatives is evoked, a network of consequences and evaluations is simultaneously evoked; subsequently, the connec-

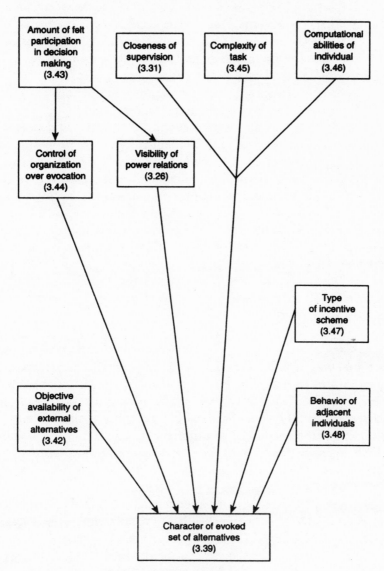

Figure 3.6 Factors affecting the evoked set.

tions relating possible choices to probable outcomes are extended
[A-3.4]. Control over the perception of consequences is one of the
crucial types of influence, and the mechanisms by which individuals
form their expectations of the consequences of action are the foci of
the present discussion.

The environment as a factor   We consider three main types of information used in forming expectations about the consequences of action. First, the external state of the environment (particularly as to potential alternatives) is of importance. Second, the pressures emanating from subgroups in the organization are a critical factor in the individual's expectations of the consequences of production. Third, the reward system specified by the organization defines an important class of consequences of production choices.

As to the effect of the environment on the perceived consequences, we can state an obvious but frequently forgotten proposition: The greater the number of *perceived alternatives to participation* (3.49) available in the external environment, the less important the consequences associated with variations in conformity to organizational demands [3.40:3.49]. The proposition can be used both to explain productivity phenomena and to interpret other related propositions (Goode and Fowler, 1949; Stone, 1952a). For example, there is an obvious relation between the general employment situation and the availability of alternatives. The greater the *number of unemployed workers* (3.50), the fewer the perceived alternatives to participation [3.49:3.50].

Individual characteristics   Next, the number of perceived alternatives is a function of characteristics of the individual. Since these characteristics are considered in the next chapter, we will not review them here. By way of specific example, we observe that perceived ease of movement to other organizations is a function of such factors as the visibility of the individual to other organizations and the visibility of other organizations to him, the propensity of the individual to search for outside alternatives, and the extent of specialization of the individual.

Because the external environment changes relatively slowly its effect on perceptions of consequences has not been given the attention it deserves. As Behrend (1953) has pointed out, it is easy to overemphasize institutional factors in studies of productivity and overlook the effects due to the external labor market. We hypothesize that market conditions are important not only for the unionized (or unionizable) work force but also the supervisory ranks, and perhaps most important for high-level management employees.

Group pressures   A factor more frequently cited as affecting productivity decisions is the pressure of subgroups and extraorganizational groups. Unlike the organisms postulated by the "machine" model of behavior, employees receive physical and emotional sustenance from groups other than the authority figures in the organization. Important consequences of their actions are controlled by subgroups within the organization or groups external to it. For example, an individual's family places constraints on his behavior in the organization (Hoppock, 1935). The precise nature of these constraints requires further investigation, but their existence is fairly well established. Similarly, the impact of the small work group on the motivations of individuals is generally acknowledged and reasonably well documented.

The perceived consequences of alternatives are (in part) a function of the *strength of group pressures* (3.51) and the *direction of group pressures* (3.52) stemming from subgroups and extraorganizational groups [3.40:3.51, 3.52]. We will return to the factors affecting the direction of group pressures later. For the moment, we focus on factors associated with the strength of such pressures on the individual participant.

First, there is the identification mechanism. The stronger the *identification with the group* (3.53), the greater the strength of group pressures [3.51:3.53].

Second, even in the absence of positive identification, the strength of group pressures increases as the *uniformity of group opinion* (3.54) increases [3.51:3.54]. An increase in opinion uniformity reduces the possibility that an individual will receive conflicting direction from the group.

Third, the strength of group pressures increases as the *range of group control over the environment* (3.55) increases [3.51:3.55]. A group that controls a large part of the environment for an individual can exert more pressure on him than can a group that controls only a small part of his environment.

The factors affecting identification with the group are considered below (pp. 83–90). With respect to uniformity of group opinion, we can specify two major mechanisms affecting uniformity. Communication among the members of the group will tend to result in shared opinions. The more *interaction within the group* (3.56), the greater the uniformity of opinion within the group [3.54:3.56]. At the same time, the effectiveness of any given amount of communication within the group is a function of the extent to which members of the group feel needs to stay within the group. Thus, the greater the *cohesiveness of the group* (3.57), the greater the uniformity of group opinion [3.54:3.57].

This small subsystem of variables affecting opinion uniformity is closely related to both the Festinger, Schachter, and Back (1950) and the Homans (1950) models of small-group behavior (Simon, 1952a;

Simon and Guetzkow, 1955a, 1955b). We can specify two major additional propositions within this subsystem. First, the interaction in the group increases as group cohesiveness increases [3.56:3.57]. Second, increases in the uniformity of group opinion result in increases in group cohesiveness [3.57:3.54]. That is, not only does group identification affect the goals of individuals who identify with the group, but also the identification of others with groups affects the strength of group pressures on the individual.

There has been less research on the effects of the extent of the group's control over the environment, but a pair of propositions can be put forth that are at least reasonable. Groups vary in their position in the society, from those with very little power and prestige to those with a great deal of both. Any given group's control over the environment depends on the *amount of intergroup competition* (3.58) for such control. The less intergroup competition, the more control over the environment exercised by a specific group [3.55:3.58]. The power position of the family *vis-à-vis* the infant child or the Communist Party *vis-à-vis* the party member tends to depend heavily on this mechanism for increasing the strength of group pressures.

Group cohesiveness also is positively related to the range of control exercised by the group [3.55:3.57]. The more cohesive the group, the more willing are its members to enforce group demands on the individual. Group cohesiveness restricts intragroup competition that would otherwise weaken the group's control over the individual member.

Although the *effectiveness* of group pressures to uniformity depends substantially on the variables already specified, the *direction* of the pressure is not dependent on these variables. We consider the important factors influencing the direction of group pressures below (see pp. 97–101).

Organizational rewards The state of the environment and the activities of suborganizational and extraorganizational groups are only partially controlled by the organization. Yet the influence they exert on perceived consequences is large. As a result, recent American students of organizational behavior have tended to relegate the explicit reward schemes of management to the background in order to examine some of the other factors we have discussed. However, a model of man that does not give a prominent place to economic incentives is, for most humans, a poor model.

For this reason we introduce here a number of propositions referring to organizational rewards. In particular, we are interested in the consequences anticipated from a decision to restrict production (or increase production). The greater the *dependence of organizational mobility on performance* (3.59), the more favorable are the perceived consequences of increased productivity [3.40:3.59]. An organization with a promotional scheme that essentially rewards seniority will be less productive than one that relates promotion to some index of production (Stone, 1952a). Similarly, we predict a productive advantage for those firms that promote on the basis of productivity over those that promote on the basis of family relationships, internal politics, or old school tie.

While promotion systems appear to have the consequences just mentioned, they also have other consequences, particularly on interpersonal relationships. Under some conditions, these will further the achievement of organizational goals, but under other conditions they will not. For example, the effect of the promotional scheme on subgroup cohesiveness will be functional or dysfunctional depending on the contribution of the subgroup to the organizational goals. Subgroups do not invariably support the organization.

The proposition, however, needs at least one word of caution. Suppose an organization establishes a promotional system that makes upward mobility depend on (a) the quantity of items produced, (b) the quality of items produced, (c) supervisory potential, and (d) punctuality. For the employee, the performance criterion has two major characteristics: First, the weights assigned to the several factors are not specified. Second, it is not stated how some of the factors are measured. Consequently, the standard offers little information about the consequences attached to specific behavior, for no connection is established between specific behavior and the "score." The greater the *subjective operationality of criteria* (3.60) used in promotion decisions, the greater the effect of the promotion system on the perceived consequences of action [3.40:3.59, 3.60] (K. Davis, 1953; Denerley, 1953).

Note that the proposition refers to "performance standards perceived" and not simply "performance standards specified." Since employees are notoriously suspicious and cynical regarding announced performance criteria, the factors affecting the subjective operationality of performance standards are an important area for future research. Some of the directions in which such research has thus far been pursued will be indicated shortly.

Promotional systems are only one of the organizational incentive programs. Most important among the others is the wage and salary system (including "fringe benefits"). We will not discuss the many wage schemes that have been devised. The details of incentive systems can be found in any one of a number of standard references (Britton, 1953; Dickinson, 1937; Louden, 1944; Lytle, 1942). Our purpose is to treat broad classes of incentive systems in terms of some simple characteristics related to the individual employee's perception of the consequences of his action. One main alternative is a system of flat hourly, weekly, or yearly payments independent of productivity. There are also systems in which pay depends on the amount of individual and/or group production. Finally, combinations of various types of systems are common.

The greater the *dependence of monetary reward on performance* (3.61), the more favorable are the consequences perceived as resulting from a decision to increase production [3.40:3.61]. In general, the introduction of an incentive wage scheme results in increased production over a straight hourly or daily rate, and the introduction of a flat rate payment in place of a former incentive system depresses production (Wyatt, 1934; Feldman, 1937; Viteles, 1953). An employment contract based on a flat rate typically is regarded as controlling the *type* of activities performed but not the *rate* at which they are performed.

We can also assert that the greater the subjective operationality of performance criteria, the greater the effect of the monetary reward system on the perceived consequences of action [3.40:3.60, 3.61] (Marriot, 1951; Byrt, 1954). Thus, individual incentive systems have a greater *direct* impact on individual motivations to produce than group systems. As in the case of mobility systems, we should interpret this assertion cautiously since the second-order effects through group pressure or the requirement of group cohesiveness are only incompletely understood (Learner, 1955).

In these propositions we have assumed a desire of participants for upward mobility in the organization and increased monetary reward. This assumption is reasonable on the whole, provided we recognize that rewards have different importance for different people. We consider this point in the next section. We can also point out that in the typical business organization there is a difference between the kinds of employees for whom the mobility system is relevant and those for whom it is largely irrelevant. For example, for a majority of blue-collar employees in most organizations, promotional rewards are almost nonexistent.

Operationality of criteria   In discussing the effects of the promotional system and the wage-payment system, we have attached most importance to the subjective operationality of performance criteria. The importance of this factor has sometimes been attributed to a need for "sense of direction" without specifying why one direction is pursued rather than another (Friedman, 1954; Krulee, 1955). Most participants in an organization probably want to evaluate the success of their actions, and standards of success undoubtedly further both learning and satisfaction (Thorndike, 1927; Elwell and Grundley, 1938; Bilodeau, 1954; Payne and Hauty, 1955; Viteles, 1955). But there is nothing particularly sacred about productivity standards; other standards can be, and frequently are, used in production situations. Consequently, the effectiveness of a given precise standard of performance depends on mechanisms that motivate its acceptance over other alternatives (e.g., a system of rewards based on the standard). Conversely, the effectiveness of a system of rewards based on a given performance standard depends on how precise (subjectively) the standard is.

A number of propositions can be or have been advanced as to factors influencing the operationality of the performance criteria. The first of these is simply the *size of the work group* (3.62). We predict that incentive schemes will work better in small than in large groups [3.60:3.62]. The greater the *extent to which activities are programmed* (3.63), the more likely that performance criteria will be subjectively operational [3.60:3.63].

If we add the proposition that the higher the *level in the organization* (3.64), the less the programming of activities [3.63:3.64], we can predict that incentive schemes will work beter at lower levels than at higher levels in the organization.

Figure 3.7 diagrams the relations we have discussed in this section. As in the case of the relations pictured in figure 3.6, this set of propositions is substantially more complicated than the set that enters into the theory of human behavior outlined in chapter 2.

3.4.3 Individual Goals

In the two previous subsections, the discussion has focused on cognitive elements of the production situation. In this section we turn to individual goals and particularly the phenomenon of identification. Humans, in contrast to machines, evaluate their own positions in relation to the value of others and come to accept others' goals as their own. In addition, individual members of an organization come to it with a prior structure of preferences – a personality, if you like – on the basis of which they make decisions while in the organization. Thus, individual goals are not "given" for the organization, but can be varied both through recruitment procedures and through organizational practices.

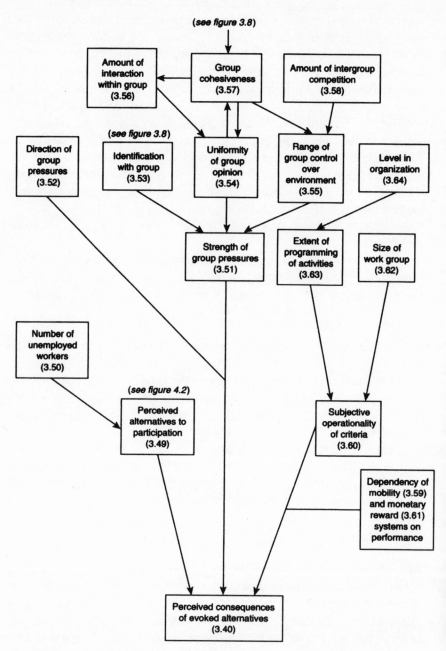

Figure 3.7 Factors affecting the perceived consequences of evoked alternatives.

There are four principal, available targets for identification: (1) organizations external to the focal organization (i.e., extraorganizational identification); (2) the focal organization itself (organizational identification), (3) the work activities involved in the job (task identification); and (4) subgroups within the focal organization (subgroup identification) [A-3.5]. Some of the phenomena that we have attributed at least partially to cognitive influences can also be explained in terms of influence over identifications. Moreover, the latter type of explanation has generally been preferred by students of worker motivation.

However, when we state a proposition about extraorganizational identifications, we cannot draw inferences about motivation to produce until we identify the factors influencing the perception of group goals. Some of these factors are indicated later in this section.

The stronger the individual's identification with a group, the more likely that his goals will conform to his perception of group norms (3.41:3.53). This basic proposition is amply supported by a variety of research findings. It directs attention to the factors affecting the strength of identification in the four alternative directions we have previously listed. We propose five basic hypotheses:

1 The greater the *perceived prestige of the group* (3.65), the stronger the propensity of an individual to identify with it [3.53:3.65]; and vice versa [3.65:3.53].

2 The greater the *extent to which goals are perceived as shared* among members of a group, the stronger the propensity of the individual to identify with the group [3.53:3.8]; and vice versa [3.8:3.53].

3 The more *frequent the interaction* between an individual and the members of a group, the stronger the propensity of the individual to identify with the group [3.53:3.56]; and vice versa [3.56:3.53].

4 The greater the *number of individual needs satisfied in the group* (3.66), the stronger the propensity of the individual to identify with the group [3.53:3.56]; and vice versa [3.66:3.53].

5 The less the *amount of competition* (3.67) between the members of a group and an individual, the stronger the propensity of the individual to identify with the group [3.53:3.67]; and vice versa [3.67:3.53].

These propositions, along with a pair of others relating interaction to perceived goal-sharing [3.56:3.8] and to the number of needs satisfied within the group [3.56:3.66], form the basic framework within which more specific propositions can be developed. That framework is portrayed in figure 3.8.

The importance of the feedback loops in the system should be obvious from the "vice versa" statements above and from the diagram.

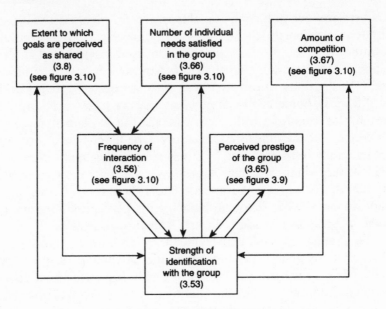

Figure 3.8 Basic factors affecting group identification.

We have not indicated all of the possible loops in the system but simply enough of them to suggest some of the dynamic features of identification phenomena. The extensive interactions among such variables as interaction, preferences, and perceptions have been explored with varying degrees of rigor in a number of areas of human behavior. Among these, perhaps the most notable are small-group and voting behavior. It is not too surprising that the same mechanisms appear to affect organizational motivation.

For convenience in presenting the propositions related to group identification, we distinguish general statements of relations from specific predictive statements. The general propositions are independent of the particular group or type of group involved. The predictions refer to specific empirical situations. This distinction is implicit throughout the book, but here it needs to be made explicit because of the variety of different groups that are relevant to productivity decisions. Because of this variety it is simplest to present the general theoretical propositions first and subsequently to review the specific hypotheses for various groups and the evidence in support of them.

Factors affecting group identification We have already specified five basic variables that affect and are affected by identification. Now we wish to describe some important factors that affect those five variables.

First, what affects the perceived prestige of the group? On the one hand, prestige will vary with the objective position of the group (i.e., its prestige with other people). On the other hand, how an individual perceives group prestige is a function not only of how other people evaluate it but of individual standards as well. Thus, perceived prestige of a group is a function of the *position of the group in the society* (3.68) and the character of *individual standards* (3.69) [3.65:3.68, 3.69].

The position of a group in a society is determined by its possession of symbols of success in the culture. We will not attempt to identify all these symbols here but will limit attention to three that are of substantial importance in identification. First, the greater the *success in achieving group goals* (3.70), the higher the position of the group in the society [3.68:3.70]. Second, the higher the average *status level* (3.71) of group members, the higher the position of the group in the society [3.68:3.71]. Third, the greater the *visibility of the group* (3.72), the higher the position of the group in the society [3.68:3.72].

Visibility, in turn, results from characteristics of the group that either distinguish it from other groups or increase the probability that it will be observed. Thus, the greater the *distinctiveness of the group* (3.73) (whether with respect to goals, membership, or practices), the greater its visibility [3.72:3.73]; the greater the *size of the group* (3.74), the greater its visibility [3.72:3.74]; the greater the *rate of growth of the group* (3.75), the greater its visibility [3.72:3.75].

Among the factors determining individual standards of prestige, two variables appear to have primary importance. First, an individual's standards will depend on the norms of the groups to which he has belonged and does now belong. Individual standards of prestige will resemble *group standards* (3.76) [3.69:3.76]. Second, standards are subject both to decay and to elaboration through personal experience. On the basis of the social comparison processes underlying aspiration-level phenomena, we would predict that the higher the *prestige level of individual experience* (3.77), the higher the individual standards of prestige [3.69:3.77]. These factors affecting the perceived prestige of the group are diagrammed in figure 3.9.

Next, we consider the major factors determining the frequency of interaction between the individual and the group. One of the most important of these factors is the feedback that connects identification with interaction. The stronger the individual's identification with the group, the greater the interaction. Increases in either the extent of goal-sharing or the number of needs satisfied in the group also result in increased interaction. What are some other factors that operate through the interaction mechanism?

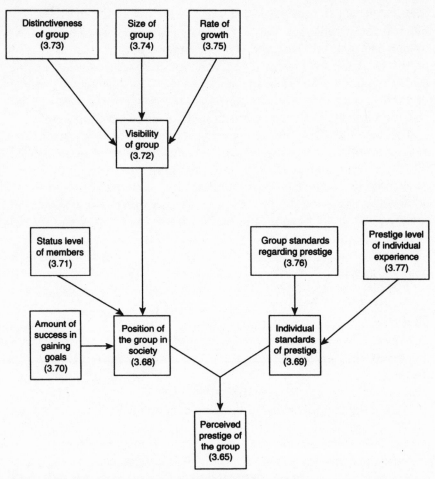

Figure 3.9 Factors affecting the perceived prestige of the group.

One such factor is simple exposure. The more *exposure to contact* (3.78), the greater the frequency of interaction between the group and the individual [3.56:3.78].

Individuals approach various groups with attitudes about them that bias the relative frequency of interaction with them. In part, these attitudes reflect norms of culture or subculture in which the individual has been reared. Hence, the stronger the *cultural pressure to participate* (3.79) in the group, the greater the frequency of interaction between the group and the individual [3.56:3.79]. In part, the attitudes are based on perceived similarities between members of the group and the individual, often derived from a common background, training, experiences, etc. The greater the *homogeneity in background* (3.80), the greater the frequency of interaction [3.56:3.80]. Finally, we will record an anomie-like hypothesis about the effect of "bigness" on interaction. The greater the *size of the community* (3.81), the less frequent the interaction between the group and the individual [3.56:3.81]. Here we use "community" as a loose term for a more or less autonomous social unit within which most individual needs are met.

We have already indicated that the greater the homogeneity of background, the greater the extent of perceived goal-sharing [3.8:3.80]. In addition, perceived goal-sharing is a function of *present* similarities in position. Doctors tend to band together not only because they share a distinctive training, but also because their activities as doctors place them in positions similar to one another. As a result, they tend to assume that this similarity leads to attitudinal similarity. The greater the *similarity of present positions* (3.82), the greater the extent to which goals are viewed as shared [3.8:3.82].

To complete this outline of factors affecting group identification, we note one variable affecting the number of individual needs satisfied in the group and a second one affecting the amount of competition between the members of the group and the individual. The greater the group's *permissiveness toward individual goal achievement* (3.83), the more individual needs will be satisfied in the group [3.66:3.83]. At least in our own culture, conformity tends to be considered a "cost" of group membership rather than a positive advantage. Since the relations among individual needs, conformity, and independence are complex and poorly understood, we state only the very weak hypothesis that nearly all individuals most of the time find a group that is permissive toward their own needs more attractive than one that is not.

The greater the *independence of individual rewards* (3.84), the less competition among group members [3.67:3.84]. Contrariwise, where individuals are, in effect, engaged in a zero-sum game in which some must lose in order for others to gain, competition is increased and identification decreased.

A diagram of these factors affecting the frequency of interaction, the extent to which goals are perceived as shared, the number of individual needs satisfied in the group, and the amount of competition between the individual and the group is provided in figure 3.10. Figures 3.8, 3.9, and 3.10 taken together represent our general conception of the variables operating on individual goals through group identification. We turn now to a discussion of how these factors function in specific types of groups.

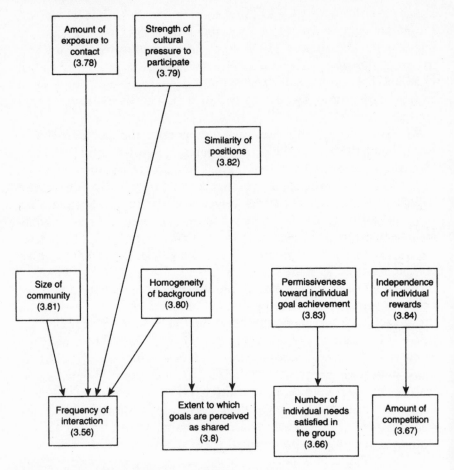

Figure 3.10   Factors affecting frequency of interaction, the extent to which goals are perceived as shared, the number of individual needs satisfied in the group, and the amount of competition.

Identification with extraorganizational groups (professional associations, community groups, family groups, trade unions). In the case of *professional associations* we predict that the greater the degree of professionalization of the individual's job, the greater his identification with a professional group. Implicit in the definition of "professionalization" are the major variables through which the prediction is realized. Professionalization implies specific formal training and thus substantial homogeneity of background. It implies formal regulation of job performance and thus similarity in positions. To the extent that a job is professionalized, techniques and standards of performance are defined by the other members of the profession. Since reference to this group and its standards is indispensable in performing a professionalized job, the group's influence on action permeates a wide class of job situations. Since there is a need to be like other members of the profession in a number of attributes, there is a tendency to extend this need to other attributes and thus to identify with the group (R. C. Davis, 1954; Moore and Renck, 1955).

With respect to *community groups*, extent of exposure appears to be of critical importance for identification. Exposure is reflected in such factors as length of residence; hence, the longer the length of residence in a community, the greater the individual's identification with community groups (Hoppock, 1935). One of the striking features of organizations like an army, where residence in a community tends to be brief, is the absence of identification with groups in the local community. On the other hand, an organization like the foreign service, in which assignment to foreign communities is often relatively extended and identification with them largely dysfunctional, uses extended vacations to bring about periodic "re-Americanization." The longer the residence, the greater the breadth and frequency of nonorganizational community contacts. Interaction results in identification.

Problems in analysis arise from our inadequate knowledge of the combined results of these several phenomena. The integration of individuals into the community has frequently been urged by organizations because it offers advantages for public relations and reduces voluntary mobility. At the same time, integration into the community gives rise to nonorganizational identifications that may be dysfunctional.

If we accept the anomie hypothesis, we will predict that the smaller the community, the more identification with community groups.

The *family* forms a third significant type of extraorganizational group. Families often have attitudes about what jobs are appropriate for their members, and those attitudes affect the orientation of individuals to their work. Similarly, family attitudes toward performance on the job are important determinants of individual performance preferences. The greater the residential mobility of the individual, the weaker his identification with family groups. Residential mobility breaks down contact with the extended family and tends to limit frequent interaction to the marital family unit (Masuoka, 1940).

Similarly, we can make a prediction based on cultural differences. The more the culture of origin utilizes the extended family as a basic social unit, the greater the identification of the individual with family groups. Thus, we would predict, for example, that an organization member of Chinese parentage would generally have stronger (and wider) family identifications than his native American counterpart (Burgess and Locke, 1953, pp. 35-6).

As an extraorganizational group, the *trade union* occupies an ambiguous position. In some cases, local unions are essentially subgroups of an organization. In other cases, locals draw their membership from several business organizations. In either case, the international union organizations and the trade union movement represent extraorganizational foci for identification. The greater the individual worker's participation in union activities, the stronger his identification with the union. This is, of course, another version of the basic Homans hypothesis. Whatever the reason an individual joins the union and participates in its functions, the participation tends to pull him more strongly into union life. There is evidence indicating that most union members become participants either more or less involuntarily or for limited special reasons, but that participation results ultimately in much deeper involvements (Sayles and Strauss, 1953; Rose, 1952b).

The greater the success of the union in its negotiations with management, the stronger the individual's identification with the union. The union's general success is, of course, related to its perceived prestige. However, variations in the "success" of the union for individual members are also relevant. The benefits gained by an individual through the union depend in part on the strategic position of an individual or his group in the manufacturing process, but they also depend on his power position in the union.

We have indicated that participation stimulates identification, but what stimulates union participation? In the first place, there are strong feedback loops from identification and felt success to participation. The stronger the identification of the individual worker with the union, the greater his participation. The greater the felt success of the union, the greater the participation. In addition, when participation is consistent with the norms of the society and of other social groups to which the individual belongs, he will participate more. Men will tend to participate in union activities more than women. Individuals from families with attitudes favorable to unions will tend to participate in union activities more than others (Rose, 1952b; Sayles and Strauss, 1953; Purcell, 1953).

Finally, since union activities imply a community of interests within a work group, pressure toward participation should depend in part on the homogeneity of that group. Groups with a common ethnic background will participate more than other groups, groups of individuals who live close together more than others, groups of individuals having similar jobs, pay, and status more than others (Rose, 1952b; Sayles and Strauss, 1953; Purcell, 1953).

Identification with the organization The second important type of group with which members tend to identify is the organization itself. We consider a few of the major predictions about the intensity of organizational identification.

Excluding the first year, the longer the service with a given organization, the stronger the identification of the individual with the organization. In most studies of the effect of length of service on identification, it is difficult to control for self-selection. Since we would predict (see chapter 4) that the stronger the identification with the organization, the weaker the propensity to leave voluntarily, a sample of participants classified according to length of service would show that those who had been members of the organization longer were stronger in identification with the organization than others (except that those who have just joined an organization might have greater identification with it than those who have been with the organization a moderate length of time). We are asserting that apart from self-selection, the length of time served itself results in increased identification. The mechanisms involved are those previously cited: The longer an individual remains in an organization, the more his interactions occur within the organization, the more his needs are satisfied within the organization, and, therefore, the more he identifies with the organization.

The greater the vertical mobility within an organization, the stronger the identification of the individual with the organization (Stone, 1952a). Expectations of vertical mobility create expectations of interaction as well as felt similarities between subordinates and superiors. On the other hand, there are a substantial number of anecdotal cases of high identification in a rigid caste system with little or no vertical mobility across castes. Perhaps one clue to the relation between mobility and identification lies in the culturally determined standards of occupational success. In a culture in which there is an expectation that ability will be rewarded by promotion, failure (or anticipated failure) to achieve higher occupational status in the organization is perceived as rejection by superiors. Identification with the organization under such circumstances accentuates the force of the rejection and, therefore, will tend to be avoided. In a culture in which the standards of success are different, failure to achieve mobility may be quite independent of felt acceptance by the organization and, therefore, not a deterrent to identification.

There is some evidence that supervisory practices affect organizational identification. In particular, it appears that the more supervisors facilitate the satisfaction of personal goals by individual members of the organization, the stronger the latter's identification with the organization (Comrey, Pfiffner, and Beem, 1952; Katz, Maccoby, Gurin, and Floor, 1951). To particularize further, the more general the supervision, the stronger the tendency of subordinates to identify with the organization; the more participation in making policy decisions, the stronger the tendency of subordinates to identify with the organization; the more supervisors are employee- rather than production-oriented, the stronger the tendency of subordinates to identify with the organization.

Finally, although specific evidence is sparse, we include a hypothesis relating organizational identification with factors that make the organization attractive to the individual. We have already argued that an individual is more likely to identify with an organization in which he has considerable interaction than one in which interaction is limited, that he is more likely to identify with an organization that he perceives as accepting him than one he perceives as rejecting him, that he is more likely to identify with an organization that permits him to satisfy personal goals than with one that frustrates the satisfaction of personal goals. Now we are arguing that an individual is more likely to identify with an organization that he perceives as high in prestige than one he perceives as low (Willerman and Swanson, 1953). Among other things, identification is a means of gaining personal status. As we will see below, prestige may adhere to subunits rather than to the organization as a whole, and thereby encourage subgroup identification rather than organizational identification. But under many conditions, identification with the organization as a whole will be a function of generalized prestige.

The more the organization produces a distinguishable product, the stronger the identification of members with it. The greater the number of high status occupations and/or individuals in the organization, the stronger the identification of individual participants with it. The larger the organization, the stronger the identification of individual participants with it. (Note that we have already specified other factors, such as breadth of interaction, that operate in an opposite direction for the large organization.) The faster the growth of the organization, the stronger the identification of individual participants with it (Payne, 1954).

In addition to such factors as these, certain factors of individual experience color personal evaluation of prestige. All of the prestige factors in an organization are judged relative to a personally determined standard of comparison. Individual participants for whom the organization has greater prestige than organizations to which other family members belong will identify more strongly with the organization. Individual participants who belong to an organization that has greater prestige than those to which individuals of the same education and experience normally belong will identify more strongly with the organization than will others. Individuals with limited experience in other organizations will identify more strongly with the organization than those with extended experience.

Identification with subgroups When we turn to subgroup identification, many of the same types of propositions can be made. For example, with slight modifications propositions similar to those just outlined can be used to relate the prestige characteristics of subgroups in the organization to the propensity of the individual worker to identify with the subgroup. In addition, the organization provides a standard – productivity – by which the prestige of subunits can be judged, and this standard also becomes a factor in identification. The more productive the subgroup in the organization, the stronger the identification of individual participants with the subgroup (Katz, Maccoby, Gurin, and Floor, 1951). Subgroup identification also depends on interaction and need-satisfaction. Consequently, those groups that facilitate interaction and satisfaction of personal goals will show greater cohesiveness than other groups. The smaller the work group, the stronger the subgroup identification of members (Marriot, 1949; Katz; 1947; Kerr, Koppelmeier, and Sullivan, 1951; Worthy 1950b; Hewitt and Parfit, 1953). The size effect apparently stems from a need for closure in interpersonal relations that (for most individuals) is more easily met in small than in large groups.

Subgroup identification implies the acceptance of, and comformity to, subgroup norms. Conversely, where factors in the situation make such acceptance and conformity difficult, identification is retarded. In particular, where external factors stimulate competition among members of a work group, subgroup identification is weakened. Where a reward system attached to individual competence excludes the possibility of everyone being rewarded, identification with subgroups will be weaker than where the reward system either is not attached to the individual competences or permits everyone to be rewarded. In other terms, the players in a zero-sum, no-partner game will be less likely to form group identifications than will players in a nonzero-sum, partnership game in which the group plays against the environment (Stone, 1952a; Babchuk and Goode, 1951).

Identification with the task group   Task identification, the last of the four major forms of identification considered here, is probably more properly thought of as identification with the class of individuals performing the same task. Of course, the task group may be either a subgroup or an extraorganizational group, depending on the nature of the task, but at least in some cases task identification appears to be a phenomenon of sufficient importance to warrant independent treatment.

First, all factors causing identification with an extraorganizational professional group apply equally to task identification. The relevant propositions will not be repeated here.

In addition, characteristics of the job, length of service in the organization, and organizational mobility affect task identification. The more a particular task is perceived as a training rather than as a terminal job, the weaker the identification with it. Thus low-level tasks in an organization do not induce identification where they are perceived as stepping-stones to higher-level positions, but they do induce task identification where mobility is not anticipated. Consequently, individuals who have held the same job for an extended period of time will be more likely to identify with the job than individuals who have held it for only a short period. If (a) perception of a task as training for a "higher" career and expectations of mobility result in job satisfaction, and (b) identification with a job as a career results in job satisfaction, and (c) perception of a task as a training job persists after expectations of upward mobility cease, then it follows that intrinsic job satisfaction associated with a less than top-level job should be high early in the service of an employee and late in the service, and that the lowest satisfaction should occur at an intermediate point when expectations of mobility have ended but task identification has not yet been achieved (Morse, 1953).

The characteristics of the job influence task identification primarily through another mechanism previously discussed. Individuals seek to satisfy personal needs through the medium of the job. When job characteristics permit such satisfactions, we predict a strong task identification. Clearly, therefore, to make general predictions one must assume a certain amount of commonality of needs within the culture from which a given organization draws its members. Some characteristics of a task have rather clear implications for a success-oriented culture like our own. Thus, the more a given task reflects a high level of technical skill, the stronger the identification of the individual participant with the task (R. C. Davis, 1954). The more a given task reflects individual autonomy in making decisions, the stronger the identification with the task. The more a given task requires the use of a number of different programs rather than a single one, the stronger the identification with the task (Morse, 1953).

The direction of group pressures In discussing suborganizational and extraorganizational identification and control over the perception of consequences above, we have been concerned with the amount of control exercised by these groups. At the same time, we have said nothing about the direction in which the control is exercised.

A suborganizational or extraorganizational group can frequently prevent production from reaching the rate specified by the management. Indeed, the literature is full of cases of this sort. At the same time, however, no good theoretical reason has thus far been advanced as to why nonorganizational groups need necessarily operate in a way incompatible with the goals of the organizational hierarchy. As Gross (1953) has pointed out, small-group controls can, under a variety of circumstances, supplement rather than hamper institutional controls. This is clearest in the case of some particular extraorganizational groups. For example, the enforcement of professional standards by professional associations frequently serves an important function for organizations employing professional technicians. Control of the employee through the wife has been cited as a common tactic of the Chinese Communist Party and American industrial firms (Dahl and Lindblom, 1953, pp. 518-19). With respect to suborganizational groups, the case is equally impressive. One problem in organizing control systems in complex organizations is to neutralize or eliminate the dysfunctional consequences of subgroup organization without destroying its ability to perform necessary functions. For example, organizations sometimes find difficulty in forcing lower-echelon leaders to conform to the demands of the hierarchy because some of the methods by which conformity can be most effectively enforced seriously undermine the leadership position of the supervisor (March, 1955b).

We have cited in this chapter obvious factors related to specific predictions of productivity and have delayed the more general discussion of organizational conflict until chapter 5. Consequently, the dependent variable in this section is the *extent to which group pressures support organizational demands* (3.85).

We wish to define the reasons for variations in the *amount of similarity between norms* (3.86) enforced by the organization on the one hand and the competing group on the other. The more similar the norms, the greater the support of group pressures for organizational demands [3.85:3.86]. To a certain extent, the similarity of norms between a given group and an organization is a "given" for the organization. Some groups will be more supportive than others, and there really is not much to be done about it. At the same time, the methods by which group norms are formed affect the content of the norms; and those methods need not be considered a "given" for the organization. We can state a few propositions reflecting both types of situations, and then indicate specific empirical predictions that stem from them.

First, the *more similar the social standing* (3.87) of the two institutions, the more similar the norms they enforce [3.86:3.87]. Second, the greater the *cultural centrality* (3.88) of the organization, the greater the similarity of its norms of those professed by other groups in the same culture [3.86:3.88]. Third, the greater the organizational control over the evocation and evaluation of alternatives in the group, the more similar will be organizational and group norms [3.86:3.44].

We can illustrate the operation of these mechanisms by specific predictions about (a) social standing, (b) cultural centrality, and (c) organization control over decision-making.

The more a particular job requires advanced formal education, the more likely that pressures from professional groups will support organizational demands in a business organization. This prediction is based on the calculation that the more highly educated a person is (up to some point in graduate education perhaps), the more likely it is that the groups to which he belongs will profess norms consistent with the norms of the business community. Both the educated group and the business group comprise generally recognized elite groups in contemporary American society and the norms of similar groups in a society are mutually supporting. Note that we are not talking of a "power elite" in the sense of influence over public policy decisions, but of a "social elite" in the "who-entertains-whom" or the "who-talks-to-whom" sense. Hence the proposition, even if true for American society, is by no means necessarily true elsewhere, since it depends on who are the elites and what is the social stratification of the culture. By contrast, in eighteenth-century England, since businessmen were not members of the social elite, the norms of educated men and businessmen were far from being mutually supportive.

The pressures from extraorganizational groups are more likely to be consistent with the demands of management if the employee is a Protestant than if he is either a Catholic or a Jew (Dalton, 1948; Collins, Dalton, and Roy, 1946; Mack, Murphy, and Yellin, 1956). In part, this proposition flows from the same general considerations as the preceding one. In general, Protestants are more likely to find their way into the social elite than are either Catholics or Jews. Therefore, the groups to which they belong are more likely to reflect norms consistent with those of businessmen. In addition, as Weber (1930) and Tawney (1937) have shown, the ideology of Protestantism strongly supports capitalist institutions.

We have been treating religious groups and professional associations as influencing the behavior of individual members of the organization but not as reciprocally influenced *by* individual behavior. The connections between the behavior of the individual employee or the firm, on the one hand, and these external groups, on the other, are virtually all "one-way" connections in which the external groups influence participants but the reverse influence chain is either non-existent or so slight as to be unobservable. If the organization cannot influence the attitudes of the outside groups or the membership of particular individuals in them, all it can do is establish criteria of selection that choose members of groups with supportive norms.

In some cases, however, suborganizational and extraorganizational groups comprise, together with the organization and its members, small social systems with strong internal interactions. In these cases we have to consider influences running in both directions – from these groups to the organization and from organization to groups.

The pressures from informal work groups are more likely to be consistent with the demands of management if the sociometry of the organization is systematically manipulated than if assignments to positions are determined more or less randomly, within technical constraints (Wyatt, 1934). The composition of informal work groups (and therefore the norms of such groups) depends partly on the physical arrangement of work locations. Physical propinquity is an important base for group membership. Consequently, the direction of subgroup pressures on an individual will depend partly on the physical location of his work.

The equilibrium that will be reached as a result of group pressures of the members on each other will depend on the cumulative effect of these pressures when they reinforce each other. At one extreme, the net pressure on any individual could be simply proportional to an unweighted average of the norms of others. In this case, the group would move toward an equilibrium norm that would also be an average of the initial positions of the members. At the other extreme, a majority norm might exert pressures on deviant minority or individual norms, but not vice versa. In this case, the group would move toward unanimity, agreeing with the norm held initially by the majority. The real situation appears to lie between these two extremes, and to be further complicated by other weighting factors, e.g., seniority in the group.

Where social contact among wives and families of members cuts across hierarchical ranks, the pressures from families are more likely to support the attitudes of management than where such contact occurs primarily "horizontally" in the hierarchy. Although questions of the ethical desirability of using influences that involve the family can be raised, these underscore rather than deny the important extent to which family relations color a wide range of individual activities. A man whose wife wishes to associate with wives of superiors will be aware of the consequences associated with rate restrictions. The consequences for business success of social failure are often the subject of comment in novels and "how-to-succeed" books. The obverse phenomenon is equally real – the consequences for social success of business failure.

Neighborhood groups, clubs, and the like serve as other sources of pressures. Some of these can be treated as independent variables like the professional association and religion; some of them, like the informal work group and the family, can be treated as part of a dynamic system of relations. In general, such evidence as is available about these group influences tends to be anecdotal, and we are not yet in a position to evaluate the correctness or the significance of our propositions.

One factor, already mentioned, affecting the direction of pressures has been explored in at least some research. Provided there is compatibility between the values pursued by the hierarchy in the organization and the other participants, the more participation of members in making policy decisions, the more likely is it that the pressures from suborganizational informal work groups will support the demands of management (Katz, Maccoby, and Morse, 1950; Katz, Maccoby, Gurin, and Floor, 1951). From the point of view of the organization, participation in decision-making is a way of enlisting the powers of the subgroup to enforce the norms of the organization. Once the organizationally dysfunctional outcomes of participation are excluded, the importance of this enforcement is manifest.

Individual goals as they affect the individual's motivation to produce reflect both the strength of his identification with available groups (including the organization) and the direction of the group pressures. They also reflect basic values derived from earlier experience. Our justification for emphasizing identification at length rather than what might be called personality factors rests on two basic considerations. First, although identification is influenced by many other factors in the organization, the more basic attitudes we call personality are less malleable. Second, those basic values that impinge on the motivation to produce require "interpretation" before they become relevant to a specific organizational situation and interpretation depends in large part on the phenomena we have discussed.

3.5 Conclusion

In this chapter we have tried to indicate one of the directions in which research on organizational behavior has expanded beyond the classical treatments of human participants as "machines." We have seen that the "machine" model of human behavior tends to ignore the wide range of roles which the participant simultaneously performs and does not effectively treat problems associated with the coordination of the roles. In particular, it should be obvious that supervisory actions based on the naïve "machine" model will result in behavior that the organization wishes to avoid.

This conclusion was, of course, one of the central hypotheses of Merton, Selznick, and Gouldner in their writing on bureaucracy. The bureacratic literature has devoted considerable attention to the problems of managing organisms whose motivations and learning behavior are much more complicated than those contemplated in the "machine" model.

In addition, we have looked at three different modes of influence over individual motivations in an organization, paying particular attention to the congruence between individual attitudes and organizational demands reflected in the motivation to produce. Our analysis suggests that influence over the motivation to produce is a function of influence over (a) the evoking of action alternatives for the individual, (b) the consequences of evoked alternatives anticipated by the individual, and (c) the values attached to consequences by the individual. Each of these aspects is partly under the control of the organization but partly also determined by extraorganizational factors. The amount of organizational control, in turn, depends partly on the behavior of the organization (e.g., supervisory practices) and partly on factors largely outside its control (e.g., general economic conditions).

As we turn now to a consideration of the other major motivational decision we will describe – the decision to participate – we will try to indicate how that decision both resembles and differs from the production decisions we have just discussed. By the end of chapter 4 we hope to have surveyed the knowledge now available on the subject of participation in organizations.

4

Motivational Constraints:
The Decision to Participate

In the last chapter we explored individual motivation to produce and described employee behavior within a general decision-making framework. We mentioned that decisions by workers to participate in an organization reflect different considerations from decisions to produce. In this chapter we explore the decision to participate.

The decision to participate lies at the core of the theory of what Barnard (1938) and Simon (1947) have called "organizational equilibrium": the conditions of survival of an organization. Equilibrium reflects the organization's success in arranging payments to its participants adequate to motivate their continued participation. In this chapter we consider first the general theory of organizational equilibrium. The theory leads us to identify the major participants in an organization and the factors affecting their participation decisions. For a number of reasons, we will direct major attention to employees, but we will show how the same general propositions also apply to other types of participants.

4.1 The Theory of Organizational Equilibrium

The Barnard–Simon theory of organizational equilibrium is essentially a theory of motivation – a statement of the conditions under which an organization can induce its members to continue their participation, and hence assure organizational survival. The central postulates of the theory are stated by Simon, Smithburg, and Thompson (1950, pp. 381–2) as follows [A-4.1]:

1 An organization is a system of interrelated social behaviors of a number of persons whom we shall call the *participants* in the organization.
2 Each participant and each group of participants receives *from* the

organization *inducements* in return for which he makes *to* the organization *contributions*.

3 Each participant will continue his participation in an organization only so long as the inducements offered him are as great or greater (measured in terms of *his* values and in terms of the alternatives open to him) than the contributions he is asked to make.

4 The contributions provided by the various groups of participants are the source from which the organization manufactures the inducements offered to participants.

5 Hence, an organization is "solvent" – and will continue in existence – only so long as the contributions are sufficient to provide inducements in large enough measure to draw forth these contributions.

The theory, like many theoretical generalizations, verges on the tautological. Specifically, to test the theory, and especially the crucial postulate 3, we need independent empirical estimates of (a) the behavior of participants in joining, remaining in, or withdrawing from organizations; and (b) the balance of inducements and contributions for each participant, measured in terms of his "utilities."

The observation of participants joining and leaving organizations is comparatively easy. It is more difficult to find evidence of the value of variable (b) that does not depend on the observation of (a). Before we can deal with the observational problem, however, we must say a bit more about the concepts of inducements and contributions.

Inducements   Inducements are "payments" made by (or through) the organization to its participants (e.g., wages to a worker, service to a client, income to an investor). These payments can be measured in units that are independent of their utility to the participants (e.g., wages and income can be measured in terms of dollars, service to clients in terms of hours devoted to him). Consequently, for an individual participant we can specify a set of inducements, each component of the set representing a different dimension of the inducements offered by the organization. Thus, each component of the inducements can be measured uniquely and independently of the utilities assigned to it by the participants.

Inducement utilities   For each component in the set of inducements there is a corresponding utility value. For the moment we will not be concerned with the shape of the utility function; but we do not exclude from consideration a step function. The utility function for a given individual reduces the several components of the inducements to a common dimension.

Contributions   We assume that a participant in an organization makes certain "payments" to the organization (e.g., work from the worker, fee from the client, capital from the investor). These payments, which we shall call contributions, can be measured in units that are independent of their utility to the participants. Consequently, for any individual participant we can specify a set of contributions.

Contribution utilities   A utility function transforming contributions into utilities of the individual contributor can be defined in more than one way. A reasonable definition of the utility of a contribution is the value of the alternatives that an individual foregoes in order to make the contribution. As we shall see below, this definition of contribution utilities allows us to introduce into the analysis the range of behavior alternatives open to the participant.

These definitions of inducements and contributions permit two general approaches to the observational problem. On the one hand, we can try to estimate the utility balance directly by observing the behavior (including responses to pertinent questions) of participants. On the other hand, if we are prepared to make some simple empirical assumptions about utility functions, we can make predictions from changes in the amounts of inducements and contributions, without reference to their utilities.

To estimate the inducement–contribution utility balance directly, the most logical type of measure is some variant of individual satisfaction (with the job, the service, the investment, etc.). It appears reasonable to assume that the greater the difference between inducements and contributions, the greater the individual satisfaction. However, the critical "zero points" of the satisfaction scale and the inducement–contribution utility balance are not necessarily identical. The zero point for the satisfaction scale is the point at which one begins to speak of degrees of "dissatisfaction" rather than degrees of "satisfaction." It is, therefore, closely related to the level of aspiration and, as has been indicated in chapter 3, is the point at which we would predict a substantial increase in search behavior on the part of the organism.

The zero point on the inducement–contribution utility scale, on the other hand, is the point at which the individual is indifferent to leaving an organization. We have ample evidence that these two zero points are not identical, but, in particular, that very few of the "satisfied" participants leave an organization, whereas some, but typically not all, of the "unsatisfied" participants leave (Reynolds, 1951).

How do we explain these differences? The explanation lies primarily in the ways in which alternatives to current activity enter into the scheme (and this is one of the reasons for defining contribution utilities in terms of opportunities foregone). Dissatisfaction is a cue for search behavior. Being dissatisfied, the organism expands its program for exploring alternatives. If over the long run this search fails, the aspiration level is gradually revised downward. We assume, however, that the change in aspiration level occurs slowly, so that dissatisfaction in the short run is quite possible. On the other hand, the inducement–contribution utility balance adjusts quickly to changes in the perception of alternatives. When fewer and poorer alternatives are perceived to be available, the utility of activities foregone decreases; and this adjustment occurs rapidly.

Consequently, we can use satisfaction expressed by the individual as a measure of the inducement–contribution utility balance only if it is used in conjunction with an estimate of perceived alternatives available. Speaking roughly, only the desire to move enters into judgments of satisfaction; desire to move *plus* the perceived ease of movement enters into the inducement–contribution utility measure. Many students of mobility (particularly those concerned with the mobility of workers) have tended to ignore one or the other of these two facets of the decision to participate (Rice, Hill, and Trist, 1950; Behrend, 1953).

Direct observation of the inducement–contribution utilities, however, is not the only possible way to estimate them. Provided we make certain assumptions about the utility functions, we can infer the utility balance directly from observations of changes in the inducements or contributions measured in nonutility terms. Three major assumptions are useful and perhaps warranted. First, we assume that the utility functions change only slowly. Second, we assume that each utility function is monotonic with respect to its corresponding inducement or contribution. Although we may not know what the utility of an increase in wages will be, we are prepared to assume it will be positive. Third, we assume that the utility functions of fairly broad classes of people are very nearly the same; within a given subculture we do not expect radical differences in values. Also, we can expect that if an increase in a given inducement produces an increase in utility for one individual, it will produce an increase for other individuals.

There are other reasonable assumptions about individual utility functions; some will be indicated below when we relate individual participation to other factors. These three assumptions, however, in themselves lead to a variety of estimation procedures. Under the first assumption the short-run effect of a change in inducements or contributions will be uncontaminated by feedback effects. By the second assumption (particularly in conjunction with the third) a host of ordinal predictions can be made on the basis of knowledge of changes in the inducements and contributions. The third assumption permits us to estimate some of the cardinal properties of the inducements-contributions balance, avoiding the problem of interpersonal comparison of utilities.

Assumptions such as those listed have some a priori validity, but it is more important that much of the evidence currently available on the behavior of participants is consistent with them. Thus, predictions are frequently and often successfully made by businessmen as to the feasibility of proposed organizational plans.

Consider the analysis of a businessman exploring the feasibility of a business venture. His first step is to construct an operating plan showing what activities and facilities are required to carry on the proposed business, including estimates of the quantities of "inputs" and "outputs" of all categories. In the language of economics, he estimates the "production function." In the language of organization theory, the production function states the rates of possible conversion of contributions into inducements (Simon, 1952-3).

His second step is to estimate the monetary inducements that will be needed to obtain the inputs in the amounts required, and the monetary contributions that can be exacted for the outputs – i.e., the prices of factors of production and of product. In estimating these monetary inducements, predictions are being made as to the inducements-contributions balances of various classes of participants. Let us give some hypothetical examples:

Salaries and wages   Information is obtained on "going rates of wages" for similar classes of work in other companies in the same area. An implicit *ceteris paribus* assumption is made with respect to other inducements, or (if the work, say, is particularly unpleasant, if proposed working conditions are particularly good or bad, etc.) the monetary inducement is adjusted upward or downward to compensate for the other factors. If the problem is to attract workers from other organizations, it is assumed that a wage differential or other inducement will be required to persuade them to change.

Capital   Information is obtained on "the money market" – i.e., the kinds of alternative investment opportunities that are available, the weight attached to various elements of risk, and the levels of interest rates. It is then assumed that to induce investment, the terms (interest rates, security, etc.) must be at least equal to the inducements available in alternative investments.

The same procedure is followed for the inducements to other participants. In each case, information is required as to the alternative inducements offered by other organizations, and these establish the "zero level" of the net inducement–contribution balance. If nonmonetary factors are not comparable among alternatives, an estimated adjustment is made of the monetary inducements by way of compensation. Of course, the adjustment may just as well be made in the nonmonetary factors (e.g., in product quality).

If the planned inducements, including the monetary inducements, give a positive balance for all groups of participants, the plan is feasible. If the plan is subsequently carried out, a comparison of the actual operations with the estimates provides an empirical test of the assumptions and the estimates. If the outcomes fail to confirm the assumptions, the businessman may still choose which of the two sets of assumptions he will alter. He may interpret the result as evidence that the basic inducements–contributions hypothesis is incorrect, or he may conclude that he has estimated incorrectly the zero points of one or more of the inducements–contributions balances. The fact is, however, that such predictions are frequently made with substantial success.

The testing of the theory is not confined to predicting the survival of new enterprises. At any time in the life of an organization when a change is made – that (a) explicitly alters the inducements offered to any group of participants; (b) explicitly alters the contributions demanded from them; or (c) alters the organizational activity in any way that will affect inducements or contributions – on any of these occasions, a prediction can be made as to the effect of the change on participation. The effects may be measurable in terms of turnover rates of employees, sales, etc., as appropriate.

4.2 The Participants

The theory of organizational equilibrium, as we have formulated it here, implies a structure – an organization – underlying the equilibrium. Specifically, there must exist a social system involving the participants that exhibits both a high degree of interrelationship and substantial differentiation from other systems within the total social milieu.

Up to this point, we have not tried to be precise in defining participation. In fact, we must necessarily be somewhat arbitrary in identifying some particular individuals as participants in a given organization. A number of individuals other than those we will identify as principal participants in a business organization receive inducements from the organization and provide contributions to its existence, and under special circumstances such "participants" may assume a dominant role in determining the equilibrium of the organization. But when we describe the chief participants of most business organizations, we generally limit our attention to the following five major classes: employees, investors, suppliers, distributors, and consumers [A-4.2].

Most obvious in any catalogue of organizational participants are the employees, including the management. Ordinarily, when we talk of organizational participants what we mean are workers, and membership in a business organization is ordinarily treated as equivalent to employment. Employees receive wages and other gratuities and donate work (production) and other contributions to the organization. As will become obvious below, employment is the area of participation in organizations in which the most extensive research has been executed.

The role of investors as participants in the organization is explicit in the economic theory of the firm but has rarely been included in other analyses of organizational behavior. A close analogue is found in some treatises on public administration where external power groups are dealt with specifically (Simon, Smithburg, and Thompson, 1950; Truman, 1951; Freeman, 1955). Although the participation of investors in the activities of business firms is frequently less active than that of political power groups in the management of governmental units, the behavior of investing participants is not so insignificant in the general American business scene as to warrant excluding them from consideration.

The distinction between units in a production–distribution process that are "in" the organization and those that are "out" of the organization typically follows the legal definition of the boundaries of a particular firm. We find it fruitful to use a more functional criterion that includes both the suppliers and the distributors of the manufacturing core of the organization (or its analogue where the core of the organization is not manufacturing). Thus, in the automobile industry it is useful to consider the automobile dealers as component parts of an automobile manufacturing organization.

Finally, the role of consumers in an organization has, like the role of investors, been generally ignored except by economic theorists. Since consumers are clearly part of the equilibrating system, organization theory must include in its framework the major components of a theory of consumption.

Taken too literally, this conception of organizations incorporates almost any knowledge about human behavior as a part of organization theory. However, we will limit our primary attention here to the participation of employees. Labor mobility has been studied at some length by both economists and social psychologists. Consequently, we will be able to find at least some evidence for the propositions cited. In general, the areas of investment behavior, supplier behavior, and middleman behavior are less well developed, and their propositions less well documented. Consumer behavior presents a somewhat different case, being the subject of considerable research (Clark, 1958). Nevertheless, we will limit ourselves in this area to the general observations made in section 4.7 below.

4.3 Employee Participation: The Participation Criterion

In one respect, an employee's relation to the organization is quite different from that of other participants. In joining the organization, he accepts an authority relation, that is, he agrees that within some limits (defined both explicitly and implicitly by the terms of the employment contract) he will accept as the premises of his behavior orders and instructions supplied to him by the organization. Associated with this acceptance are commonly understood procedures for "legitimating" communications and clothing them with authority for employees. Acceptance of authority by the employee gives the organization a powerful means for influencing him – more powerful than persuasion, and comparable to the evoking processes that call forth a whole program of behavior in response to a stimulus.

On the assumption that employees act in a subjectively rational manner, we can make some predictions about the scope of the authority relation from our knowledge of the inducements and contributions of the employees and other organization members (Simon, 1952–3). An employee will be willing to enter into an employment contract only if it does not matter to him "very much" what activities (within the area of acceptance agreed on in the contract) the organization will instruct him to perform, or if he is compensated in some way for the possibility that the organization will impose unpleasant activities on him. It will be advantageous for the organization to establish an authority relation when the employee activities that are optimal for the organization (i.e., maximize the inducement utility to other participants of the employee's activity) cannot be predicted accurately in advance.

These propositions can be restated in a form that permits them to be tested by looking at terms of the employment contract. A particular aspect of an employee's behavior can be (a) specified in the employment contract (e.g., as the wage rate usually is), (b) left to the employee's discretion (e.g., sometimes, but not always, whether he smokes on the job), or (c) brought within the authority of the employer (e.g., the specific tasks he performs within the range fixed by the job specification). The conditions that make it advantageous to stipulate an aspect of behavior in the contract are sharp conflict of interest (e.g., as to wage level) and some uncertainty as to what that interest is. It is advantageous to leave to the employee's discretion those aspects that are of little interest to the employer but great interest to the employee; and to subject the employee to the organization's authority in those aspects that are of relatively great interest to the employer, comparatively unimportant to the employee, and about which the employer cannot make accurate predictions much in advance of performance.

We have already noted in chapter 3 that the authority relation is not a simple one. The problems of defining and enforcing the "employment contract" are a matter of concern and potential conflict for all organizational participants. We will make a series of similar observations in this chapter and in chapter 5 before returning (in chapter 6) to the importance of authority relations in programmed organizational activity.

To construct a series of hypotheses relating employee participation to external variables, we must first establish a criteron for "participation." Three methods of measuring participation yield substantially different results. First, we can measure the quantity of production by the individual worker. This criterion makes chapter 3 a special case of participation phenomena. Second, we can use an absence criterion. Permanent physical absence associated with leaving the company payroll represents the extreme value on the low side. Differences in on-the-job productivity are not captured by the absence criterion but employees are distinguished by their absence rates as well as their turnover rates. Third, we can use a turnover criterion: we can identify participation with the all-or-none phenomena of being on or off the organization payroll.

Although it may appear at first blush that these measures simply reflect different degrees of disassociation from the organization and, therefore, are simply different points on a common continuum, the available empirical evidence indicates no consistent relation among measures of production, absences, and voluntary turnover (Acton Society Trust, 1953; Morse, 1953; Brayfield and Crockett, 1955). The correlations are sometimes high, sometimes low; and the antecedent conditions for each result are difficult to specify. Some reasons for these findings are suggested by the available research, although substantiation is difficult.

First, under what conditions should we expect to find low absence (and/or productivity) associated with high voluntary turnover? We might expect that if extreme penalties are imposed for absence (relative to those generally expected in the group employed), absence rates will tend to be low among those who choose to stay on the job. But we should also expect to find a high rate of exit from the job. Similarly, where the ability to leave the organization is restrained (e.g., by government fiat), we should expect to find low voluntary turnover rates but (particularly if labor is scarce) relatively high absence rates (Mayo and Lombard, 1944).

Second, under what conditions should we expect to find a positive relation between absence and turnover? Assume (1) that motivation to avoid the demands (i.e., contributions) of the job situation stems primarily from dissatisfaction with the inducements–contributions balance, (2) that for most people motivation to seek relief through temporary absence occurs at a point related consistently to the point at which motivation to quit occurs, and (3) that the factors contributing to individual dissatisfaction are general to the population of workers rather than specific to individual workers. Under these assumptions, absence and voluntary turnover will be positively related when the penalties associated with absence and withdrawal are "normal."

Although we have scarcely touched the complexity of the relation among absenteeism, sickness, and turnover, we can see that the choice of a criterion of participation will significantly affect the propositions about participation. We propose here to use a turnover criterion, both because there is some intuitive sense in which such a criterion is most meaningful and because we have already dealt with the production criterion (which is closely related, at least conceptually, to the absence criterion) in the previous chapter. At the same time, however, we will attempt to point out how an absence criterion would support similar or different propositions.

4.4   Employee Participation: The General Model

Our general orientation to the problem of turnover has already been indicated in section 4.1. We make the general postulate that increases in the *balance of inducement utilities over contribution utilities* (4.1) decrease the *propensity of the individual participant to leave* (4.2) the organization, whereas decreases in that balance have an opposite effect [4.2:4.1].

The inducements–contributions balance, it was pointed out, is a function of two major components: the *perceived desirability of leaving the organization* (4.3) and the *perceived ease of movement from the organization* (4.4) (i.e., the utility of alternatives foregone [4.1: 4.3, 4.4]). Although these are not completely independent factors, most of the propositions below are statements about variations in either one or the other of them. The satisfaction (or motivation to withdraw) factor is a general one that holds for both absences and voluntary turnover. Differences between absences and turnover stem not from differences in the factors including the initial impulse but primarily from differences in the consequences of the alternative forms of withdrawal. The perceived ease of withdrawal from the organization, on the other hand, frequently is quite different for permanent withdrawal than for absenteeism or sick leave.

4.5   Factors Affecting the Perceived Desirability of Movement from the Organization

Some of the factors listed here affect the perceived desirability of movement and others the perceived ease of movement. However, in most cases the intervening variables are not made explicit in the available research and hence at least some of the structure of the theory is not tested directly. Nevertheless, there is sufficient information available to support the existence of two distinct mechanisms. One of the advantages of retaining the intervening variables is that it permits us to use data on absenteeism as possibly relevant to questions of turnover even though (as has been previously indicated) we have theoretical reasons and empirical evidence for believing that absenteeism and turnover are not in all respects well correlated. The reader who wishes to question this assumption will, of course, also wish to question the propositions cited here that depend significantly on data gathered from studies of absences.

The literature on the factors associated with employee motivation to leave an organization suggests that the primary factor influencing this motivation is employee satisfaction with the job as defined by him. The greater the individual's *satisfaction with the job* (4.5), the less the perceived desirability of movement [4.3:4.5]. A fairly wide range of job characteristics is relevant, since individual discontent with employment may reflect any of a number of relatively distinct aspects of the job. To identify these dimensions has been one of the major goals of the research conducted at the University of Michigan (Katz, Maccoby, and Morse, 1950; Katz, Maccoby, Gurin, and Floor, 1951; Mann and

Baumgartel, 1952; Morse, 1953). Our purpose is not to identify these dimensions in a factor-analysis sense but to specify the psychological mechanisms that operate to produce work satisfaction.

The most reasonable hypotheses about an individual's motivation to withdraw from employment are closely related to the conflict phenomena discussed in chapter 5. We can state three major propositions. First, the greater the *conformity of the job characteristics to the self-characterization held by the individual* (4.6), the higher the level of satisfaction [4.5:4.6]. Dissatisfaction arises from a disparity between reality and the ego-ideal held by the individual. The greater the disparity, the more pronounced the desire to escape from the situation.

Second, the greater the *predictability of instrumental relationships on the job* (4.7), the higher the level of satisfaction [4.5:4.7]. Ability to predict the cost of attaining a specified volume of production would be an example of such predictability in the job of factory manager. As will be indicated in chapter 5, one form of decision-making conflict stems from incomplete predictability. In general and up to a fairly extreme point, increased predictability yields increased satisfaction for most people – particularly in activities that are primarily instrumental. For example, one would predict that the satisfaction of the driver of an automobile would increase monotonically with the predictability of other drivers and of road conditions when he was driving to work, but not necessarily when he was engaged in a race. Similarly, in the work situation predictability is valued in most relationships but probably not all (Reynolds, 1951; Coch and French, 1948).

Third, the greater the *compatibility of work requirements with the requirements of other roles* (4.8), the higher the level of satisfaction [4.5:4.8]. As Curle (1949a) has pointed out, one of the major reasons for interpersonal differences in work satisfaction is that groups in a society do not always make mutually compatible demands on the individual worker. One would predict that an organizational participant would try to select his group memberships so as to keep at a low level the conflict imposed by differences in the demands made upon him.

Each of the three propositions specifies prior conditions for decision-making conflict; to the extent that withdrawal from one of the groups in the situation represents a solution to this type of conflict, we can infer the relations we have specified. Specific studies, however, have been aimed at the relations between primary factors and turnover (or absenteeism) without clearly defining the intervening factors we have identified; and it is from the propositions that follow that we infer support for the mechanisms proposed above.

Consider first empirical data relating to variations in the conformity of the job to the employee's self-characterization. Three types of individual evaluations of self appear to be significant: estimates of one's independence, one's worth, and one's specialized competences or interests. The greater the *consistency of supervisory practices with employee independence* (4.9), the less the conflict between job characteristics and individual self-image [4.6:4.9]. Thus, Reynolds and Shister (1949) have found that the most frequently cited reason for job dissatisfaction is an adverse conception of the independence and control provided by the work situation. So long as an individual desires independence in decision-making, the more authoritarian the supervisory practices, the greater the dissatisfaction aroused and the greater the pressure to withdraw (Morse and Reimer, 1955; Morse, 1953). Where physical egress is blocked, there is some evidence that withdrawal through rejection and in some cases psychoneurosis is stimulated (Stouffer *et al.*, 1949).

We have previously discussed (chapter 3) the independence norm in American culture that makes such a proposition reasonable. Where we deal with aggregate data, we may assume a generally pervasive norm of this sort. Where individual predictions are desired, we must try to distinguish individual differences in the strength of the independence norm.

The larger the *amount of rewards* (4.10) offered by the organization (in terms of status or money), the less the conflict between the job and the individual's self-image [4.6:4.10]. This proposition (other things being equal) is almost universally accepted, but the mechanisms through which it operates need to be specified. It is not as obvious a proposition as marginal economic analysis suggest. Recent studies of the labor market have cast considerable doubt on the traditional description of that market, particularly the extent to which wage and salary information is widely shared among employees (Reynolds, 1951). We are suggesting here that an employee has a conception of what he is worth in money and status, that his conception is not totally unrelated to the labor market value of his services, but that it is far from totally dependent on the market value. To cite one obvious example, the contemporary discontent of the teaching profession with its share of the national income is only partially explicable in terms of the economic model.

The greater the *individual's participation in job assignment* (4.11), the less the conflict between the job and the individual's self-image [4.6:4.11]. Studies in both army and industrial units suggest the not-surprising finding that, although the act of joining the organization commits the individual momentarily to whatever task is assigned him (since that is the nature of his employment contract) and all such tasks are perceived initially as yielding a favorable inducements–contributions balance, the employee is not indifferent to the several alternatives but prefers some to others (Bolanovich, 1948; Stouffer *et al.*, 1949). Consequently, an employee assigned according to personal preference will have a more favorable inducements–contributions balance than an employee not so assigned.

Self-conceptions change. In particular, they respond to environmental conditions as aspiration levels do. Status, wage, and job activity aspirations change as a function of experience and comparison with others whom the individual considers comparable. What can we say about changes in the perceived desirability of movement from our knowledge about aspiration-level changes?

Within a given occupational level, the higher the *level of education* (4.12), the greater the conflict between the job and the individual's self-image [4.6:4.12]. Some evidence for this hypothesis is reported by Reynolds (1951). He found that in a group of manual workers those with a high school education were more likely to want to leave their present jobs than those without a high school education. Similar findings were obtained in the army during World War II (Stouffer *et al.*, 1949; Morse 1953). Whether the relation holds at a higher level in an organization is not clear.

Within a given promotional ladder, the greater the *rate of change* of status and/or income (4.13) in the past, the greater the disparity between the job and the individual's self-image [4.6:4.13]. Using such a precise term as the "rate of change" may overstate what is meant. Individual participants make estimates of their worth on the basis of some projection of past achievement. For example, where promotions or salary increases occur regularly, the extrapolation is made in terms of future similar increases. Where, at some point in a promotional ladder, there is a substantial decrease in either the percentage or absolute increment, we would predict that discontent, voluntary withdrawal, or both would be produced (Stockford and Kunze, 1950; Morse, 1953). In a nonbusiness context, Brinton (1952) argues that this mechanism accounts for a major source of revolutionary pressure in a political system. Comparability of the job with the self-characterization of the individual bears a close relation to the compatibility of the job with other roles demanded by society. Many features of a self-characterization are based on pressures from other groups. In self-characterization, demands made by the society have been internalized so that they persist even though conformity is no longer enforced by existing membership groups. However, many role demands are enforced not through internalization but through the immediate rewards and punishments provided by the environment and in particular by other individuals and groups. To cite one instance, a man who has to work on a holiday will be reminded by his family and associates of what he (and they) must forego so that he can work.

Consequently, we would predict that the greater the extent to which the activities demanded by the job make it difficult or impossible to fulfill ordinary expectations in other social groups, the greater the perceived desirability of movement (Bullock, 1952). To generate specific predictions from this generalization, we need some estimate of the "normal" from which deviations are to be measured. Most obvious among these are work schedules. The greater the *congruence of work–time patterns with those of other roles* (4.14), the greater the compatibility of the job and other roles [4.8:4.14]. Problems arise when the requirements of the job deviate significantly from the expectation of an 8-hour day and 5-day week, a holiday on Sunday, and normal daylight work hours. All of these, and particularly the latter, are clearly artifacts of a particular culture. To the extent that this is a correct characterization of a cultural pattern, we can make specific predictions: The perceived desirability of movement will be greater among workers on the night shift than among workers on the day shift (Brissenden and Frankel, 1922). The perceived desirability of movement will be greater among workers who must be absent from their homes for periods of time greater than a normal working day than among others. The perceived desirability of movement will be greater among workers whose jobs involve frequent geographical moves than among others.

These and a host of similar propositions serve as common rules of thumb for determining wage differentials. In general, the propositions are so "obvious" that there have been few attempts at direct proof. If we can assume a long-run tendency of business firms to adjust to reality, the continued existence of wage differentials offers some indirect proof of the propositions.

Propositions like those just cited are based on cultural norms and the pressures they exert through institutions like the family or the community. The norms are taken as given and the compatibility of the work with them is evaluated. However, there are many roles (e.g., friendship roles) where the compatibility of job with other activities depends as much on the characteristics of the other groups as it does on the characteristics of the job. For the individual, potential problems arise from the demands of overlapping group membership. Where the job stimulates the development of a number of single-purpose groups with overlapping membership, workers can be expected to find the work less pleasant than where a multipurpose integrated group exists. Thus, we are led to a pair of anomie-like hypotheses: The smaller the *size of the work group* (4.15), the greater the compatibility of organizational and other roles [4.8:4.15]. The smaller the *size of the organization* (4.16), the greater the compatibility of organizational and other roles [4.8:4.16]. The hypotheses may well not hold in the extreme ranges: A work group of one individual will not be a very satisfactory group for most individuals. The differences between a group of one (or two) and a group of ten have not been investigated and may reverse the relation. Similarly, differences between groups of 100 and groups of 200 have not been investigated. It is quite possible that there exist critical "optimal" group sizes. With this proviso, there is a fair amount of empirical evidence supporting the hypothesis, particularly if we use data on absences interchangeably with turnover data (Acton Society Trust, 1953; Blackett, 1928; Reynolds and Shister, 1949).

Finally, one further hypothesis may shed light on an important difference between absences and turnover. We have argued that the larger the organization, the higher the probability that the individual will become involved in overlapping and conflicting group memberships. From this, we have argued, there stems a desire to leave the organization. In general, the proposition is supported by the available data on absences. However, the data on turnover fail to support the proposition with any consistency at all. How can we explain this difference? It is probably caused by the arbitrary nature of our turnover data. The larger the organization, the greater the *perceived possibility of intraorganizational transfer* (4.17) [4.17:4.16], and therefore, the less the perceived desirability of leaving the organization [4.3:4.17] (Brissenden and Frankel, 1922; Rice, 1951). Typically turnover is defined as leaving the formally defined organization (e.g., the business firm). Thus, leaving a job in manufacturing to take a job in distribution will be classified as turnover if there is a change of company, but not otherwise. A substantial amount of what would be called turnover in smaller firms is classified as "interdepartmental transfer" in larger firms.

The structure of these propositions relating to the individual participant's perceived desirability of movement is pictured in figure 4.1.

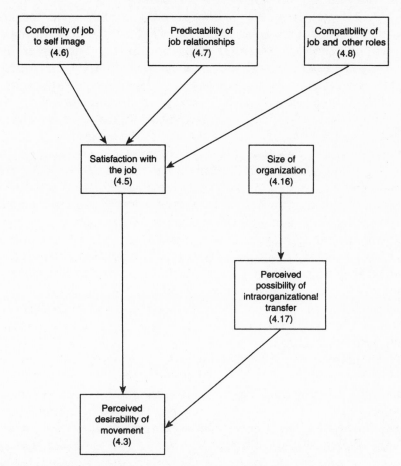

Figure 4.1 Major factors affecting perceived desirability of movement.

4.6 Factors Affecting the Perceived Ease of Movement from the Organization

Under nearly all conditions the most accurate single predictor of labor turnover is the state of the economy. Even such a gross aggregate statistic as the national quit rate shows a strong negative relationship with the aggregate rate of discharges and layoffs. When jobs are plentiful, voluntary movement is high; when jobs are scarce, voluntary turnover is small. It is the object of this section to suggest some possible refinements of these propositions.

We will hypothesize that perceived ease of movement for an individual depends on the availability of jobs for which he is qualified (and willing to accept) in organizations visible to him. The greater the *number of perceived extraorganizational alternatives* (4.18), the greater the perceived ease of movement [4.4:4.18]. We wish to explore the factors associated with both the visibility of organizations and the availability of jobs. But first, some preliminary remarks are in order.

Let us suppose that we have a population of organizations and a population of potential employees. Each potential employee has a number of attributes primarily, but not exclusively, related to his special competences as a worker. Each organization can rank combinations of such attributes so that workers can be correspondingly ranked in terms of their desirability as employees (almost independently of specific job requirements). From this it follows that when organizations expand, they do no (i.e., virtually no) firing; when they contract, they do no hiring. Even where one would not expect such a relationship to hold, in a change of political administration, it is extremely difficult to make new appointments while attempting to reduce the over-all size of the organization (e.g., the Republican administration in 1953).

Under these conditions, an individual's perception of the ease of moving from a given organization will depend on (a) the number of organizations whose rankings he can scan, (b) his level in these rankings, and (c) the ranking that corresponds to the current hire–fire point. The first of these factors is the visibility factor; the other two are different aspects of the job availability factor. The lower the *level of business activity* (4.19), the less the number of extraorganizational alternatives [4.18:4.19]. When unemployment figures are used as a criterion of the state of business, this proposition becomes almost a tautology. And since virtually all of the standard measures of business activity show a relatively high correlation with each other, it is not surprising that voluntary turnover rates should decrease when business turns downward. Shifts in business can be conceived as shifting the critical "cutoff" points on each industry's ranking of jobs, and hence changing the alternatives open to an employee. For specific predictions in specific industries, differences in the impact of the business cycle may result in differences in turnover, but the impact of a recession in one area spreads beyond that area, since the change in the cutoff point in one industry alters the alternatives open to individuals not only in that industry but also in related industries.

The evidence for the proposition is substantial. Reynolds (1951) reports that in the 1948–9 recession, the average voluntary separations in 39 companies surveyed fell from 3.5 percent per month to 1.6 percent per month and that, in general, market demand for labor is a dominant factor in voluntary turnover. Similar results are reported by Behrend (1953), Blackett (1928), Brissenden and Frankel (1922), Palmer (1954), and Woytinsky (1942).

Not all of the variance in behavior, however, can be explained in this fashion. Individual attributes define the individual's employability rank and, therefore, determine differential effects of changes in the state of business. Consequently, we wish to be able to specify factors that affect individual ranks.

The perceived availability of outside alternatives is a function of the *sex of the participant* (4.20) [4.18:4.20]. Male workers will perceive movement to be easier than will female workers. In general, studies have reported a higher turnover rate among males than among females, although a careful study should probably distinguish between marriageable and nonmarriageable females. Myers and MacLaurin (1943), Brissenden and Frankel (1922), Palmer (1954) and Bakke *et al.*, (1954) have reported data supporting the proposition (in Palmer's case the differences are slight). Yoder (Bakke *et al.*, 1954), however, failed to find a significant difference. Hauser (Bakke *et al.*, 1954) has some data that indicate a close relationship between female turnover rates and marriage. For the female worker the family organization is an alternative to work.

The perceived availability of outside alternatives is a function of the *age of the participant* (4.21) [4.16:4.21]. The older the worker, the less the perceived ease of movement. A second way in which age affects the perceived ease of movement is indicated below. The mechanism just cited is clearly important. In ranking job attributes, age is a negatively valued characteristic. Consequently, turnover among younger persons will be higher than among older persons – even when skill and other attributes are held constant (Myers and MacLaurin, 1943; Reynolds, 1951; Bakke *et al.*, 1954).

The perceived availability of outside alternatives is a function of the *social status of the participant* (4.22) [4.18:4.22]. Members of low-status groups will perceive movement to be more difficult than will members of high-status groups. Thus, we would predict lower voluntary turnover among Negroes than among whites, lower among Jews than among Gentiles, lower among foreign-born than among native-born citizens.

All the propositions just cited refer to more or less static conditions in organizations operating within the contemporary American culture. However, some important features influencing the employability of an individual reflect somewhat more dynamic characteristics. The perceived availability of outside alternatives is a function of the *technology* of the economy (4.23) [4.18:4.23] (Palmer and Ratner, 1949; Jaffe and Stewart, 1951). For example, recent changes in technology have tended to raise the relative ranks of female workers and white-collar employees by increasing the range of jobs for which they are employable. Automation will presumably have a quite similar shuffling affect on the rankings.

The longer the *length of service* (4.24) of the employee, the greater his *specialization* (4.25) [4.25:4.24]; the greater his specialization, the fewer the extraorganizational alternatives perceived [4.18:4.25]. Where the previous proposition dealt with changes in the ratings of attributes, the present one depends on changes in the attributes of a given individual. When an individual remains in an organization for a long time, his skills become more and more specific to the organization in question. Consequently, he becomes more and more indispensable to that organization but more and more dispensable to other organizations. In specialization we approach a theoretically very interesting limiting case where the demand and supply of a particular bundle of abilities tends to decrease until we have an organization that can find a replacement only at prohibitive cost and an employee who can find another job only at prohibitive loss. At executive levels this case of bilateral monopoly is probably quite common, with salaries determined by bargaining and/or rules of thumb. Data on the compensation of business executives are consistent with this characterization of the situation (Roberts, 1956; Simon, 1957). A number of studies substantiate the negative relationship between skill level and voluntary turnover (Brissenden and Frankel, 1922; Reynolds, 1951; Morse, 1953).

All of the propositions thus far listed operate through changes (or differences) in the actual availability of jobs – either through differences in the hire–fire point, or through individual differences in employability. However, these are not the only factors involved. The perception of alternatives depends partly on the actual alternatives available and partly on evoking mechanisms. As a result, the range of organizational alternatives visible to a particular potential participant varies from individual to individual, from organization to organization, and from situation to situation (Reynolds, 1951).

The larger the *number of organizations visible* (4.26) to the participant, the greater the number of perceived extraorganizational alternatives [4.18:4.26]. This is one of the basic propositions stemming from our conception of the labor market. The greater the number of organizations scanned, the higher the probability that the scanning will include an alternative job that is above the cutoff point. What factors affect the visibility of organizations to participants? Certain characteristics of organizations make some more visible than others, and certain characteristics of individuals make more organizations visible to them than to other individuals. With respect to the latter, we can specify a simple mechanism that leads to a number of specific propositions. The greater the *prestige of the organization* (4.27), the greater the *visibility of the organization* (4.28) [4.28:4.27]. If we now apply the propositions relating to organizational prestige that were cited in chapter 3, we can use these to generate a series of specific predictions. The larger the organization, the more visible it will be. The more the organization produces a distinguishable product, the more visible it will be (Reynolds and Shister, 1949). The greater the number of high–status occupations and/or individuals in the organization, the more visible it will be. The faster the rate of growth of the organization, the more visible it will be.

Individuals who are valued by organizations with high visibility will, in general, perceive movement to be easier than will individuals whose skills are demanded by less visible organizations.

It has been found that typical scanning procedures for potential members of business organizations are limited by geography (Reynolds, 1951). Scanning for job opportunities is typically largely word of mouth, and depends on the range of organizations included in the individual's usual contacts. Knowledge of organizations decreases rapidly with distance, except for special cases of individuals with relatively high–mobility expectations or preferences.

Thus, the greater the *heterogeneity of personal contacts* (4.29) for the employee, the greater the number of organizations visible to him [4.26:4.29] (Reynolds, 1951). From this, one can make a number of subsidiary predictions, for which, however, there appear to be no data. For example, the perceived ease of movement will be greater among residents of suburbs than among residents of central cities (on the assumption that bedroom communities exhibit somewhat greater organizational heterogeneity than comparable central areas). There will be an increase over time in the perceived ease of movement because of increased commuting. The more nonwork organizations in which the individual participates, the greater his perceived ease of movement. For example, it has been observed that craft union members frequently use their union to learn about available jobs (Reynolds 1951).

Organizational recruitment, however, is not simply a matter of individual scanning of alternatives. Simultaneously, organizations are searching for personnel. The job seeks the man as well as vice versa. Consequently, factors that determine the mode of search used by organizations will affect the success of the individual's search.

The greater the *visibility of an individual* (4.30) to organizations, the greater the number of organizations visible to him [4.26:4.30]. With available data there is no certain way to define the important factors that affect the visibility of an individual in a job market. However, there is every reason to assume a strong feedback relationship between organizational visibility to the individual and that individual's visibility to the organization. Thus, the greater the number of organizations visible to an individual, the greater his visibility to relevant organizations [4.30:4.26]. The scanning process involved in the job market is necessarily, at least in part, a two-way scanning in which it is probable that if one sees, he will be seen. However, the mechanism is not a typical case of feedback, for with a change in either visibility of the individual or visibility of organizations to him, the other adjusts immediately to an equilibrium position, remaining fixed until one variable or the other is changed by some independent factor.

We have already specified at least some of the independent factors that might affect the visibility of organizations. Now we shall indicate some characteristics of individuals that would affect their visibility. The greater the range of organizations in which an individual has personal contacts, the more visible he is [4.30:4.29]. The higher the social status of an individual, the more visible he is [4.30:4.22]. The greater the *uniqueness of the individual* (4.31), the more visible he is [4.30:4.31]. In the absence of empirical evidence, little can be said about these propositions except that they conform to our own experience and intuitions.

Finally, we need to consider an explicitly motivational factor: the individual's propensity to engage in search activities. At any point, the individual must decide not only what alternative to choose on the available evidence, but also whether he should search for additional evidence (or alternatives). The greater the *individual's propensity to search* (4.32), the greater the number of organizations visible to him [4.26:4.32]. In the literature, we can distinguish two major mechanisms by means of which search propensities are varied. Both of them are discussed elsewhere in more general terms, but the present case represents an important specific instance. On the one hand, search is generated by dissatisfaction. On the other hand, it is regulated by the habituation of the individual to the situation.

The greater the individual's satisfaction with his job, the less the propensity to search for alternative jobs; in general, there will be a critical level of satisfaction above which search is quite restricted and below which search is quite extensive [4.32:4.5] (Reynolds, 1951). We have argued previously that there is a critical level on the satisfaction-dissatisfaction scale at which the individual commences to scan alternatives not previously considered. Indeed, the whole section on the perceived desirability of movement can be viewed as a set of propositions bearing on this problem. Although the perceived desirability of movement and the perceived ease of movement are two distinct factors, the propositions relating to search show that they have considerable interdependence. Dissatisfaction makes movement more desirable and also (by stimulating search) makes it appear more feasible.

Habit also operates to restrict search. The greater the *habituation to a particular job or organization* (4.33), the less the propensity to search for alternative work opportunities [4.32:4.33] [Hill and Trist, 1955). In a sense, this is included in the prior proposition, since habitual choice of an alternative indicates that it is an acceptable alternative. However, it may be desirable to separate current satisfactoriness from historical satisfactoriness – particularly where we allow some adjustments in aspiration levels. Thus, if search is restricted in a mildly unsatisfactory situation, adjustment to the situation can occur before the factors restricting search are overcome (or recognized). Habituation serves to narrow severely the range of alternatives considered. It tends to remove the particular decision (in this case the choice of organization) from the realm of evaluation and choice so that the job comes to be treated less as a variable in the control of the individual than as a constant defined for him.

Unfortunately, the specific propositions relating to habituation are somewhat contaminated by other factors. For example, we would hypothesize that habituation is a function of both the length of service and the age of the participant [4.32:4.21, 4.24]. But results relating length of service and age to turnover are susceptible to a number of different explanations and this is only one of the mechanisms at work.

The major propositions in this section (i.e. those relating to the perceived ease of movement) are summarized in figure 4.2. Along with those previously indicated in figure 4.1, they constitute the major factors affecting employee participation in an organization.

4.7   Extension to Other Participants

We have discussed at some length the factors affecting employee job decisions. We cannot undertake a similar detailed treatment of the

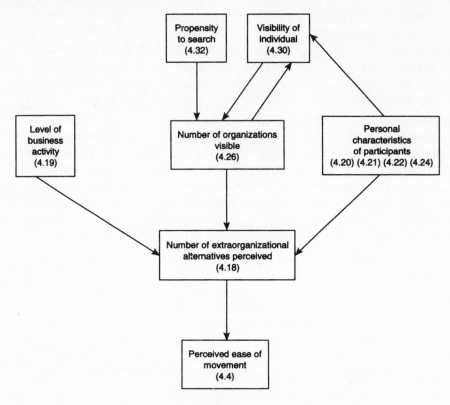

Figure 4.2 Major factors affecting perceived ease of movement.

participation decisions of other participants – buyers, suppliers, agents, or investors. In view of their importance to the organizational system, however, we will indicate briefly how propositions on employee decisions to participate can be extended to these other areas.

Our treatment of employee participation specified two major variables:

1 the perceived desirability of movement, and
2 the perceived ease of movement.

Similar major mechanisms operate in other areas. A consumer's decision to switch brands can be analyzed in terms of propensity to change, determined by experience with the present and past brands and the ease of change (i.e., market structure). A dealer's decision to change his franchise depends on both a perceived desire to do so and the availability of alternatives.

That a similar framework appears to serve in these different areas is not surprising in view of their common features. This does not mean, however, that there are direct analogues of each proposition cited above for all areas of participation. For example, investment behavior and employee behavior differ with respect to the relative comparability of alternatives. Although investment decisions are not made in terms of easily compared dimensions and under conditions of certain knowledge, we may hypothesize that the subjective uncertainty of investors (at least major investors) tends to be less than that of employees. In such a situation, we would predict that aspiration levels would adjust more rapidly to the external environment for investors than for employees.

An important difference between consumer behavior and employee behavior lies in the extent to which "inaction" is an alternative. An employee is rarely placed in the position of a consumer who has exhausted his inventory. If he does "nothing," he continues in his present job. If the typical consumer does "nothing," he starves to death. The difference between the two situations is partially reflected in the premium that manufacturers are prepared to pay to secure the "inaction" situation with consumers (e.g., in selling magazine subscriptions).

The mention of such differences is a necessary preface to a brief discussion of how the general framework and the major variables in this chapter can be extended to participants other than employees. Considering only the major hypotheses, we have been concerned with four basic variables:

• the visibility of alternatives;
• the propensity to search for alternatives;
• the level of satisfaction with the existing alternative;
• the availability of acceptable alternatives to leaving the organization.

Visibility of alternatives We have argued that the employment market is not a "perfect market" in the sense that all alternatives are always known to all buyers and sellers. Similarly, advertising is a monument to the proposition that the visibility of alternatives is a factor in consumer behavior. Factors associated with visibility, such as advertising and outlet characteristics, comprise a major source of concern for firms dealing in ordinary retail markets (Howard, 1957).

Search propensities A basic factor in determining employee job decisions is the rate of the employee's search activity. Similarly, in the case of participants other than employees, search propensities appear to be of substantial importance. For example, we would predict that one of the characteristic features of a "captive" supplier would be his disinclination to seek new alternatives through active search. Brand loyalty of consumers and the behavior of small investors with respect to AT&T stock are similar phenomena reflecting rather low search activity.

Satisfaction In discussing employee mobility, we indicated that satisfaction affected both the perceived desirability of movement and (by stimulating or retarding search activity) the perceived ease of movement. In particular, we noted that shifts in levels of aspiration had important affects on employee participation. If we examine investment behavior and the behavior of organizations seeking funds, we observe a similar concern. For example, there is a tendency for firms to pay out extra profits in good years as supplementary rather than regular dividends in order to avoid expectations about future payments that might be difficult to realize (Walter, 1957). Organizations with franchised dealers also find that substantial downward shifts in payments to dealers after a "temporary" boom period result in considerable dealer resistance and threats of withdrawal.

Alternatives to movement The final important feature of our model of employee participation is the importance of alternatives that represent a change without leaving the organization. Such alternatives exist frequently – sometimes more in one organization than in another or more for one participant than for another. Similarly, recent market research has emphasized the importance of the distribution structure of the market for brand shifting (Kuehn, 1958). In other areas (e.g., investors, suppliers, dealers) major participants frequently use their power position to force an acceptable policy on the organization. Thus, a major stockholder's first reaction to an unacceptable organization policy is likely to be an attempt to change the policy rather than a withdrawal from the organization.

4.8 Opportunism and Organizational Survival

When the conditions within or surrounding an organization change in such a way as to affect adversely its inducements–contributions balance and endanger its survival, members of the organization may initiate changes in activities and new activities to restore a favorable balance. (The initiating processes themselves will be considered in more detail in chapter 7.) Ordinarily, it is the group of participants called the "management" or the "administrators" who take responsibility for the adjustment, but on occasion this function may be performed by other groups. For example, banks or investors frequently assume active management of enterprises that are failing financially, and groups of employees threatened with unemployment may do so also (e.g., the willingness of the ILGWU to take on management responsibilities in small garment factories which are facing difficulties).

The identity of the individuals or groups who are active in this adaptive or "opportunistic" process is significant, for it largely determines the kinds of changes that will be attempted and the order in which they will be tried. In general, there is not a single, unique set of conditions for organizational survival (Simon, 1952-3), but various sets of alternative conditions that would produce a favorable inducements–contributions balance. Adaptation of the organization for survival may move it in the direction of any one of these alternatives.

Opportunistic changes in the inducements–contributions balance of an organization will tend to leave untouched those inducements and contributions that are objects of identification of the individuals initiating the change. In particular, these individuals may be identified with the organization goals or with a social group in the organization, or may be motivated primarily by personal inducements. To the extent that they are identified with the organizational goals, they will seek to preserve these while modifying other inducements and contributions; to the extent that they are identified with a group or with personal goals, they will be primarily concerned with the survival of the organization on whatever terms this is most easily achieved (Simon, Smithburg, and Thompson, 1950, p. 389).

We can particularize these propositions by making use of what we know about the specific identifications of specific kinds of people (see chapter 3). For instance, we would expect the salaried full-time executives of a voluntary organization (e.g., a welfare organization) to be more willing to change the organization's goals to ensure its survival than the volunteer workers in the same organization (Messinger, 1955).

For those groups that can influence the organization's activities, opportunism is an alternative to leaving the organization that may be evoked when satisfaction is low. We would predict a greater probability of the former being evoked before the latter to the extent that (a) a participant perceives himself as influential in determining the organization's activities, (b) substitute inducements are not perceived as readily available from other organizations, and (c) possibilities are seen of restoring a favorable inducements–contributions balance without destroying those particular inducements that are important to the individual. Variables (b) and (c) frequently operate in opposing directions; i.e., those persons who are most closely identified with aspects of the organization's current pattern of activity – hence resistive to change in the pattern – are generally also those who have the fewest opportunities for substitute satisfaction in other organizations.

4.9 Conclusion

Decisions to participate in the organization – either to enter or to withdraw – are a second major class of decisions made by the organizational members that focus attention on the motivational problems involved in using human beings to perform organizational tasks. Like the decisions considered in chapter 3, participation decisions are both more complex and more important to the organization than their position in classical theory would suggest. In this chapter we have examined the inducements–contributions postulate originally formulated by Barnard and the evidence on labor turnover. We have suggested some extensions of the general model for employee participation to participants other than employees.

Testing the inducements–contributions postulate requires procedures for measuring (in terms of individual utilities) the inducements offered by the organization and the contributions made by the participant. The difficulty of the measurement problem depends on the extent to which three critical assumptions are satisfied: (a) that individual utilities change only slowly; (b) that utility functions are monotone; (c) that broad groups of people have roughly the same utility functions. We have suggested that such assumptions are reasonable even though they have not really been verified. The inducements–contributions balance has two major components: the perceived desirability of leaving the organization and the utility of alternatives foregone in order to stay in the organization (i.e., the perceived ease of leaving the organization). The perceived desirability of movement is a function of both the individual's satisfaction with his present job and his perception of alternatives that do not involve leaving the organization. We have discussed some factors that affect these variables. The perceived ease of leaving the organization is a function of the number of extraorganizational alternatives perceived; and we have discussed the factors affecting such perceptions.

Whether dissatisfaction with the organization leads to withdrawal depends on whether the participant perceives the "employment contract" as given or as subject to change. Where the contract is viewed as unchangeable, the only options are to "accept" or "reject."

Where the contract can be changed, participation by no means precludes internal conflict and bargaining. Internal bargaining as an alternative to movement is a factor in several types of organizational participation. Because of the importance of this phenomenon, and of organizational conflict in general, to organization theory, we turn now in chapter 5 to the conditions under which conflict arises in an organization, the consequences of conflict, and the organizational reactions to it. Increasingly, we will be moving from the semiconscious motivational factors considered in chapters 3 and 4 to more conscious and deliberate power phenomena.

5

Conflict in Organizations

Conflict is a term of many uses. Most generally, the term is applied to a breakdown in the standard mechanisms of decision-making so that an individual or group experiences difficulty in selecting an action alternative. This general definition will be adopted here. Thus, conflict occurs when an individual or group experiences a decision problem. We will shortly introduce specific types of conflict defined in terms of the decision-making model we described earlier.

We can identify three main classes of conflict phenomena:

1 individual conflict: conflict in individual decision-making;
2 organizational conflict: individual or group conflict within an organization;
3 interorganizational conflict: conflict between organizations or groups.

These three classes generally arise from rather different basic mechanisms, although there is a partial overlap. Our primary interest is in the second class – organizational conflict. We will also attempt, however, to state some major propositions about the other classes. We cannot entirely ignore individual conflict, because one type of organizational conflict arises from individual decision problems. Nor can we ignore interorganizational conflict entirely, because conflict between groups frequently occurs within a larger organization.

Our objective in this chapter is to consider three main features of conflict:

1 Under what conditions does conflict arise? We wish to be able to predict when and where organizational or individual conflict will occur.
2 What are the reactions of individuals and organizations to conflict? In general, we expect the response to conflict to be an attempt to resolve it, and we wish to be able to specify what form this attempt will take.
3 What is the outcome of conflict? Particularly in a bargaining situation, we are interested in who gets what.

Because the last of these questions concerns interorganizational conflict primarily, our major interest will be in the first two. What we have to say on the theory of bargaining will be found in section 5.5.

5.1 Individual Conflict

To characterize how individual conflict arises, we start by indicating the conditions under which decision-making is uncomplicated. A simple decision situation exists if (a) among the evoked alternatives of action one is clearly better than all others, and (b) the preferred evoked alternative is good enough to be acceptable. Under these conditions a decision will be made quickly and there will be no *ex post facto* evaluations of the decision. If, on the other hand, no alternative is clearly better than the others, or if the best alternative is not "good enough," there will be delay in decision-making and *ex post facto* re-evaluations and rationalizations.

Conflict arises in three major ways, which we can distinguish as *unacceptability, incomparability,* and *uncertainty.* In the case of *unacceptability,* the individual knows at least the probability distributions of outcomes associated with each alternative of action. In addition, he may be able to identify a preferred alternative without difficulty, but the preferred alternative is not good enough, i.e., it does not meet a standard of satisfactoriness. In the case of *incomparability,* the individual knows the probability distributions of outcomes, but cannot identify a most preferred alternative. In the case of *uncertainty,* the individual does not know the probability distributions connecting behavior choices and environmental outcomes.

How can we describe the major types of individual decision situations? In order to avoid an overly elaborate typology, we limit ourselves to five kinds of perceived outcomes of choice. They are described in terms of the probability, u, of a choice resulting in a positively valued state of affairs, and the probability, w, of the choice resulting in a negatively valued state of affairs.

1 A *good* alternative is one that has a high u-value and a small w-value. The critical values for u and w are subjectively determined and vary from one individual to another. A good alternative is above the acceptable level defined by the individual, and thus is "viable."

2 A *bland* alternative is an alternative for which u and w are both small. It has little likelihood of producing a state of affairs having either positive or negative value to the individual.

3 A *mixed* alternative is one that has a high probability of producing both positively and negatively valued outcomes. In this case u and w are both large.

4 A *poor* alternative is one that is unlikely to result in a desirable outcome and likely to result in an undesirable outcome (i.e., u is small and w is large).

5 An alternative is *uncertain* if the individual does not have a conception of the probabilities attached to it. Under these conditions u and w are unknown either because the outcomes themselves are unknown or because the subjective utility of the outcomes is unknown.

To construct a typology of individual conflict we imagine a choice situation involving two alternatives, A and B, each of which can assume any of the five values indicated above. There will be, then, 25 different choice situations, of which 10 are mirror images of another 10. Hence, there are 15 distinct situations, which produce the three types of conflict as follows:

	Alternatives		
	A	B	Type of Conflict
1	Good	Good	Incomparability
2	Good	Bland	No conflict
3	Good	Mixed	No conflict
4	Good	Poor	No conflict
5	Good	Uncertain	No conflict
6	Bland	Bland	Unacceptability and incomparability
7	Bland	Mixed	Unacceptability and incomparability
8	Bland	Poor	Unacceptability
9	Bland	Uncertain	Uncertainty
10	Mixed	Mixed	Unacceptability and incomparability
11	Mixed	Poor	Unacceptability
12	Mixed	Uncertain	Uncertainty
13	Poor	Poor	Unacceptability and incomparability
14	Poor	Uncertain	Uncertainty
15	Uncertain	Uncertain	Uncertainty

In a number of cases (2 through 5) no conflict is anticipated. In these cases, one alternative is acceptable and the other is not, so that there is negligible difficulty in decision-making. The other cases represent various forms of incomparability, unacceptability and uncertainty.

The relation between these categories and the Miller and Dollard (Hunt, 1944; Miller, 1951; Miller and Dollard, 1941) typology of conflict situations is obvious. Our category 1 is equivalent to an "approach–approach" situation. Categories 6–12 represent various forms of an "approach–avoidance" situation. Category 13 is an "avoidance–avoidance" conflict. Categories 14–15 introduces a dimension (uncertainty) that is not important in the Miller-Dollard theory. What most sharply distinguishes the conflict theory outlined here and below from the classical conflict theories is the emphasis we place on conflict as a generator of search behavior. Although there clearly are situations that fit the classical model of choice from a fixed set of action alternatives, we will argue that the commonest reaction of the organism to a conflict situation is to look for a way out of the dilemma. This is, of course, consistent with some of the major propositions both of Miller and Dollard and of Lewin (1935).

Reaction to conflict

We will not treat extensively the propositions on reactions to individual conflict, but we will identify some major propositions that will be relevant for the extension to organizational conflict.

We have now specified that *perceived conflict* (5.1) is a function of the *subjective uncertainty of alternatives* (5.2), the *subjective incomparability of alternatives* (5.3), and the *subjective unacceptability of alternatives* (5.4) [5.1:5.2, 5.3, 5.4]. We assume that where conflict is perceived, *motivation to reduce conflict* (5.5) is generated [5.5:5.1]. This assumption that conflict represents a disequilibrium in the system is implicit in all treatments of the phenomenon.

Reaction to conflict depends on its source. Where the source of conflict is uncertainty, the individual will first increase his *search for clarification* (5.6) of the consequences of alternatives already evoked [5.6:5.5, 5.2]. Failing in that, he will increase his *search for new alternatives* (5.7) [5.7:5.5, 5.2]. That is, there is a tendency to evaluate a few alternatives thoroughly before searching for new ones. This priority in effort admits several interpretations. First, if the world is perceived as benign and providing many good alternatives, only a few alternatives need be examined to find a satisfactory one. The rationalistic flavor of the interpretation can be reduced by viewing the process of evoking alternatives as involving an unconscious screening mechanism that rejects obviously poor alternatives. Finally, to carry the explanation all the way from a quasi-economic theory to a quasi-learning one, we may suppose that the individual has learned from past experiences in similar situations to generate responses that have a relatively high probability of being acceptable. On this analysis, the tendency for an individual to resolve uncertainty before searching for alternatives will be stronger in "ordinary" situations than in "unusual" situations. This follows from a general learning proposition about the generalization of learned responses. However, even where the situation is entirely new and the subliminal screening largely ineffective, the individual decision maker may react to the situation in the standard way if he generalizes not to the substantive content of the situation but to its problem-solving character.

Where the source of conflict is unacceptability, the individual will search for new alternatives [5.7:5.5, 5.4]. The strength of the motivation to reduce conflict (and thus the rate of search) depends on the *availability of bland alternatives* (5.8) and the *time pressure* (5.9) [5.5:5.8, 5.9]. As in the previous case, recognition of the unacceptability of available alternatives triggers search activity. Repeated failure to discover "acceptable" alternatives leads generally to a redefinition of "acceptable" (Hunt, 1944, pp. 333–78). The proposition above, therefore, is essentially a statement about how much failure is required to produce a shift in aspiration. The proposition is weak, since it simply asserts that *some* search will occur before adjustment of aspirations. As in the preceding proposition, the inclination to search depends on an underlying expectation that the world is essentially benign.

The second part of the hypothesis suggests that the speed of search is variable, depending both on time pressure and the availability of a bland alternative as an escape hatch. In general, search will be more vigorous the greater the time pressure; it will also be more vigorous when no bland alternative is available (Lewin, 1935). This is the usual proposition relating creativity to stress. The evidence suggests that (at least for some individuals) search becomes less fruitful as stress and time pressure are pushed to the limit. Search may then be extremely vigorous but largely stereotyped. (Birch, 1945; Lazarus, Deese, and Osler, 1952.)

Where the source of conflict is incomparability (but not unacceptability), *decision time* (5.10) will be short [5.10:5.3, 5.4]. Under such conditions choice will depend on attention and the sequence in which alternatives are presented. Without arguing that individuals never assess marginal differences between alternatives, we think that the choice between several satisfactory alternatives depends more on attention cues and the order of presentation than it does on indifference curves. The literature of market research, for example, is full of evidence susceptible to this interpretation.

Our major hypotheses on individual reaction to conflict are summarized in figure 5.1.

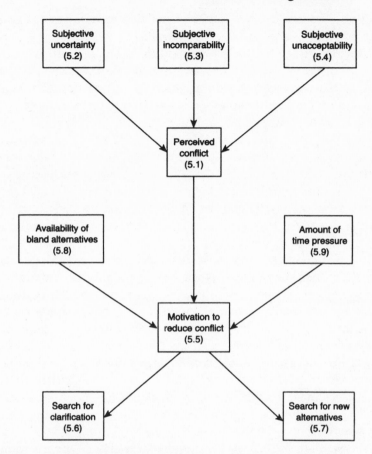

Figure 5.1 Factors affecting individual conflict and individual reactions to conflict.

5.2 Organizational Conflict: Individual Conflict Within an Organization

At several places in this volume, particularly in the discussions of productivity and turnover, we examined specific problems of individual conflict that arise in organizations. Conflict is also implicit in some of the propositions on bureaucratic transformation of goals. In this chapter, we will see how these phenomena affect conflict within an organization, how conflict arises, and how organizations react to it. These are the subjects to which we now turn.

In an organization, each member can evaluate the alternatives open (or apparently open) to the organization. Thus, we can characterize the situation by describing the states of the individual members and the decision rules operating in the organization.

Difficulty in decision-making in an organization is at least partly a function of the prescribed decision procedures. It makes a difference whether the group operates under dictatorial, majority, or unanimity rules. In our discussion, however, we assume that the group functions under at least an implicit unanimity rule. By this we mean that the group deems it important generally to arrive at a decision agreeable to all members, even though it may operate formally under another decision rule for resolving a deadlock. It is our impression that this restriction is not particularly severe, since most task-oriented organizations have strong tendencies to seek consensus. Although these tendencies vary in strength, we will probably not go far wrong if we proceed on the unanimity model.

How can conflict, as we have defined it, arise in an organization? We distinguish two major types of organizational conflict. First, decision problems may arise that at the outset are primarily intraindividual – inside the individual members. In this case, the organizational problem is that none (or very few) of the members has a known acceptable alternative in terms of his own goals and perceptions. The second type of organizational conflict arises not from the problems of individuals in making up their minds, but from differences between the choices made by different individuals in the organization. In this case, the individual participants are not in conflict but the organization as a whole is.

These are not the only possible types of situations. Various combinations of inter- and intraindividual conflict can and will occur. We wish, however, to distinguish situations in which organizational conflict is generally of one type or the other and to indicate differences in the reaction of organizations to decision problems according to the type of conflict involved. Our concern in this section is individual conflict as it occurs in an organization. In the next section we will consider intergroup conflict.

In the brief discussion of individual conflict above, three types were indicated: uncertainty, incomparability, and unacceptability. In order for organizational conflict to be of an intraindividual type, the decision problem must put all (or nearly all) of the relevant members of the organization in one of three types of personal conflict. Conversely, interindividual conflict requires (a) that each individual participant have an acceptable alternative of action, and (b) that different participants prefer different alternatives. Thus, we need to consider the incidence of intraindividual conflict, organizational reaction to such conflict, and attitudes about such conflict as well as the more commonly discussed interindividual conflict.

From the earlier hypotheses we can predict directly that organizational conflict of the intraindividual type is most likely to occur when the conditions surrounding the organizational decision involve widespread uncertainty or a scarcity of acceptable alternatives of action. Naturally, there will be individual variation, but many features of an environment have general affects on individual judgments along these dimensions. It is meaningful to characterize environments or decision situations as "uncertain" or "bad", meaning by the first that the subjective certainty of individuals in such a situation tends to be lower than in other situations and by the second that individuals generally perceive the environment as offering few or no good alternatives.

Factors affecting uncertainty

We can make two hypotheses: The greater the *amount of past experience* (5.11) with a decision situation, the less probable that intraindividual organizational conflict will arise [5.2:5.11]. The less the *complexity of the decision situation* (5.12), the less probable that intraindividual organizational conflict will arise [5.2:5.12]. From these propositions, we deduce that organizational conflict of the intraindividual type will be more frequent in determining the price on a new product or in choosing production equipment for a new production line involving substantial changes in basic technology than in determining price on a standard product under a stable environment or in selecting production equipment on a line having no significant changes in technology. The evidence for these propositions does not really exist, although they are consistent with a reasonable extension of available data on decision time by individuals as a function of complexity and prior experience (Cartwright, 1941a, 1941b; Festinger 1943a, 1943b; Cartwright and Festinger, 1943).

At the same time, organizational characteristics affect the amount of uncertainty within the organization. For example, an organizational policy of frequent interdepartmental transfer of personnel tends to keep experience at a low level. Organizational policies producing an inadequate or inaccessible "memory" tend to accentuate uncertainty.

Factors affecting unacceptability

When we turn to factors leading to a more or less general sense of "unacceptability" of available alternatives, we must again rely largely on inferences from introspection and from extrapolation of individual behavior, particularly the behavior cited in chapter 4 on individual dissatisfaction with the organizational alternatives. A general disparity between aspirations and possible achievement produces individual conflict within the organization. Since we know that aspirations tend to adjust to achievement after a time lag, conflict will occur when the lag in that adjustment is appreciable. The greater the *disparity between aspiration levels and achievement* (5.13), the higher the probability of individual conflict within the organization [5.4:5.13].

Such disparities occur most frequently when the *munificence of the environment* (5.14) undergoes a sudden downward shift [5.13:5.14]. The most obvious example of a sudden unfavorable shift in the environment of a business organization is a business recession. In a recession, individual aspiration levels will be rather consistently higher than can be satisfied. As a result, many individuals will find themselves in personal conflict of the unacceptability variety (Argyris, 1952). Consequently, we would predict that this type of organizational conflict would increase during an economic recession and decrease during relatively good business years.

A similar result can occur without an actual downward economic trend. We would predict that aspiration levels would outrun satisfaction if the rate of increase in achievement were suddenly checked; for aspiration levels can become attached to rates of change, and an environment that is "getting better all the time" but at a decreasing rate is likely to give rise to conflict of the unacceptability type. Thus not only a recession but also a slowdown in a boom may increase the frequency of intraindividual organizational conflict (Stockford and Kunze, 1950).

We can also specify types of organizations that will be particularly prone to conflict. For example, an organization that is relatively unsuccessful in a growing industry will be more prone to intraindividual organizational conflict than will other organizations.

The major propositions of this section are outlined in figure 5.2.

5.3 Organizational Conflict: Intergroup Conflict Within an Organization

So long as there is widespread individual conflict, one of the necessary conditions for intergroup conflict in an organization – to wit, differing individual commitments – is not met and, consequently, such conflict

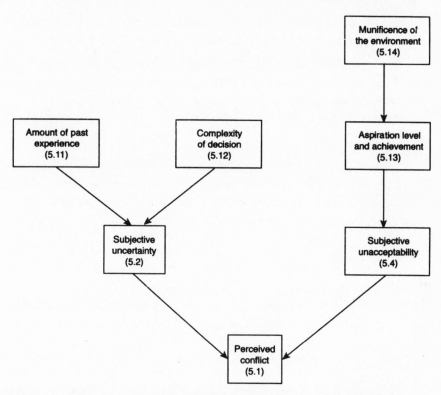

Figure 5.2 Factors affecting individual conflict within organizations.

is minimized. On the other hand, the absence of uncertainty and unacceptability is not a sufficient condition for intergroup conflict. We need to specify the mechanisms that, given unambiguous choices at the individual level, produce disagreement among the participants in an organization and thus organizational conflict of that type.

The conditions necessary for intergroup conflict in addition to the general absence of individual conflict can be summarized in terms of three variables. The existence of a positive *felt need for joint decision-making* (5.15) and of either a *difference in goals* (5.16) or a *difference in perceptions* of reality (5.17) or both among the participants in the organization are necessary conditions for *intergroup conflict* (5.18) [5.18:5.15, 5.16, 5.17]. Thus, we argue that there are three major factors influencing intergroup conflict and that they do not enter into the scheme in a strictly additive fashion, although shifts in any of the three will generally have positive affects on the amount of potential conflict.

Factors affecting the felt need for joint decision-making

A more detailed consideration of organizational interdependence will be found in chapter 6. An organization (if one can be imagined) with no joint decision-making needs could tolerate widespread disagreement among its participants. At the other extreme, where many individual decisions become joint organizational decisions, the potential areas of conflict are substantial (Schachter, 1951).

The felt need for joint decision-making in an organization can arise from a number of factors. Two seem particularly critical. The need for joint decision-making in an organization arises through two central problems in organizational decision-making: resource allocation and scheduling. The greater the *mutual dependence on a limited resource* (5.19), the greater the felt need for joint decision-making with respect to that resource [5.15:5.19]. The greater the *interdependence of timing of activities* (5.20), the greater the felt need for joint decision-making with respect to scheduling [5.15:5.20]. The mechanisms underlying these propositions are readily apparent. So long as there are interdependencies associated with scarce resources or scheduling problems, any internal pressure on a participant to control his environment leads to a desire to control the allocation of resources and the timing of activities that impinge on his own (Sherif and Sherif, 1956). This gives rise to a pressure toward participation in the relevant decisions made by other participants and thus to pressure toward joint decision-making.

Selecting an appropriate area for joint decision-making is itself a decision on which organizational conflict is quite possible. For example, if the pressure for joint decision-making is essentially unilateral, we would anticipate resistance to it with resulting conflict. One area of conflict that is important in large task-oriented organizations is the area of authority and power relations. In chapters 3 and 4 we noted the interpersonal problems that arise from a disparity between the egalitarian norms of American culture and authority hierarchies in an organization. The intensity of such problems should (according to the present hypothesis) be a function of the amount of interdependence between levels in the hierarchy. One feature of organizational conflict is particularly obvious in this instance: Subjective judgments about departmental interdependence may vary; the superior and subordinate will not necessarily view the same external situation as demanding the same amount of coordination. We return to this point below.

The general propositions lead to a number of specific predictions for which, unfortunately, we have little reliable data. There will be more conflict between units sharing a common service unit than there will be between units and that do not share a common service unit and the conflict will center on the resource provided by the service unit. There will be more conflict between units adjacent to one another in a flow-chart sense than between other units, and the conflict will center on the resource, product, etc., that are represented in the flow (Whyte, 1947). Conflict among subunits in an organization will be particularly acute with respect to budgeting and the allocation of money and less acute (in general) in other aspects of organizational decision-making (Argyris, 1952).

Although these are critical points for joint decision-making and thus focal points for organizational conflict, it is possible to restrain the operation of the mechanisms involved. Where the pressure toward joint decision-making stems from scheduling problems, at least some of it can be relieved through building buffer inventories so that the activities of the units are not so critically time-dependent. We would predict, therefore, that conflict would be less where such inventories are used than where they are not. Similarly, where a service unit organizes itself in such a way as to distinguish more or less permanently among the subunits that serve the different operating units, pressure for coordination is decreased. In this case, the joint decision problems are transformed into less frequent decisions about the allocation of personnel in the service unit. Thus, we would predict more conflict among individuals drawing upon a secretarial pool where there is no semipermanent assignment of secretaries than where such assignments are made.

Finally, as to the conflict centering on budget allocations, intensity of the pressure toward joint decision-making will depend on how limited funds are for the organization as a whole. There is no particular problem associated with dividing an unlimited pie, and so long as the available resources of the organization permit allocations as large or larger than the allocations in the preceding budget period, organizational subunits do not feel any great pressure toward coordination and discussion. So long as such a condition obtains, conflict about budget is probably considerably less than where the supply of money resources is tight (Kornhauser, Dubin, and Ross, 1954). This leads to a proposition relating the felt need for joint decision-making to the state of the environment. The greater the munificence of the environment, the less the felt need for joint decision-making [5.19:5.14].

The general level of departmental "interconnectedness" that enters through resource supply and scheduling overlap also has affects (primarily those related to interpersonal interaction) that decrease conflict, as will be indicated below.

As we noted earlier, the pressure toward joint decision-making operates through individual judgments of the need for coordination. Our propositions have ignored interpersonal variation in such judgments. Under some conditions we may not be able to ignore personal factors in perception. For example, we hypothesize that the interdependence between two sections within a single department will seem less to the section chiefs than it will to the head of the department. In general, the higher the *organization level* (5.21), the greater the felt need for joint decision-making [5.15:5.21]. We would expect such a result because the rationale for the existence of a department lies largely in the need for coordination of its parts. The head of the department is thus alerted to see problems of coordination when they exist and motivated to imagine them when they are absent. Although the mechanism is obscured somewhat by upward identification and aspiration, we would expect organizational executives at any level to view units under them as highly interdependent and their own unit as largely self-contained.

Pressure toward joint decision-making supplies one of the necessary conditions for intergroup conflict. If, in addition, uncertainty is low and acceptable alternatives frequent, so that individual conflict is not dominant, the possibility of intergroup disagreement and conflict arises.

Factors affecting differentiation of goals

As has been indicated above, if there is pressure toward joint decision-making, interindividual conflict arises either when there are differences among individual goals or when there are differences among individual perceptions of reality. One reason why intergroup conflict in an organization has received so little attention in economic theories of the firm is that those theories have assumed away differences either in goals or in perceptions within the organization (Black, 1948). Most commonly, the goal of the organization has been assumed as given (e.g., profit maximization for the business firm), and the possibility that there might be different interpretations of the goal or that other goals might impinge on the behavior of individual participants has been ignored. Similarly (as we will note in chapter 6), interpersonal differences in knowledge are not considered.

The variability of individual motivations has been assumed away by focusing on the employment contract. Granting that individual motivations differ, participants in an organization are induced to conform to organizational goals by payments (most commonly thought of as money payments) by means of which their individual goals are satisfied. Thus, it is argued, individual goals are attached to organizational goals as hunger or thirst drives are attached to particular behaviors in a learning experiment.

"Learning" of this sort, however, depends on a number of variables in the stimulus situation and in the individual participant. Money is a very effective generalized means to a wide variety of specific goals but it does not suffice for some. Thus, the effectiveness of monetary rewards varies from individual to individual.

We will describe some characteristics of organizations that facilitate (or retard) goal differentiation among individual participants or among subunits. These characteristics fall naturally into three broad types:

1 those that affect the commonality of individual goals within the organization;
2 those that affect the clarity and consistency of the reward structure and, therefore, the reinforcement system, and
3 those that affect the compatibility of individual rewards.

The factors associated with a commonality of goals among individual participants in an organization have been discussed elsewhere (see chapter 3). The sharing of goals tends to be a function largely of the recruitment procedures and interaction patterns of the organization. First, it is possible to vary the homogeneity of goals by varying the requirements for "admission." Thus, an organization that hires its engineers from particular colleges is hiring a more homogeneous group of participants than an organization that does not have such requirements. An organization that consists entirely of accountants has a great deal more homogeneity of individual goals than an organization containing accountants, engineers, psychologists, and artists.

Once the participants have been recruited, variations in the homogeneity of individual goals result from variations in the extent to which reference group identifications are established on the premises. These in turn depend on the extent and character of the interaction patterns within the organization (see chapter 3). In addition, they tend to be a function of time; differentiation of subunit goals is characteristic of organizational maturation.

The organizational reward structure is explicitly designed to overcome the problems associated with diverse individual goals. The employment contract specifies implicitly that in exchange for monetary and other remuneration employees will pursue organizational objectives. The effectiveness of the reward system in preventing differences in goals depends, however, on some other features of the organization.

First, rewards that are linked to vague criteria will be ineffective in coordinating individual goals. The less the *subjective operationality of organizational goals* (5.22), the greater the differentiation of individual goals in the organization [5.16:5.22]. We have already noted in chapter 3 a number of factors that affect the subjective operationality of goals. These factors include the type of organization (the extent to which its activities are routinely programmed), the size of the organization, and the level in the organization with which you are dealing. Thus, we predict greater conflict stemming from goal differentiation in research organizations than in production organizations, more conflict in General Motors than in Sam's Economy Market, more conflict at high levels than at low.

At the same time, goal conflict can be stimulated by a reward system that, though fully operational, places individual members or subgroups in competition for scarce resources. We have already noted that unlimited resources tend to decrease the demand for joint decision-making. They also should increase the differentiation of goals [5.16:5.19]. Organizations functioning in a benign environment can satisfy their explicit objectives with less than a complete expenditure of organizational "energy". As a result, a substantial portion of the activities in the organization is directed toward satisfying individual or subgroup goals. The "organizational slack" thus generated has several consequences.

It means that organizations typically can find ways of surviving during crisis periods despite their difficulty in discovering possible economies during better periods (Cyert and March, 1956).

Further, organizational slack has direct significance for intergroup conflict within the organization. When resources are relatively unlimited, organizations need not resolve the relative merits of subgroup claims. Thus, these claims and the rationalizations for them tend not be challenged; substantial differentiation of goals occurs within the organization (Simon, 1953b). When resources are restricted and this slack is taken up, the relations among individual members and subgroups in the organization become more nearly a strictly competitive game. From this we predict that as resources are reduced (e.g., in a business recession for a business organization; after a legislative economy move in a governmental organization), intergroup conflict tends to increase.

Finally, reward systems in organizations are rarely internally consistent. One reason is that most systems are "designed" by bargaining and piecemeal engineering in which consistency is not always a clearly recognized virtue. Another reason is that no single institution defines the reward system. As we have noted in earlier chapters, the formal hierarchy is not the only agency rewarding and punishing behavior. The classical accountant's attitude about the relative desirability of over- and under-estimation of costs is partly learned in his professional training, partly enforced by his professional group, and (usually) partly reinforced by the organizational hierarchy. A major area for organizational research is the behavior of organizations in which there exists a partial conflict of interests.

Factors affecting differentiation of individual perceptions

Not all conflict within an organization is goal conflict. As we will see in chapters 6 and 7, the cognitive processes underlying organizational decision-making are major factors. In an organization of any size at all, there will be different amounts and types of information at different points. This incomplete sharing of information leads to intraorganizational disagreement where there is pressure toward joint decision-making within the organization (Cartwright and Zander, 1953).

Most of the propositions relating to goal differentiation are to be found in chapter 3; most of the propositions on differentiation of individual perceptions are cited in chapters 6 and 7. Consequently, we will include here only the major factors of relevance for the present discussion.

First, there is a substantial interaction between individual goals and cognition. The greater the differentiation of individual goals, the greater the differentiation of individual perceptions [5.17:5.16]; and vice versa [5.16:5.17]. This pressure toward consistency of values with expectations has been noted by many observers of human behavior. In an organization the pressure is accentuated by departmentalization and the consequent structure of social influence within subgroups (Dearborn and Simon, 1958).

In addition, there are three major ways in which organizational characteristics affect the commonality of information among participants: (1) organization members may share a common source of information; (2) the formal techniques for processing information within an organization may provide for wide communication; (3) informal information channels may provide widespread sharing of information.

The greater the *number of independent information sources* (5.23), the greater the differentiation of perceptions within the organization

[5.17:5.23]. Thus, we would expect less perceptual conflict in an organization when one outside individual or group of individuals holds an acknowledged monopoly of relevant information than where there are a number of external sources. This means that in some areas (e.g., medical care) there will be fewer cognitive differences than in other areas (e.g., political tactics). It also means that the extent of conflict in an organization may depend on the extent to which it (collectively) seeks information from a homogeneous outside group. If the personnel in an organization seeking outside information about potential markets are all economists, they are likely to secure a more homogeneous picture of the world than if they include both economists and psychologists.

The greater the *channelling of information-processing* (5.24), the greater the differentiation of perceptions within the organization [5.17:5.24]. By channelling information we mean limiting the number of organization members to whom any given bit of information is transmitted. The amount of channelling can be affected by formal organizational procedures. For example, the extent to which the raw data for a cost estimate are known to parts of the organization other than the unit in which they were collected depends on standard operating procedures for transmitting such data and on the time pressures facing persons reviewing the estimates. Similarly, the informal communication structure of the organization affects the sharing of information. Where departments are closely "connected" (spatially, in terms of work, in terms of types of employees, etc.), we would predict less differentiation of individual perceptions than where they are relative remote. That is, if interaction occurs between two units (for whatever reason), it will tend to stimulate other interaction and increased sharing of information. An organization of largely autonomous departments will have greater perceptual conflict than a less decentralized one (Simon, Kozmetsky, and Tyndall, 1954).

We have now specified three ways in which departmental interconnections affect intergroup organizational conflict. The closer the connections, the greater will be the felt need for joint decision-making, the less the differentiation of goals, and the less the differentiation of perceptions. Since two of these factors retard and the third stimulates conflict, a specific prediction depends on the strength of the individual effects and interactions among them. Thus, for prediction we need an explicit specification not only of gross relationships but also of their functional form and the values of their critical parameters.

An outline of our major propositions is provided in figure 5.3.

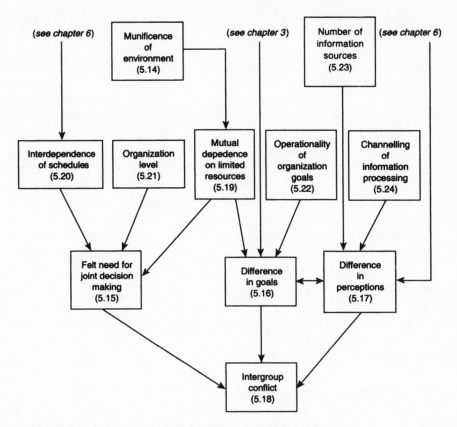

Figure 5.3 Factors affecting intergroup conflict within an organization.

5.4 Organizational Reaction to Conflict

Thus far we have taken conflict as the dependent variable and have indicated the conditions under which it is likely to arise. We can now consider propositions in which organizational conflict is the independent variable. As in the case of the individual, we assume that internal conflict is not a stable condition for an organization and that effort is consciously directed toward resolving both individual and intergroup conflict.

An organization reacts to conflict by four major processes:

1 problem-solving;
2 persuasion;

3 bargaining, and
4 "politics."

In problem-solving, it is assumed that objectives are shared and that the decision problem is to identify a solution that satisfies the shared criteria. Thus, in the problem-solving process the importance of assembling information is stressed, search behavior is increased, and considerable emphasis is placed on evoking new alternatives.

In the case of persuasion, it is assumed that individuals goals may differ within the organization but that goals need not be taken as fixed. Implicit in the use of persuasion is the belief that *at some level* objectives are shared and that disagreement over subgoals can be mediated by reference to common goals. There is less reliance on information-gathering than in problem-solving and a greater emphasis on testing subgoals for consistency with other objectives. As in the case of problem-solving, however, evoking phenomena are of considerable importance – in this instance evoking relevant criteria (i.e., unconsidered objectives).

Where bargaining is used, disagreement over goals is taken as fixed, and agreement without persuasion is sought. One of the major questions in current bargaining theory is the extent to which bargaining "solutions" represent appeals to shared values of "fairness" or "obviousness" (and thus – in our terms – persuasion) rather than a struggle in terms of persistence, strength, etc. (Schelling, 1957). In either case, we can identify a bargaining process by its paraphernalia of acknowledged conflict of interests, threats, falsification of position, and (in general) gamesmanship.

By "politics" we mean a process in which the basic situation is the same as in bargaining – there is intergroup conflict of interest – but the arena of bargaining is not taken as fixed by the participants. A basic strategy of small powers (whether organizational subunits or nation states) in their relations with large powers is not to allow those relations to be defined as bilateral but to expand the relevant parties to include potential allies. The tendency for the organizational conflict of collective bargaining to expand to include governmental institutions is well known, as are the less frequent but equally dramatic instances of stockholder disputes. The use of politics within the organization proper is also an important technique for resolving intergroup conflict (Selznick, 1949; Lipset, 1950).

The first two of these processes (problem-solving and persuasion) represent attempts to secure private as well as public agreement to the decisions. Such processes we will call *analytic*. The last two (bargaining and politics), which do not, we will call *bargaining*. Our objective is to specify when the organization will tend to use analytic processes to resolve conflict and when it will resort to bargaining.

The extent of *use of analytic processes to resolve conflict* (5.25) is a function of the *type of organizational conflict* (5.26) involved [5.25:5.26]. The more organizational conflict represents individual rather than intergroup conflict, the greater the use of analytic procedures. That is, when the organization cannot reach a decision because the individual participants in the organization cannot do so, we expect the behavior in the organization to parallel our propositions about the reaction to individual conflict. The organization members initiate search for additional information on the alternatives available to them and the consequences attached to those alternatives. Conversely, the more organizational conflict represents intergroup differences, the greater the use of bargaining.

These tendencies to resolve intergroup conflict through bargaining and individual conflict through analysis are not invariable, however. The two major processes have different effects on the organization. In particular, bargaining has some potentially disruptive consequences as a decision-making process. Bargaining almost necessarily places strains on the status and power systems in the organization. If those who are formally more powerful prevail, this results in a more forceful perception of status and power differences in the organization (generally dysfunctional in our culture). If they do not prevail, their position is weakened. Furthermore, bargaining acknowledges and legitimizes heterogeneity of goals in the organization. Such a legitimation removes a possible technique of control available to the organizational hierarchy.

Because of these consequences of bargaining, we predict that the organizational hierarchy will perceive (and react to) all conflict as though it were in fact individual rather than intergroup conflict. More specifically, we predict that almost all disputes in the organization will be defined as problems in analysis, that the initial reaction to conflict will be problem-solving and persuasion, that such reactions will persist even when they appear to be inappropriate, that there will be a greater explicit emphasis on common goals where they do not exist than where they do, and that bargaining (when it occurs) will frequently be concealed within an analytic framework.

Unfortunately, although each of these predictions appears to be testable, we do not know of explicit evidence testing them.

5.5   Interorganizational Conflict

For reasons that were indicated earlier, we shall not deal at length with interorganizational conflict. Many of the phenomena of intergroup conflict within organizations are almost indistinguishable from the phenomena that we might consider under the present heading. The distinction between internal and external relations for an organization is frequently a cloudy one. However, there will generally be more pressure toward use of analytic techniques within the organization than in relations between organizations. Of course, this pressure will operate through broad social institutions and reference groups, but with substantially reduced effect.

For this reason, the literature on interorganizational conflict has been particularly concerned with the resolution of conflict through bargaining processes – with who gets what. Although there have been, particularly in economics, a variety of approaches to problems of interorganizational conflict (Zeuthen, 1930; Hicks, 1932; Harsanyi, 1956), in recent years the theory of bargaining has been of particular interest to game theorists. Attempts have been made to apply game theory to conflict among firms in an oligopolistic industry (Shubik, 1956) among political parties in a democratic nation state (Luce and Rogow, 1956), and among nations (Deutsch, 1954). Without attempting to review the entire literature that has grown around game theory since it was first presented by von Neumann (1928, 1937) and subsequently von Neumann and Morgenstern (1944), we can indicate briefly what kinds of problems in the theory of conflict it has attacked and what directions of current development in game theory are most promising. For an excellent general review, see Luce and Raiffa (1957).

The area of game theory that is most satisfactorily developed is also the least relevant to the major questions of interorganizational conflict: two-person, zero-sum theory has not, on the whole, yielded much for bargaining theory. On the other hand, the theories of two-person and n-person cooperative games are both more relevant and less well developed. Mathematically, they have proved much less tractable; and while game theorists have been pointing out the importance of psychological and sociological assumptions to generate solutions to such games, neither psychological nor sociological research has provided these assumptions. Nevertheless, there are a number of significant post-1944 developments in n-person and nonzero-sum theory.

The developments of particular significance to interorganizational conflict turn upon two questions about the bargaining process: (1)

which coalitions among players are likely to be formed, or – if formed – likely to be stable? (2) What will be the outcome of the bargaining? We will consider each question briefly.

Coalition structure

When there are more than two participants in the game, the problem of probable and stable coalitions arises. Who will coalesce with whom? And for how long? In the von Neumann and Morgenstern discussion, coalition formation is a central part of n-person theory. In their treatment it is assumed that all possible coalitions are considered, that each player has perfect knowledge of the game (except for the strategies of the other players), that each player has a well-defined preference ordering over the outcomes and attempts to maximize expected utility, and that payments are made in terms of an infinitely divisible, unrestrictedly transferable commodity. Given these assumptions, it is possible to derive some "reasonable" qualitative propositions about coalition formation. However, the assumptions have been challenged both on a priori grounds and on the basis of a few bits of experimental evidence (Kalish, Milnor, Nash, and Nering, 1952). As a result of these challenges, attempts have been made to relax or change the critical assumptions. Consideration of all of the modifications that have been explored would take us far afield. Of particular interest, however, is the effort to impose restrictions on the set of coalitions considered. Luce (1954, 1955a, 1955b) has suggested that changes in coalitions will ordinarily involve only small local shifts (e.g., the transfer of one person at a time). If we make such a restriction and allow the existence of more than one stable coalition, it will in general be true that what coalition is ultimately formed depends not only on the game characteristics but also on what coalition exists at the outset. Game theory has traditionally focused on the evaluation of alternative coalitions, whereas actual behavior may depend at least as much on which coalitions are considered. Luce's equilibrium theory can be viewed as a theory of search behavior (specifically, search for alternative coalitions). If we were to add to it a mechanism controlling the intensity of search, it would come close to being another example of the type of behavior model we have discussed at several points in the present volume.

Bargaining outcome

Game theory in its original form was no more satisfactory than traditional economic theory in providing an exact prediction of the outcome of a bargaining situation. What it offered was a specification of a set of feasible outcomes – the "solution" of the game. For example, in the case of a highly specialized executive bargaining with his organization over salary, the salary paid will be somewhere between the value of the best alternative available to the executive elsewhere (i.e., what the executive can guarantee to himself without cooperation) and the cost to the organization of hiring and training a replacement (i.e., what the organization can guarantee to itself without cooperation). Since this range may be quite wide, the theory is not overly helpful.

A number of suggestions have been made for improving the determinateness of a bargaining outcome prediction. These attempts represent possible responses to the following problem: Given a conflict of the sort described above, what would be a "fair" outcome? When the problem is viewed in this way, it is sometimes described as the arbitration problem since it reflects the point of view of the impartial arbiter. Moreover, if we assume that there are general standards of fairness in the culture to which the parties must (in the long run) conform, it is possible to argue that bargaining is implicit arbitration with the norms of society serving as the enforcing mechanisms for fairness. The better known procedures for arriving at unique outcomes in bargaining situations – those of Nash (1950, 1953), Shapley (Kuhn and Tucker, 1953), and Raiffa (Kuhn and Tucker, 1953) – all satisfy some "reasonable" definition of fairness. Nash's procedure, which is perhaps the best known, defines the fair outcome as that one which maximizes the product of individual utilities. This outcome depends substantially on the participants' attitudes toward risk. In general, a participant will achieve a more favorable bargain the more willing he is to take risks. Additional implications of the Nash solution have been derived both for the general case and for some special instances such as the duopoly situation (Mayberry, Nash, and Shubik, 1953).

Game theoretic approaches have been supplemented in recent years by somewhat different conceptions of the bargaining process. Perhaps the most interesting of these recent nongame attacks on the problem is that of Schelling (1957). He argues that the outcome of a bargaining situation depends on some qualities of "obviousness" that commend it to the parties involved. If we imagine that bargaining situations are rarely perceived as unique, we can anticipate that individuals in a culture will build up "normal" responses to such situations. These responses are then evoked in new situations. The relation between "obviousness" and "fairness" is not clear. On the whole, Schelling's solutions depend less on the participants' attitudes toward risks – and thus their abilities to use threats – than the solutions proposed by game theorists. One way of reconciling Schelling's conceptions with game theory is to view Schelling's theory as determining what set of bargaining alternatives will be considered. A game theory approach (e.g., Nash's) could then be applied to select a solution from within this newly-defined set.

It is on this note that we will leave the discussion of bargaining. With rare exceptions, bargaining theory has operated in an empirical vacuum. The assumptions about human motivations and behavior have usually been made on the basis of introspection, inspection of special cases, and mathematical tractability. In general, we would have more confidence in the future development of the theory if serious empirical research were to match, in terms of energy and competence, the mathematical efforts of the past 10 years. In the absence of such an effort, we are reluctant to pursue in greater detail the possible outcomes of bargaining or to comment in detail on the common allegation that in the "real world" bargaining situations are so complex and unstandardized that nothing approximating a general theory of bargaining can be developed. Our own judgment is that a counsel of despair is premature but that we need a good deal more confrontation of theory and evidence. It may well turn out that the factors determining which alternatives (i.e., of coalitions and solutions) are considered may be quite different from the factors determining which of the considered alternatives is chosen as solution.

5.6   Conclusion

In this chapter we have indicated how conflict arises within an organization and what types of behavior result from conflict. We have discussed two quite distinct kinds of organizational conflict:

1 conflict that is essentially intraindividual, where organization members themselves have difficulty making a choice;
2 conflict among individuals, where the members of the organization have choices that are mutually inconsistent.

We have seen how individual conflict can arise from the incomparability of alternatives, from the unacceptability of alternatives, or from uncertainty about the consequences of alternatives. We have shown how both the organizational environment and the characteristics of the organization contribute to the amount of individual conflict within an organization.

Similarly, we have discussed intergroup conflict within an organization, the conditions under which it arises, and organizational reactions to it. We have argued that a felt need for joint decision-making, and the existence of differences in goals or differences in perceptions or both, are necessary for intergroup conflict, and that the conditions under which these conditions occur are (in part) predictable from a knowledge of the organization.

Because organizational conflict leads to such phenomena as bargaining and power struggles, the present chapter differs from the earlier chapters on motivational factors in organizational behavior. Here the motivations are frequently made more explicit and the problem of conflict of interests is met (albeit somewhat reluctantly by the organization) head-on. Thus, we have moved all the way from the avoidance of motivational factors in the scientific management movement to the central role of interpersonal conflict in game theory. We have tried to indicate at several points in our discussion that the interaction between motivational and cognitive factors is substantial. In order to complete our description of "organizational man," we must focus directly on his attributes as a decision maker attempting to be rational. That is the subject to which we turn next.

6

Cognitive Limits on Rationality

In the three previous chapters, we have considered how motivations and goals affect human behavior in organizations. The content of these chapters constitutes an important amendment to the "classical" thoery of organization, which regards the employee as an "instrument." In the present chapter and the following one we shall focus on a different set of qualities of the organization member – his characteristics as a rational man. When, at the end of chapter 7, we conclude our study of these characteristics and their implications for organization theory, we will have completed the main tasks we set ourselves:

1 to eliminate, one by one, the artificialities of the classical description of the employee as an instrument;
2 to replace this abstraction with a new one that recognizes that members of organizations have wants, motives, and drives, and are limited in their knowledge and in their capacities to learn and to solve problems.

First, we take note of some characteristics of human rationality that bear upon decision-making processes in organizations. Next, we see how organizational decision-making is organized into "programs" or strategies. In the third section we re-examine the phenomenon of organizational identification in the light of the introductory analysis to see to what extent identification is an intellective rather than a motivational process. The fourth section considers the implications of the decision-making process for the division of work; and the fifth section discusses the communications requirements and processes that arise out of the division of work. In the final section we state some of the broader propositions about organization structure that can be derived from the analysis of decision-making processes.

6.1 The Concept of Rationality

How does the rationality of "administrative man" compare with that
of classical "economic man" or with the rational man of modern
statistical decision theory? The rational man of economics and
statistical decision theory makes "optimal" choices in a highly
specified and clearly defined environment:

1 When we first encounter him in the decision-making situation, he already
   has laid out before him the whole set of alternatives from which he will
   choose his action. This set of alternatives is simply "given"; the theory does
   not tell how it is obtained.
2 To each alternative is attached a set of consequences – the events that will
   ensue if that particular alternative is chosen. Here the existing theories fall
   into three categories:

   (a) *Certainty*: theories that assume the decision maker has complete and
       accurate knowledge of the consequences that will follow on each
       alternative.
   (b) *Risk*: theories that assume accurate knowledge of a probability
       distribution of the consequences of each alternative.
   (c) *Uncertainty*: theories that assume that the consequences of each
       alternative belong to some subset of all possible consequences, but that
       the decision maker cannot assign definite probabilities to the occur-
       rence of particular consequences.

3 At the outset, the decision maker has a "utility function" or a "preference-
   ordering" that ranks all sets of consequences from the most preferred to the
   least preferred.
4 The decision maker selects the alternative leading to the preferred set of
   consequences.

In the case of *certainty*, the choice is unambiguous. In the case of *risk*,
rationality is usually defined as the choice of that alternative for which
the expected utility is greatest. Expected utility is defined here as the
average, weighted by the probabilities of occurrence, of the utilities
attached to all possible consequences. In the case of *uncertainty*, the
definition of rationality becomes problematic. One proposal that has
had wide currency is the rule of "minimax risk": consider the worst set
of consequences that may follow from each alternative, then select the
alternative whose "worst set of consequences" is preferred to the worst
sets attached to other alternatives. There are other proposals (e.g., the
rule of "minimax regret"), but we shall not discuss them here.

Some difficulties in the classical theory

There are difficulties with this model of rational man. In the first place, only in the case of certainty does it agree well with common-sense notions of rationality. In the case of uncertainty, especially, there is little agreement, even among exponents of statistical decision theory, as to the "correct" definition, or whether, indeed, the term "correct" has any meaning here (Marschak, 1950).

A second difficulty with existing models of rational man is that it makes three exceedingly important demands upon the choice-making mechanism. It assumes (1) that all the alternatives of choice are "given"; (2) that all the consequences attached to each alternative are known (in one of the three senses corresponding to certainty, risk, and uncertainty respectively); (3) that the rational man has a complete utility-ordering (or cardinal function) for all possible sets of consequences.

One can hardly take exception to these requirements in a normative model – a model that tells people how they *ought* to choose. For if the rational man lacked information, he might have chosen differently "if only he had known." At best, he is "subjectively" rational, not "objectively" rational. But the notion of objective rationality assumes there is some objective reality in which the "real" alternatives, the "real" consequences, and the "real" utilities exist. If this is so, it is not even clear why the cases of choice under risk and under uncertainty are admitted as rational. If it is not so, it is not clear why only limitations upon knowledge of consequences are considered, and why limitations upon knowledge of alternatives and utilities are ignored in the model of rationality.

From a phenomenological viewpoint we can only speak of rationality relative to a frame of reference; and this frame of reference will be determined by the limitations on the rational man's knowledge. We can, of course, introduce the notion of a person observing the choices of a subject, and can speak of the rationality of the subject relative to the frame of reference of the observer. If the subject is a rat and the observer is a man (especially if he is the man who designed the experimental situation), we may regard the man's perception of the situation as objective and the rat's as subjective. (We leave out of account the specific difficulty that the rat presumably knows his own utility function better than the man does). If, however, both subject and observer are men – and particularly if the situation is a natural one not constructed for experimental purposes by the observer – then it becomes difficult to specify the objective situation. It will be safest, in such situations, to speak of rationality only relative to some specified frame of reference.

The classical organization theory described in chapter 2, like classical economic theory, failed to make explicit this subjective and relative character of rationality, and in so doing, failed to examine some of its own crucial premises. The organizational and social environment in which the decision maker finds himself determines what consequences he will anticipate, what ones he will not; what alternatives he will consider, what ones he will ignore. In a theory of organization these variables cannot be treated as unexplained independent factors, but must themselves be determined and predicted by the theory.

Routinized and problem-solving responses

The theory of rational choice put forth here incorporates two fundamental characteristics: (1) Choice is always exercised with respect to a limited, approximate, simplified "model" of the real situation [A-6.1]. We call the chooser's model his "definition of the situation." (2) The elements of the definition of the situation are not "given" – that is, we do not take these as data of our theory – but are themselves the outcome of psychological and sociological processes, including the chooser's own activities and the activities of others in his environment [A-6.2] (Simon, 1947, 1955; March, 1955a; Cyert and March, 1955, 1956; Newell, Shaw, and Simon, 1958).

Activity (individual or organizational) can usually be traced back to an environmental stimulus of some sort, e.g., a customer order or a fire gong. The responses to stimuli are of various kinds. At one extreme, a stimulus evokes a response – sometimes very elaborate – that has been developed and learned at some previous time as an appropriate response for a stimulus of this class. This is the "routinized" end of the continuum, where a stimulus calls forth a performance program almost instantaneously.

At the other extreme, a stimulus evokes a larger or smaller amount of problem-solving activity directed toward finding performance activities with which to complete the response. Such activity is distinguished by the fact that it can be dispensed with once the performance program has been learned. Problem-solving activities can generally be identified by the extent to which they involve *search*; search aimed at discovering alternatives of action or consequences of action. "Discovering" alternatives may involve inventing and elaborating whole performance programs where these are not already available in the problem solver's repertory (Katona, 1951).

When a stimulus is of a kind that has been experienced repeatedly in the past, the response will ordinarily be highly routinized [A-6.3]. The stimulus will evoke, with a minimum of problem-solving or other computational activity, a well-structured definition of the situation that will include a repertory of response programs, and programs for selecting an appropriate specific response from the repertory. When a stimulus is relatively novel, it will evoke problem-solving activity aimed initially at constructing a definition of the situation and then at developing one or more appropriate performance programs [A-6.4].

Psychologists (e.g., Wertheimer, Duncker, de Groot, Maier) and observant laymen (e.g., Poincaré, Hadamard) who have studied creative thinking and problem-solving have been unanimous in ascribing a large role in these phenomena to search processes. Search is partly random, but in effective problem-solving it is not blind. The design of the search process is itself often an object of rational decision. Thus, we may distinguish substantive planning – developing new performance programs – from procedural planning – developing programs for the problem-solving process itself. The response to a particular stimulus may involve more than performance – the stimulus may evoke a spate of problem-solving activity – but the problem-solving activity may itself be routinized to a greater or lesser degree. For example, search processes may be systematized by the use of check lists.

Satisfactory versus optimal standards

What kinds of search and other problem-solving activity are needed to discover an adequate range of alternatives and consequences for choice depends on the criterion applied to the choice. In particular, finding the optimal alternative is a radically different problem from finding a satisfactory alternative. An alternative is *optimal* if:

1 there exists a set of criteria that permits all alternatives to be compared, and
2 the alternative in question is preferred, by these criteria, to all other alternatives.

An alternative is *satisfactory* if:

1 there exists a set of criteria that describes minimally satisfactory alternatives, and
2 the alternative in question meets or exceeds all these criteria.

Most human decision-making, whether individual or organizational, is concerned with the discovery and selection of satisfactory alternatives; only in exceptional cases is it concerned with the discovery and selection of optimal alternatives [A-6.5]. To optimize requires processes several orders of magnitude more complex than those required to satisfice. An example is the difference between searching a haystack to find the sharpest needle in it and searching the haystack to find a needle sharp enough to sew with.

In making choices that meet satisfactory standards, the standards themselves are part of the definition of the situation. Hence, we need not regard these as given – any more than the other elements of the definition of the situation – but may include in the theory the processes through which these standards are set and modified. The standard-setting process may itself meet standards of rationality: for example, an "optimizing" rule would be to set the standard at the level where the marginal improvement in alternatives obtainable by raising it would be just balanced by the marginal cost of searching for alternatives meeting the higher standard. Of course, in practice the "marginal improvement" and the "marginal cost" are seldom measured in comparable units, or with much accuracy. Nevertheless, a similar result would be automatically attained if the standards were raised whenever alternatives proved easy to discover, and lowered whenever they were difficult to discover. Under these circumstances, the alternatives chosen would not be far from the optima, if the cost of search were taken into consideration. Since human standards tend to have this characteristic under many conditions, some theorists have sought to maintain the optimizing model by introducing cost-of-search considerations. Although we doubt whether this will be a fruitful alternative to the model we are proposing in very many situations, neither model has been used for predictive purposes often enough to allow a final judgment.

Performance programs

We have seen that under certain circumstances the search and choice processes are very much abridged. At the limit, an environmental stimulus may evoke immediately from the organization a highly complex and organized set of responses. Such a set of responses we call a performance program, or simply a program. For example, the sounding of the alarm gong in a fire station initiates such a program. So does the appearance of a relief applicant at a social worker's desk. So does the appearance of an automobile chassis in front of the work station of a worker on the assembly line.

Situations in which a relatively simple stimulus sets off an elaborate program of activity without any apparent interval of search, problem-solving, or choice are not rare. They account for a very large part of the behavior of all persons, and for almost all of the behavior of persons in relatively routine positions. Most behavior, and particularly most behavior in organizations, is governed by performance programs.

The term "program" is not intended to connote complete rigidity. The content of the program may be adaptive to a large number of characteristics of the stimulus that initiates it. Even in the simple case of the fire gong, the response depends on the location of the alarm, as indicated by the number of strokes. The program may also be conditional on data that are independent of the initiating stimuli. It is then more properly called a performance strategy. For example, when inventory records show that the quantity on hand of a commodity has decreased to the point where it should be reordered, the decision rule that governs the behavior of the purchasing agent may call upon him to determine the amount to be ordered on the basis of a formula into which he inserts the quantity that has been sold over the past twelve months. In this case, search has been eliminated from the problem, but choice – of a very routinized kind, to be sure – remains.

We will regard a set of activities as routinized, then, to the degree that choice has been simplified by the development of a fixed response to defined stimuli. If search has been eliminated, but a choice remains in the form of a clearly defined and systematic computing routine, we will still say that the activities are routinized. We will regard activities as unroutinized to the extent that they have to be preceded by program-developing activities of a problem-solving kind.

6.2 Performance Programs in Organizations

There are several ways to determine what programs a particular organization uses:

1 Observing the behavior of organization members. In relatively routine positions, where the same situations recur repetitively and are handled in terms of fairly definite programs, it is easy to infer the program from behavior. This is a common method for inducting new members of an organization into its procedures.

2 Interviewing members of the organization. Most programs are stored in the minds of the employees who carry them out, or in the minds of their superiors, subordinates, or associates. For many purposes, the simplest and most accurate way to discover what a person does is to ask him.

3 Examining documents that describe standard operating procedures. Programs may be written down, more or less completely and more or less accurately. The relation of a written operating procedure to the actual program that is carried out is complex, for the program may have been written down:

(a) as an instruction to initiate a new program and communicate it to those who will carry it out;
(b) as a description of an existing program to instruct new organization members; or
(c) as an exposition (with or without amendments) of an existing program to legitimize or "formalize" it.

There are other possibilities besides these three. In any event, when a document is used as a source of information about a program, the purposes for which it was prepared are relevant to its interpretation.

A person who has been trained in the observation of organizations can extract by these and other techniques a large part of the program that governs routine behavior. This is such a common-sense fact that its importance has been overlooked: Knowledge of the program of an organization permits one to predict in considerable detail the behavior of members of the organization. And the greater the *programming* (6.1) of individual activities in the organization, the greater the *predictability* (6.2) of those activities [6.2:6.1].

To be sure, prediction of behavior from the knowledge of a program has none of the element of "surprise" that we commonly associate with scientific prediction – any more than prediction of the lines that will be uttered by a Hamlet on the stage. It is no less important for its common-sense obviousness.

In general, we would anticipate that programs will be generated by past experience and in expectation of future experience in a given situation. Thus, the greater the *repetitiveness* (6.3) of individual activities, the greater the programming [6.1:6.3]. From this one would predict that programming will be most complete for clerical and factory jobs, particularly when the work is organized largely by process.

The prediction of behavior from a program when tasks are relatively simple and routine is illustrated by findings of Guetzkow and Simon (1955) using five-man experimental groups in the Bavelas network. Employing methods-analysis techniques, they were able to predict average trial times of groups to within 10 percent from a knowledge of the methods the groups were using to perform the task.

If the program determines in some detail the behavior of individuals and groups performing relatively routine tasks, then we can predict behavior to the extent that we can answer the following questions: (1) What motivates members of the organization to accept a program as a determinant of their behavior? What processes, other than motivation, are involved in implementation of programs? This question has already been examined in earlier chapters. (2) What determines the content of a program? To what extent can the program be predicted uniquely from the requirements of the task? How are programs invented and developed, and what are the determinants of this process? (3) What are the consequences of programs, as developed and executed, for the goal and subgoal structure of the organization? (4) What are the predictors of behavior in areas that are not routinized and are unprogrammed? This question will be taken up in the next chapter.

We turn now to the second and third of these questions.

Program content

The extent to which many human activities, both manual and clerical, can be programmed is shown by the continuing spread of automation to encompass a wider and wider range of tasks. In order to substitute automatic processes for human operatives, it is necessary to describe the task in minute detail, and to provide for the performance of each step in it. The decomposition of tasks into their elementary program steps is most spectacularly illustrated in modern computing machines which may carry out programs involving thousands of such steps. The capabilities of computers have now been extended to many tasks that until recently have been thought to be relatively complex, involving problem-solving activities of a fairly high order. Some examples are several existing computer programs for the automatic design of small electric motors and transformers, a program that enables a computer to discover proofs for certain kinds of mathematical theorems, and a program for translating languages.

Even on routine jobs, *program content* (6.4) varies. We have already mentioned the extreme case: the detailed specification of output, methods, and pace in a man-paced assembly operation. But not all programs are of this type. They may not contain detailed time specifications (e.g., in typical machine-paced operations). In fact, programs usually specify the content of an activity more closely than its timing [A-6.6]. They may specify the properties of the product (e.g., in blueprints, tolerances, etc.) rather than the detail of the methods to be used. We need propositions that will explain variations in program content along these dimensions:

1 The extent to which pacing rules are built into the program.
2 The extent to which work activities are detailed in the program.
3 The extent to which product specifications are detailed in the program.

Since performance programs are important aspects of the organizational system, their content will presumably tend to be related to the functions they perform. We can identify two major functions that such programs fulfill, or at least are intended to fulfill. First, they are a part of the control system in the organization. Organizations attempt to control employees by specifying a standard operating procedure and attaching organizational rewards and penalties to it. Second, performance programs are important parts of the coordination system in the organization. They help fulfill the needs for interdepartmental predictability [A-6.7] (Blau, 1955).

Insofar as they are to function as controls, the programs must be linked to variables that are observable and measurable. We would expect program content to be a function of the *ease of observing job activities* (6.5), the *ease of observing job output* (6.6), and the *ease of relating activities to output* (6.7) [6.4:6.5, 6.6, 6.7]. Thus, we would predict that programs will contain activity specifications in preference to product specifications to the extent that: (a) the activity pattern is easily observed and supervised, (b) the quantity and quality of output are not easily observed and supervised; (c) the relations between activity pattern and output are highly technical, and are matters of scientific and engineering knowledge, better known to specialists in the organization than to the operatives (Ridley and Simon, 1938).

Conversely, programs will contain specifications of quality and quantity of output to the extent that: (a) the activity pattern is difficult to observe and supervise; (b) the quantity and quality of output are easily observed and supervised; (c) the relations between activity pattern and output are matters of common sense, are matters of skill in the specific occupation for which the operatives are trained, or are highly variable, depending upon circumstances of the individual situation that are better known to the operatives than to supervisors and specialists.

For performance programs to serve as coordinative devices, they must be linked to the coordination needs that are felt by the organization. Consequently, we would hypothesize that program content will be a function of the *need for activity coordination* (6.8) and the *need for output coordination* (6.9) [6.4:6.8. 6.9]. The more minutely other members of the organization need to synchronize or coordinate their activities with the activities of a particular member, the more completely will the program specify the activity pattern and/or the pacing of those activities. But to the extent that the activities of the former depend on the characteristics of the output of the latter, rather than on his activities, the program will specify product characteristics.

These propositions about program content are derived from the assumption that the program will be rationally adapted to the organization's objectives. To the extent that this assumption actually determines program, program content becomes a technological question in exactly the same way as the form of the production function is a technological question. In the experiment with the Bavelas network, mentioned previously, determining the most efficient program for performing the task is an exercise in methods study resting upon knowledge of human physiological constants – the times required to perform certain simple acts. If we assume that over some period of time an organization will actually arrive at an efficient program, we can predict its long-run behavior from our technical analysis.

Suppose, however, that we substitute for the maximizing assumption implicit in this method of prediction the assumption that behavior is rational in the more limited sense described earlier: that programs are sought that will operate "satisfactorily," and that the "best" program is not necessarily sought or found. In this case, predicting the program becomes more difficult. Which of the (presumably numerous) satisfactory potential programs the organization will adopt depends, under these circumstances, upon the procedures it employs to construct new programs and to improve existing ones. These procedures will provide the principal subject matter for the next chapter.

The structure of programs

To illustrate further the structure of programs for handling recurrent events, we will describe some formal procedures often used by business concerns for controlling inventory. We will analyze first the common "two-bin" system of inventory control, then a more elaborate system.

In the two-bin system of inventory control, two quantities are established for each item kept in stock: (1) the order quantity (the amount to be purchased on a single order), (2) the buffer stock (the amount that should be on hand when a new order is placed). The program is very simple:

"1 When material is drawn from stock, note whether the quantity that remains equals or exceeds the buffer stock. If not:
"2 Write a purchase order for the specified order quantity."

Let us call the first step the "program-evoking" step, and the second step the "program-execution" step. The bifurcation is characteristic of programs – a program includes a specification of the circumstances under which the program is to be evoked [A-6.8]. In the example just cited, the program specifies certain observations, which are to be made (whether the buffer stock is intact) whenever a certain event occurs (withdrawal of material from stock). A decision to act or not to act (to apply or not to apply the program) is based on the result of the observation.

The program-evoking step may involve only observation auxiliary to some other activity (as in this example), or it may invoke systematic scanning of some part of the environment (e.g., the activity of a quality inspector). Further, a program-execution step by one member of an organization may serve as a program-evoking step for another member. In the example above, the receipt of a purchase order from the inventory clerk is a program-evoking step for the purchasing department.

In our very simple example, the program-execution step requires neither discretion nor problem-solving. In more complicated situations, the program will be a strategy; i.e., action will be contingent on various characteristics of the situation. For example, in a more elaborate inventory control scheme, the purchase quantity may depend on a forecast of sales. Then the program might look like this:

"1 When material is drawn from stock, note whether the quantity that remains equals or exceeds the buffer stock. If not:
"2 Determine from the sales forecast provided by the sales department the sales expected in the next k months.
"3 Insert this quantity in the 'order quantity formula,' and write a purchase order for the quantity thus determined."

This program, although it is contingent on certain changing facts (the sales forecast), does not allow discretion to the person who executes it – at least in ordinary meanings of the word "discretion." If, however, the organization does not provide the inventory clerk with an official sales forecast, or does not establish a specific order quantity, we would say that the clerk's activity was, to that extent, discretionary. We might discover by observation and interview that the clerk was in fact following a very definite and invariable program, but one stored in his own memory and not recorded in official instructions.

The nature of discretion

The amounts and kinds of *discretion* (6.10) available to the organizational participant are a function of his performance program and in particular the extent to which the program specifies activities (means) and the extent to which it specifies product or outcome (ends) [6.10:6.4]. The further the program goes in the latter direction, the more discretion it allows for the person implementing the program to supply the means-end connections. Compare the programs cited earlier with the following alternative program:

"1 It is the duty of the inventory clerk to determine when each item should be reordered and in what quantity, and to place orders with the purchasing department. He should perform this function with attention to the costs of holding inventories, the costs of shortages, and the economies associated with bulk orders."

If we interpret the last sentence as enjoining the clerk to minimize the sum of the specified costs, we see that this program specifies a goal, but leaves the means undetermined. To construct a "rational" program starting from these premises requires the following steps:

1 defining the total cost function in specific terms;
2 estimating the coefficients that appear in the cost function;
3 deriving a formula or "strategy" that specifies the ordering rules as functions of:

   (a) the coefficients that appear in the cost function,
   (b) the sales forecasts (i.e., finding the policy that minimizes step 1), and

4 inserting in the formula the coefficients estimated in step 2, and the sales forecasts.

It is difficult to find a place for discretion within the framework of traditional theories of rational behavior. In the present theory, however, a whole host of phenomena fall under this heading.

First, when a program involves search activities, the actual course of action depends on what is found. We may regard the choice of a course of action after search as discretionary.

Second, when a program describes a strategy, application of the strategy to specific circumstances requires forecasts or other estimates of data. We may regard the application of the strategy to select a course of action as discretionary.

Third, a program may exist in the memory of the individual who is to apply it, having arrived there either as a result of extraorganizational training (e.g., professional training or apprenticeship), or as a product of learning from experience rather than as a result of formal instructions. Under these circumstances we often regard him as behaving in a discretionary fashion.

In all of the cases listed above, the decision process may in fact be highly routinized – the term "discretionary" referring in these instances to the form of the performance program or the source from which it was acquired. These cases need to be distinguished from a fourth meaning of "discretionary": A program may specify only general goals, and leave unspecified the exact activities to be used in reaching them. Moreover, knowledge of the means-ends connections may be sufficiently incomplete and inexact that these cannot be very well specified in advance. Then "discretion" refers to the development and modification of the performance program through problem-solving and learning processes. Although it is difficult to draw a perfectly sharp line between changing a program and changing a datum in applying a strategy, we have already argued that there is an important difference of degree here. With these several meanings of the term "discretionary" in mind, we do not need separate propositions about the amount of discretion, for these will be subsumed under the propositions already noted that specify the form, content, and completeness of programs.

Interrelation of programs

A program, whether simple or complex, is initiated when it is evoked by some stimulus. The whole pattern of programmed activity in an organization is a complicated mosaic of program executions, each initiated by its appropriate program-evoking step [A-6.9].

Insofar as the stimuli that evoke programs come from outside the organization, the individual pieces of this mosaic are related to each other only in making claims on the same time and resources, and hence in posing an allocation problem. Nevertheless, if the goal of optimizing is taken seriously, this allocation problem will usually complicate the problem-solving process greatly, for it requires the marginal return from activity in response to any particular stimulus to be equated with the marginal return from activities in response to all other stimuli. Hence, all programs must be determined simultaneously.

When the goal is to respond to stimuli in a satisfactory, but not necessarily optimal, fashion, choice is much simpler; for the standards may be set at levels that permit a satisficing response to each stimulus without concern for the others. The organization, under these circumstances, normally has some slack that reduces the interdependence among its several performance programs.

Apart from resource-sharing, there may be other and more integral connections among programs. Program A may be a *higher-level* program, i.e., a problem-solving activity whose goal is to revise other programs, either by constructing new ones, reconstructing existing ones, or simply modifying individual premises in existing programs. In this case, the *content* of the lower-level programs that are related to A will depend on A. Or, program A may be a program one of whose execution steps serves as an initiating stimulus for program B.

The inventory example illustrates both possibilities. As to the first, program A may be a forecasting program, or a program for periodic revision of the coefficients in the cost function. As to the second possibility, the order that goes from the inventory clerk to the purchasing department serves to initiate one of the purchasing programs of the latter.

Program and organization structure

In organizations there generally is a considerable degree of parallelism between the hierarchical relations among members of the organization and the hierarchical relations among program elements. That is to say, the programs of members of higher levels of the organization have as their main output the modification or initiation of programs for individuals at lower levels [A-6.10].

Any organization possesses a repertory of programs that, collectively, can deal in a goal-oriented way with a range of situations. As new situations arise, the construction of an entirely new program from detailed elements is rarely contemplated. In most cases, adaptation takes place through a recombination of lower-level programs that are already in existence [A-6.11]. An important objective of standardization is to widen as far as possible the range of situations that can be handled by combination and recombination of a relatively small number of elementary programs.

Limitation of high-level action to the recombination of programs, rather than the detailed construction of new programs out of small elements, is extremely important from a cognitive standpoint. Our treatment of rational behavior rests on the proposition that the "real" situation is almost always far too complex to be handled in detail. As we move upwards in the supervisory and executive hierarchy, the range of interrelated matters over which an individual has purview becomes larger and larger, more and more complex. The growing complexity of the problem can only be matched against the finite powers of the individual if the problem is dealt with in grosser and more aggregative form. One way in which this is accomplished is by limiting the alternatives of action that are considered to the recombination of a repertory of programs (Simon, 1953b).

We may again illustrate this point with the inventory example. Top management decides upon the total dollar inventories without controlling the distribution of inventories among individual items. Specific inventory control programs are found at lower levels of the organization.

6.3 Perception and Identifications

We have seen that humans, whether inside or outside administrative organizations, behave rationally, if at all, only relative to some set of "given" characteristics of the situation. These "givens" include knowledge or assumptions about future events or probability distributions of future events, knowledge of alternatives available for action, knowledge of consequences attached to alternatives – knowledge that may be more or less complete – and rules or principles for ordering consequences or alternatives according to preference.

These four sets of givens define the situation as it appears to the rational actor. In predicting his behavior, we need this specification and not merely a specification of the situation as it "really" is, or, more precisely, as it appears to an outside observer.

The steps that lead, for an actor, to his defining the situation in a particular way involve a complex interweaving of affective and cognitive processes. What a person wants and likes influences what he sees; what he sees influences what he wants and likes.

In the three previous chapters we have examined primarily motivational and affective factors. We have considered the relation between individual goals and organizational goals, the ways in which goals are acquired from reference groups, and the motivational bases for conformity with group goals. Cognition enters into the definition of the situation in connection with goal attainment – determining what means will reach desired ends. But cognition enters into the goal-formation process also, because the goals used as criteria for choice seldom represent "final" or "ultimate" values. Instead, they too reflect the perceived relations of means to ends and hence are modified by changing beliefs about these relations. Since goals provide the principal bridge between motivations and cognition, we will begin our consideration of cognitive elements in the definition of the situation with the topic of subgoal formation.

Cognitive aspects of subgoal formation

An individual can attend to only a limited number of things at a time. The basic reason why the actor's definition of the situation differs greatly from the objective situation is that the latter is far too complex to be handled in all its detail. Rational behavior involves substituting for the complex reality a model of reality that is sufficiently simple to be handled by problem-solving processes.

In organizations where various aspects of the whole complex problem are being handled by different individuals and different groups of individuals, a fundamental technique for simplifying the problem is to factor it into a number of nearly independent parts, so that each organizational unit handles one of these parts and can omit the others from its definition of the situation [A-6.12]. This technique is also prominent in individual and small-group behavior. A large complex task is broken down into a sequence of smaller tasks, the conjunction of which adds up to the accomplishment of the larger. The factorization of a large task into parts can be more elaborate for an organization than for an individual, but the underlying reason is the same: the definition of the situation at any one moment must be sufficiently simple to be encompassed by a human mind.

The principal way to factor a problem is to construct a means-end analysis. The means that are specified in this way become subgoals which may be assigned to individual organizational units [A-6.13]. This kind of jurisdictional assignment is often called "organization by purpose" or "departmentalization by purpose."

The motivational aspect of this particular process of subgoal formation is rather simple. Whatever will motivate individuals and groups to accept the task assigned them through the legitimate (formal and informal) processes of the organization will provide motivation for subgoals. For the subgoals are implicit or explicit in the definition of the situation as it is incorporated in the task assignment.

When tasks have been allocated to an organizational unit in terms of a subgoal, other subgoals and other aspects of the goals of the larger organization tend to be ignored in the decisions of the subunit. In part, this bias in decision-making can be attributed to shifts in the *focus of attention* (6.11). The definition of the situation that the subunit employs is simplified by omitting some criteria and paying particular attention to others. In particular, we expect the focus of attention to be a function of the *differentiation of subgoals* (6.12) and the *persistence of subgoals* (6.13) [6.11:6.12, 6.13].

The tendency of members of an organizational unit to evaluate action only in terms of subgoals, even when these are in conflict with the goals of the larger organization, is reinforced by at least three cognitive mechanisms. The first of these is located within the individual decision maker, the second within the organizational unit, and the third in the environment of the organizational unit.

In the individual there is reinforcement through selective perception and rationalization. That is, the persistence of subgoals is furthered by the focus of attention it helps to generate [6.13:6.11]. The propensity of individuals to see those things that are consistent with their established frame of reference is well established in individual psychology. Perceptions that are discordant with the frame of reference are filtered out before they reach consciousness, or are reinterpreted or "rationalized" so as to remove the discrepancy. The frame of reference serves just as much to validate perceptions as the perceptions do to validate the frame of reference.

Within the organizational unit there is reinforcement through the *content of in-group communication* (6.14). Such communication affects the *focus of information* (6.15) [6.15:6.14], and thereby increases subgoal persistence [6.13:6.15]. The vast bulk of our knowledge of fact is not gained through direct perception but through the second-hand, third-hand, and nth-hand reports of the perceptions of others, transmitted through the channels of social communication. Since these perceptions have already been filtered by one or more communicators, most of whom have frames of reference similar to our own, the reports are generally consonant with the filtered reports of our own perceptions, and serve to reinforce the latter. In organizations, two principal types of in-groups are of significance in filtering: in-groups with members in a particular organizational unit, and in-groups with members in a common profession [A-6.14]. Hence, we may distinguish *organizational* identifications and *professional* identifications. There are others, of course, but empirically these appear to be the most significant.

Finally, there is reinforcement through selective exposure to environmental stimuli. The *division of labor in the organization* (6.16) affects the information that various members receive [6.15:6.16]. This differentiation of information contributes to the differentiation of subgoals [6.12:6.15]. Thus perceptions of the environment are biased even before they experience the filtering action of the frame of reference of the perceiver. Salesmen live in an environment of customers; company treasurers in an environment of bankers; each sees a quite distinct part of the world (Dearborn and Simon, 1958).

There is one important distinction between this source of reinforcement and the two mentioned previously. Reinforcement through selective perception and rationalization and reinforcement through in-group communication serve to explain how a particular definition of the situation, once it becomes established in an individual or group, maintains itself with great stability and tenacity. These mechanisms do not explain, however, what particular definitions of the situation will *become* established in particular environments – they explain behavior persistence and not the origins of behavior. In order to predict what particular subgoals we are likely to find in particular parts of an organization, we must take as our starting point (a) the system of subgoal assignment that has resulted from analysis of the organization's goals, and (b) the kinds of stimuli to which each organizational unit is exposed in carrying out its assignments. Under the last heading we must include the selective feedback to organizational units of those consequences of action that relate to their particular subgoals.

Through these mechanisms of subgoal formation and subgoal perception, there is selective attention to particular consequences of proposed alternatives, and selective inattention to others. The magnitude of these effects depends in part on variations in the "capacity" of the individual participants in the organization. The smaller the *span of attention* (6.17), the narrower the focus of attention and the more critical the screening mechanisms cited above [6.11:6.17]. One variable of particular importance in determining the span of attention is, of course, the *time pressure* (6.18) involved [6.17:6.18]. In general, we would expect selective perception to be most acute where time is shortest. The relations among these variables are indicated in figure 6.1.

Other cognitive aspects of the definition of the situation

All the statements of the last section apply, *mutatis mutandis*, to the other elements of the definition of the situation besides goals and values. That is to say, the definition of the situation represents a simplified, screened, and biased model of the objective situation, and filtering affects all of the "givens" that enter into the decision process: knowledge or assumptions about future events; knowledge of sets of alternatives available for action; knowledge of consequences attached to alternatives; goals and values (Levin, 1956; Gore, 1956).

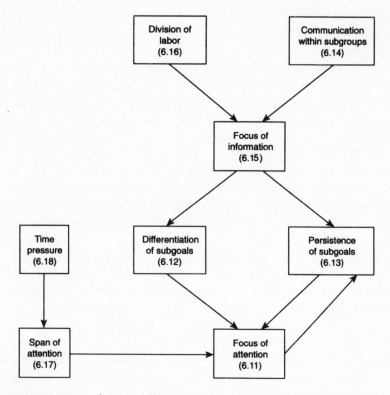

Figure 6.1 Some factors affecting selective attention to subgoals.

Consider just knowledge and assumptions about future and present events – "stipulated facts," "absorption of uncertainty." What the sales of the ABC Company are going to be in 1961 is a question of fact. But this matter of fact may become a matter of organizational stipulation – all action within the organization to which the 1961 sales figure is relevant being based upon an "official" sales forecast. Organizational techniques for dealing with uncertain future and present facts will be discussed in a later section of this chapter.

A related phenomenon is the summarizing of raw information to communicate it further in the organization. The weatherman makes observations of temperature, humidity, barometric pressure, but may communicate only his conclusions in the form of a weather forecast. In organizational communication, evidence is replaced with conclusions drawn from that evidence, and these conclusions then become the "facts" on which the rest of the organization acts [A-6.15]. One partic-ular form or summarization is classification. When a particular thing has been classified as belonging to a species, all the attributes of the species can be ascribed to the individual instance of it. Priority systems are an example of an important kind of formal classification device.

Similarly, individuals and organizations develop repertories of programs of action suited to different situations. These are frequently combined with classification systems so that once a situation has been assigned to a particular class the appropriate action program can be applied to it. Such repertories of performance programs, and the requisite habits and skills for their use, appear to make up the largest part of professional and vocational training.

Knowledge of consequences is intimately related to selective attention to subgoals, and does not require further elaboration here.

The goals that are included in the definition of the situation influence choice only if there are some means, valid or illusory, for determining the connections between alternative actions and goal satisfaction – only if it can somehow be determined whether and to what extent these goals will be realized if particular courses of action are chosen. When a means of testing actions is perceived to relate a particular goal or criterion with possible courses of action, the criterion will be called *operational*. Otherwise the criterion will be called nonoperational. This distinction has already been made in discussing the effects of organizational reward systems.

For some purposes we will need to make the further distinction between cases where means–end relations can be evaluated prior to action, and those where they can be evaluated only after the fact. We will call operational goals in the former case *operational ex ante*, in the latter case *operational ex post*.

The goal of "promoting the general welfare" is frequently a part of the definition of the situation in governmental policy-making. It is a nonoperational goal because it does not provide (either *ex ante* or *ex post*) a measuring rod for comparing alternative policies, but can only be related to specific actions through the intervention of subgoals. These subgoals, whose connection with the broader "general welfare" goal is postulated but not testable, become the operational goals in the actual choice situation. (Speaking strictly, whether a goal is operational or nonoperational is not a yes–no question. There are all degrees of "operationality." It will often be convenient, however, to refer simply to the two ends of the continuum.)

An important circumstance causing the substitution of subgoals for more general goals as criteria of decision is that the former are perceived as operational, the latter as nonoperational [A-6.16]. For example, a business firm may understand to some degree how its specific actions affect its share of market, but may understand less surely how its actions affect long-range profits. Then the subgoal of maintaining a particular share of market may become the effective criterion of action – the operational goal.

The distinction between operational and nonoperational goals, combined with the generalization that behavior in organizations is intendedly rational, leads to the consideration of two qualitatively different decision-making processes associated with these two kinds of goals. When a number of persons are participating in a decision-making process, and these individuals have the same operational goals, differences in opinion about the course of action will be resolved by predominately analytic processes, i.e., by the analysis of the expected consequences of courses of action for realization of the shared goals. When either of the postulated conditions is absent from the situation (when goals are not shared, or when the shared goals are not operational and the operational subgoals are not shared), the decision will be reached by predominately bargaining processes. These are, of course, a distinction and prediction made in chapter 5 and lead to a proposition previously suggested: Rational, analytic processes take precedence over bargaining processes to the extent that the former are feasible. The condition of feasibility is that there be shared operational goals. The proposition, while it has not been much tested, is eminently testable. The goal structure of participants in a decision-making process can be determined by observation of their interaction or by interviewing or opinion-polling techniques. Their understanding of the means–end connections, and of possible methods for testing these connections, can be ascertained in the same way. It is not difficult to code their actual interaction in such a way as to detect the amount of bargaining.

The distinction between operational and nonoperational goals has been made the basis for the distinction between unitary and federal organization units (Simon, Smithburg, and Thompson, 1950, pp. 268–72). This distinction will be explored in the next chapter.

The distinction between operational and nonoperational goals also serves to explain why a theory of public expenditures has never developed a richness comparable to that of the theory of public revenues. The economic approach to a theory of public expenditures would postulate some kind of "utility" or "welfare" function. A rational expenditure pattern would be one in which the marginal dollar of expenditure in each direction would make an equal marginal contribution to welfare. Although statements of this kind are encountered often enough in the literature of public finance, they are infrequently developed. The reason is that, in the absence of any basis for making the welfare maximization goal operational (because of the absence of an operational common denominator among the subgoals of governmental service), the general statement leads neither to description nor to prescription of behavior (Simon, 1943).

In the literature on organizations, identification with subgoals has generally been attributed to motivation. Hence, in an analysis of conflict among organizational units, the affective aspects of the conflict have been stressed. In the present section, we have seen that cognitive processes are extremely important in producing and reinforcing subgoal identification. Subgoals may replace broader goals as a part of the whole process of replacing a complex reality with a simplified model of reality for purposes of decision and action (Blau, 1955).

What difference does it make whether subgoal identification is motivationally or cognitively produced – whether the attachment to the subgoal has been internalized or is only indirect, through a cognitive link to some other goal? It may make very little or no difference in the short run; indeed, it may be difficult to find evidence from short-run behavior that would distinguish between these mechanisms. But it may make a great deal of difference in the processes for changing identifications. The greater *the dependence of the identification on cognitive links* to other goals (6.19), the greater the *effectiveness of attention-directing stimuli in changing goal emphasis* (6.20) [6.20:6.19]. By the same token, where identification depends on cognitive links, the invention of new techniques for evaluating the means–ends connections between action alternatives and goals will transform bargaining processes into processes of rational analysis. These hypotheses can be tested empirically.

6.4   The Division of Work

Insofar as tasks are highly programmed, the division of work is a problem of efficient allocation of activities among individuals and among organizational units – a version of the assignment problem already discussed in chapter 2. However, we need to make two distinctions that tend to be overlooked in the classical theory: First, there is a problem of specialization among individual employees, and a problem of specialization among organizational units. There is no reason to suppose that both sets of problems have the same answers or that the same general principles apply to both. Second, the division of work that is most effective for the performance of relatively programmed tasks need not be the same as that which is most effective for the performance of relatively unprogrammed tasks. In the present discussion, we shall be concerned primarily with programmed tasks; the subject of unprogrammed tasks will be reserved for the next chapter.

The economies of individual specialization arise principally from opportunities for using programs repetitively [A-6.17]. To develop in a person the capacity to carry out a particular program requires an investment in training. In automatic operations, there is an analogous capital investment in machinery capable of carrying out the program. In the case of a computing machine, a substantial part of this investment actually consists of the cost of programming the machine for the particular operations in question. In all of these cases there are economies to be derived, *ceteris paribus*, from assigning the work so as to minimize this investment cost per unit of program execution.

Programs that are built into machines or acquired by humans usually take the form of generalized means – skills or processing capacities that can be used in executing a wide variety of tasks. Typing skill, for example, is a skill of transforming any manuscript into type–written form, and typing occurs as a subprogram in a wide range of programs. Similarly, a drill press is a bundle of capacities for drilling holes; the program can be called into play whenever the fabrication of some product requires holes to be drilled.

This rather obvious point underlies the central problem in specializing highly programmed activities. Consider an organization that performs a large number of tasks, each consisting of the fabrication of a product. If we analyze the fabrication process into subprograms, we find that it becomes economical to arrange the work so that there will be specialized means (machines and trained employees) for performing some of these subprograms. But since a number of these specialties will be required for the manufacture of each product, we create in this way considerable interdependence and need for coordination among them. The greater the *specialization by subprograms* (6.21) (process specialization), the greater the *interdependencies among organizational subunits* (6.22) [6.22:6.21].

Interdependence does not by itself cause difficulty if the pattern of interdependence is stable and fixed. For in this case, each subprogram can be designed to take account of all the other subprograms with which it interacts. Difficulties arise only if program execution rests on contingencies that cannot be predicted perfectly in advance. In this case, coordinating activity is required to secure agreement about the estimates that will be used as the basis for action, or to provide information to each subprogram unit about the relevant activities of the others. Hence, we arrive at the proposition that the more repetitive and predictable the situation, the greater the *tolerance for interdependence* (6.23) [6.23:6.3]. Conversely, the greater the elements of variability and contingency, the greater is the burden of coordinating activities that are specialized by process (MacMahon, Millett, and Ogden, 1941).

Thus, we predict that process specialization will be carried furthest in stable environments, and that under rapidly changing circumstances specialization will be sacrificed to secure greater self-containment of separate programs [A-6.18]. A second prediction is that organizations, in order to permit a greater degree of process specialization, will devise means for increasing stability and predictability of the environment [A-6.19].

Three important devices come under this heading. All of these devices may be regarded as instances of the more general practice of standardization – of reducing the infinite number of things in the world, potential and actual – to a moderate number of well-defined varieties. The greater the *standardization of the situation* (6.24), the greater the tolerance for subunit interdependencies [6.23:6.24].

The first step in almost all major manufacturing sequences that lead from natural raw materials to finished goods is refining. In steel manufacture, a complex of natural materials – ores, coke, and flux – is reduced to a relatively homogeneous, standard material – pig iron. In the natural textile industries, fibers are transformed into threads of uniform size, strength, and elasticity by carding and spinning processes. In all such cases, the complexity of subsequent manufacturing processes and their contingency on raw materials is reduced by transforming highly variable natural materials into much more homogeneous semimanufactured products [A-6.20]. After homogeneity has been attained, subsequent steps in the manufacturing process may again produce great variety in the product – alloy steels in the first example, dyed fabrics in the second. But it is often difficult and expensive to program this subsequent elaboration unless the processing begins with a simple, homogeneous material of known properties.

A second important device for dealing with the interdependencies created by specialization is the use of interchangeable parts [A-6.21]. When the fit of two parts is assured by setting minimum and maximum size limits, the interdependency between the units that make them is decreased and the burden of coordination partly removed.

Third, the need for coordinated timing between successive process steps is reduced by holding buffer inventories [A-6.22]. If process A precedes process B in the manufacture of some item, then the effect of variations in the rate of process A upon process B can be largely removed by maintaining an inventory of products on which process A has been completed.

Even with such devices, the need for coordination typically remains. The most common device for securing coordination among subprograms where there is a high degree of process specialization is scheduling. A schedule is simply a plan, established in advance, that determines what tasks will be handled and when. It may have greater or less detail, greater or less precision. The *type of coordination* (6.25) used in the organization is a function of the extent to which the situation is standardized [6.25:6.24]. To the extent that contingencies arise, not anticipated in the schedule, coordination requires communication to give notice of deviations from planned or predicted conditions, or to give instructions for changes in activity to adjust to these deviatons. We may label coordination based on pre-established schedules *coordination by plan*, and coordination that involves transmission of new information *coordination by feedback*. The more stable and predictable the situation, the greater the reliance on coordination by plan; the more variable and unpredictable the situation, the greater the reliance on coordination by feedback.

Insofar as coordination is programmed and the range of situations sufficiently circumscribed, we would not expect any particularly close relation between the coordinative mechanisms and the formal organizational hierarchy. That is to say, scheduling information and feedback information required for coordination are not usually communicated through hierarchical channels. Hierarchy may be important in establishing and legitimizing programs, but the communication involved in the execution of highly programmed activities does not generally follow the "lines of command" [A-6.23] (Bakke, 1950).

In addition, from the standpoint of any particular organization, specialization and the structure of subprograms is as much sociological as it is technological. The organization depends to a great extent upon the training that employees bring to it – training acquired by apprenticeship or in schools. Hence the boundaries of specialization of individual jobs tend to be determined by the structure of trades and professions in the broader social environment [A-6.24].

6.5 Communication

On the basis of the foregoing analysis, we may classify the occasions for communication as follows:

1 Communication for nonprogrammed activity. This is a catchall category that will need further analysis later.
2 Communication to initiate and establish programs, including day-to-day adjustment or "coordination" of programs.
3 Communication to provide data for application of strategies (i.e., required for the execution of programs).
4 Communication to evoke programs (i.e., communications that serve as "stimuli").
5 Communication to provide information on the results of activities.

The distinction between the first two categories and the last three is the familiar distinction between communication relating to procedural matters and communication relating to substantive content.

Empirical evidence for the distinction among the last three categories was obtained from a study of the use of accounting data by operating departments in manufacturing concerns. It was found that accounting information was used at various executive levels to answer three different kinds of questions: (a) Problem-solving questions: Which course of action is better? This corresponds to our category three. (b) Attention-directing questions: What problems shall I look into? This corresponds to category four. (c) Score-card questions: How well am I (or is he) doing? This corresponds to category five. Some of the accounting information was also used in connection with less programmed activity (Simon, Guetzkow, Kozmetsky, and Tyndall, 1954). We will consider this point below.

Communication and coordination

The capacity of an organization to maintain a complex, highly interdependent pattern of activity is limited in part by its capacity to handle the communication required for coordination. The greater the *efficiency of communication* (6.26) within the organization, the greater the tolerance for interdependence [6.23:6.26]. The problem has both quantitative and qualitative aspects.

As we noted earlier, it is possible under some conditions to reduce the volume of communication required from day-to-day by substituting coordination by plan for coordination by feedback. By virtue of this substitution, organizations can tolerate very complex interrelations among their component parts in the performance of repetitive activities. The coordination of parts is incorporated in the program when it is established, and the need for continuing communication is correspondingly reduced. Each specific situation, as it arises, is largely covered by the standard operating procedure.

A different method for increasing the organization's tolerance for interdependence is to increase the efficiency of communication by making it possible to communicate large amounts of information with relatively few symbols. An obvious example is the blueprint, which provides a common plan stated in extreme detail. The blueprint employs a carefully defined, highly developed "language" or set of symbolic and verbal conventions. Because of this standardized language, it can convey large quantities of information. The same attention to standardization of language is seen in accounting systems and other reporting systems that employ numerical data.

Accounting definitions and blueprint conventions are examples of a still more general phenomenon: technical languages, whose symbols have definite and common meanings to the members of an organization. Prominent in these technical languages are categories for classifying situations and events.

The role of unambiguous technical terms in permitting coordination by feedback is shown by the Christie–Luce–Macy experiments (Macy, Christie, and Luce, 1953) with "noisy marbles" in the Bavelas network. Participants in the experiment were given some colored marbles, and they were required to discover what color was held by all of them. Control groups were given marbles that had solid colors like "red," "yellow," etc. Experimental groups were given streaked marbles whose colorings did not correspond in any simple way to color designations in common language. Comparison of the performance of the control with the experimental groups showed (a) that the latter were much hindered by the lack of adequate technical vocabulary, and (b) that their performance became comparable to that of the control groups only when they succeeded in inventing such a vocabulary and securing its acceptance throughout the group.

Classification schemes are of particular significance for the program-evoking aspects of communication. When an event occurs that calls for some kind of organization response, the question is asked, in one form or other: "What *kind* of event is this?" The organization has available a repertory of programs, so that once the event has been classified the appropriate program can be executed without further ado. We can make this process more specific with a pair of examples.

The oil gauge on the dashboard of an automobile is an example of the use of classification in program-evoking. For most drivers, the oil pressure is either "all right" or "low." In the first case, no action is taken; in the second case a remedial program is initiated (e.g., taking the automobile to a repair shop). Some auto manufacturers have substituted a red light, which turns on when the oil pressure is not in the proper range, for the traditional gauge. This example also illustrates how substituting standards of satisfactory performance for criteria of optimization simplifies communication.

Similarly, inspection activities often involve dichotomous decisions. In these cases, the choice is not usually between evoking a program or not evoking one (action or inaction), but between different programs. Thus, if the item being inspected meets the standards, one program is evoked (it is passed on for further processing); if it fails to meet standards, another program is evoked (scrapping, or reworking, as the case may be).

One reason that classifying is so economical of communication is that most of the coordination can be preprogrammed; the organization has a repertory of responses to stimuli, and it only needs to know what kind of stimulus it is confronted with in order to execute an elaborate program. On the other hand, if the communication system could handle a more complete description of the program-evoking event, and if the action part of the organization had the capacity to develop programs on the spot to meet present needs, no doubt one could conceive tailor-made programs that would be more accurately adapted to each separate situation than are the preprogrammed responses.

Here again the normative or adaptive problem of organization design is one of balance. If its model of reality is not to be so complex as to paralyze it, the organization must develop radical simplifications of its responses. One such simplification is to have (a) a repertory of standard responses, (b) a classification of program-evoking situations, (c) a set of rules to determine what is the appropriate response for each class of situations. The balance of economies and efficiencies here is exactly the same as it is in all cases of standardization. Note that what we have described in an organizational framework is quite comparable to discrimination learning in individuals. In the individual case, as in the organizational, there is a close relationship between the categories used in the cognitive code and the operational decision rules (Whorf, 1956).

In our culture, language is well developed for describing and communicating about concrete objects. The blueprint has already been mentioned as an important technical device for this purpose. Language is also very effective in communicating about things that can be classified and named, even if they are intangible. Thus, when there are standard repertories of programs, it is easy to refer to them.

On the other hand, it is extremely difficult to communicate about intangible objects and nonstandardized objects. Hence, the heaviest burdens are placed on the communications system by the less structured aspects of the organization's tasks, particularly by activity directed toward the explanation of problems that are not yet well defined. We shall see in the next chapter that this difference in communication difficulty has important implications for the organization of nonprogrammed activities.

Where the available means of communication are primitive – relative to the communication needs – so will be the system of coordination. There will tend to be less self-containment of organizational units and a greater reliance on coordination through communication the greater the efficiency of communication [6.12:6.26]. This relation may sometimes be obscured by the fact that pressure toward coordination (e.g., under conditions of rapid change) may compel attempts at feedback coordination even though available communication is inefficient. It should also be noted that self-containment decreases and interdependencies increase the likelihood of developing an efficient communication code [6.26:6.21].

The absorption of uncertainty

The use of classification schemes in communication has further consequences, some of which go back to our earlier discussion of perception and identification. The technical vocabulary and classification schemes in an organization provide a set of concepts that can be used in analyzing and in communicating about its problems. Anything that is easily described and discussed in terms of these concepts can be communicated readily in the organization; anything that does not fit the system of concepts is communicated only with difficulty. Hence, the world tends to be perceived by the organization members in terms of the particular concepts that are reflected in the organization's vocabulary. The particular categories and schemes of classification it employs are reified, and become, for members of the organization, attributes of the world rather than mere conventions (Blau, 1955).

The reification of the organization's conceptual scheme is particularly noticeable in *uncertainty absorption* (6.27). Uncertainty absorption takes place when inferences are drawn from a body of evidence and the inferences, instead of the evidence itself, are then communicated. The successive editing steps that transform data obtained from a set of questionnaires into printed statistical tables provide a simple example of uncertainty absorption.

Through the process of uncertainty absorption, the recipient of a communication is severely limited in his ability to judge its correctness. Although there may be various tests of apparent validity, internal consistency, and consistency with other communications, the recipient must, by and large, repose his confidence in the editing process that has taken place, and, if he accepts the communication at all, accept it pretty much as it stands. To the extent that he can interpret it, his interpretation must be based primarily on his confidence in the source and his knowledge of the biases to which the source is subject, rather than on a direct examination of the evidence.

By virtue of specialization, most information enters an organization at highly specific points. Direct perception of production processes is limited largely to employees in a particular operation on the production floor. Direct perception of customer attitudes is limited largely to salesmen. Direct evidence of the performance of personnel is restricted largely to immediate supervisors, colleagues, and subordinates.

In all of these cases, the person who summarizes and assesses his own direct perceptions and transmits them to the rest of the organization becomes an important source of informational premises for organizational action. The "facts" he communicates can be disbelieved, but they can only rarely be checked. Hence, by the very nature and limits of the communication system, a great deal of discretion and influence is exercised by those persons who are in direct contact with some part of the "reality" that is of concern to the organization. Both the amount and the *locus of uncertainty absorption* (6.28) affect the *influence structure of the organization* (6.29) [6.29:6.27, 6.28].

Because of this, uncertainty absorption is frequently used, consciously and unconsciously, as a technique for acquiring and exercising power. In a culture where direct contradiction of assertions of fact is not approved, an individual who is willing to make assertions, particularly about matters that do not contradict the direct perceptions of others, can frequently get these assertions accepted as premises of decision.

We can cite a number of more or less "obvious" variables that affect the absorption of uncertainty. The more complex the data that are perceived and the less adequate the organization's language, the closer to the source of the information will the uncertainty absorption take place, and the greater will be the amount of summarizing at each step of transmission. The locus of absorption will tend to be a function of such variables as: (a) the needs of the recipient for raw as against summarized information (depending upon the kinds of data used in selecting the appropriate program), (b) the need for correction of biases in the transmitter, (c) the distribution of technical competence for interpreting and summarizing raw data, and (d) the need for comparing data from two or more sources in order to interpret it.

The way in which uncertainty is absorbed has important consequences for coordination among organizational units. In business organizations, expected sales are relevant to decisions in many parts of the organization: purchasing decisions, production decisions, investment decisions, and many others. But if each organizational unit were permitted to make its own forecast of sales, there might be a wide range of such estimates with consequent inconsistencies among the decisions made by different departments – the purchasing department, for example, buying raw materials that the production department does not expect to process. It may be important in cases of this kind to make an *official* forecast and to use this official forecast as the basis for action throughout the organization.

Where it is important that all parts of an organization act on the same premises, and where different individuals may draw different conclusions from the raw evidence, a formal uncertainty absorption point will be established, and the inferences drawn at that point will have official status in the organization as "legitimate" estimates. The greater the need for coordination in the organization, the greater the *use of legitimized "facts"* (6.30) [6.30:6.8, 6.9].

The communication network

Associated with each program is a set of information flows that communicate the stimuli and data required to evoke and execute the program. Generally this communication traverses definite channels, either by formal plan or by the gradual development of informal programs. Information and stimuli move from sources to points of decision; instructions move from points of decision to points of action; information of results moves from points of action to points of decision and control.

Rational organization design would call for the arrangement of these channels so as to minimize the communication burden. But insofar as the points of origin of information and the points of action are determined in advance, the only mobile element is the point of decision. Whatever may be the position in the organization holding the formal authority to legitimize the decision, to a considerable extent the effective discretion is exercised at the points of uncertainty absorption.

In large organizations, specialization of communication functions will be reflected in the division of work itself. Among the specialized communication units we find are (a) units specializing in the actual physical transmission of communications: a telephone and teletype unit, messenger group, or the like; (b) units specializing in recording and report preparation: bookkeeping and other record-keeping units; (c) units specializing in the acquisition of raw information, usually referred to as intelligence units, sometimes as research units; (d) units specializing in the provision of technical premises for decision: research units, technical specialists; (e) units specializing in the interpretation of policy and organizational goals, a function usually not much separated from the main stem of the hierarchy; and (f) units specializing in the retention of information: files, archives units [A-6.25].

In part, communication channels are deliberately and consciously planned in the course of programming. In part, they develop through usage. We will make two hypotheses about such development. First, the greater the communication efficiency of the channel, the greater the *communication channel usage* (6.31) [6.31:6.26]. The possession by two persons, or two organization units, of a common, efficient language facilitates communication. Thus, links between members of a common profession tend to be used in the communication system. Similarly, other determinants of language compatibility – ethnic background, education, age, experience – will affect what channels are used in the organization.

Second, channel usage tends to be self-reinforcing [6.31:6.31]. When a channel is frequently used for one purpose, its use for other unrelated purposes is encouraged. In particular, formal hierarchical channels tend to become general-purpose channels to be used whenever no special-purpose channel or informal channel exists or is known to the communicator. The self-reinforcing character of channel usage is particularly strong if it brings individuals into face-to-face contact. In this case (the Homans hypothesis) informal communication, much of it social in character, develops side-by-side with task-oriented formal communication, and the use of the channel for either kind of communication tends to reinforce its use for the other.

In part, the communication network is planned; in part, it grows up in response to the need for specific kinds of communication; in part, it develops in response to the social functions of communication. At any given stage in its development, its gradual change is much influenced by the pattern that has already become established. Hence, although the structure of the network will be considerably influenced by the structure of the organization's task, it will not be completely determined by the latter.

Once a pattern of communication channels has become established, this pattern will have an important influence on decision-making processes, and particularly upon nonprogrammed activity. We may anticipate some of the analysis of the next chapter by indicating briefly the nature of this influence.

The existing pattern of communication will determine the relative frequency with which particular members of the organization will encounter particular stimuli, or kinds of stimuli, in their search processes [6.11:6.31]. For example, a research and development unit that has frequent communication with sales engineers and infrequent communication with persons engaged in fundamental research will live in a different environment of new product ideas than a research and development unit that has the opposite communication pattern.

The communication pattern will determine how frequently and forcefully particular consequences of action are brought to the attention of the actor. The degree of specialization, for example, between design engineers, on the one hand, and installation and service engineers, on the other, will have an important influence on the amount of awareness of the former as to the effectiveness of their designs.

From our previous propositions concerning time pressure effects, we would predict that the pattern of communication would have a greater influence on nonprogrammed activities carried out with deadlines and under time pressure than upon activities that involve relatively slow and deliberate processes of decision. For, given sufficient time, if particular information is available anywhere in an organization, its relevance to any particular decision is likely to be noticed. Where decisions are made relatively rapidly, however, only the information that is locally available is likely to be brought to bear. We see here another reason why specialization (in this case specialization with respect to possession of information) is tolerated to a greater degree under "steady-state" conditions than when the organization is adapting to a rapidly changing environment.

6.6 Organization Structure and the Boundaries of Rationality

It has been the central theme of this chapter that the basic features of organization structure and function derive from the characteristics of human problem-solving processes and rational human choice. Because of the limits of human intellective capacities in comparison with the complexities of the problems that individuals and organizations face, rational behavior calls for simplified models that capture the main features of a problem without capturing all its complexities.

The simplifications have a number of characteristic features:

1 Optimizing is replaced by satisficing – the requirement that satisfactory levels of the criterion variables be attained.
2 Alternatives of action and consequences of action are discovered sequentially through search processes.
3 Repertories of action programs are developed by organizations and individuals, and these serve as the alternatives of choice in recurrent situations.
4 Each specific action program deals with a restricted range of situations and a restricted range of consequences.
5 Each action program is capable of being executed in semi-independence of the others – they are only loosely coupled together [A-6.26].

Action is goal-oriented and adaptive. But because of its approximating and fragmented character, only a few elements of the system are adaptive at any one time; the remainder are, at least in the short run, "givens." So, for example, an individual or organization may attend to improving a particular program, or to selecting an appropriate program from the existing repertory to meet a particular situation. Seldom can both be attended to simultaneously.

The notion that rational behavior deals with a few components at a time was first developed extensively in connection with economic behavior by John R. Commons (1951), who spoke of "limiting factors" that become the foci of attention and adaptation. Commons's theory was further developed by Chester I. Barnard (1938), who preferred the term "strategic factor."

This "one-thing-at-a-time" or "*ceteris paribus*" approach to adaptive behavior is fundamental to the very existence of something we can call "organization structure." Organization structure consists simply of those aspects of the pattern of behavior in the organization that are relatively stable and that change only slowly. If behavior in organizations is "intendedly rational," we will expect aspects of the behavior to be relatively stable that either (a) represent adaptations to relatively stable elements in the environment, or (b) are the learning programs that govern the process of adaptation.

An organization is confronted with a problem like that of Archimedes: in order for an organization to behave adaptively, it needs some stable regulations and procedures that it can employ in carrying out its adaptive practices. Thus, at any given time an organization's programs for performing its tasks are part of its structure, but the least stable part. Slightly more stable are the switching rules that determine when it will apply one program, and when another. Still more stable are the procedures it uses for developing, elaborating, instituting, and revising programs.

The matter may be stated differently. If an organization has a repertory of programs, then it is adaptive in the short run insofar as it has procedures for selecting from this repertory a program appropriate to each specific situation that arises. The process used to select an appropriate program is the "fulcrum" on which short-run adaptiveness rests. If, now, the organization has processes for adding to its repertory of programs or for modifying programs in the repertory, these processes become still more basic fulcra for accomplishing longer-run adaptiveness. Short-run adaptiveness corresponds to what we ordinarily call problem-solving, long-run adaptiveness to learning.

There is no reason, of course, why this hierarchy of mechanisms should have only three levels – or any specified number. In fact, the adaptive mechanisms need not be arranged hierarchically. Mechanism A may include mechanism B within its domain of action, and vice versa. However, in general there is much asymmetry in the ordering, so that certain elements in the process that do not often become strategic factors (the "boundaries of rationality") form the stable core of the organization structure.

We can now see the relation between Commons's and Barnard's theories of the "limiting" or "strategic" factor and organization structure. Organization will have structure, as we have defined the term here, insofar as there are boundaries of rationality – insofar as there are elements of the situation that must be or are in fact taken as givens, and that do not enter into rational calculations as potential strategic factors. If there were not boundaries to rationality, or if the boundaries varied in a rapid and unpredictable manner, there could be no stable organization structure. Some aspects of structure will be more easily modified than others, and hence we may need to distinguish short-run and long-run structure.

In this chapter, we have been concerned mostly with short-run structure – with programs to respond to sequences of situations requiring adaptive action. The "boundaries of rationality" that have been the source of our propositions have consisted primarily of the properties of human beings as organisms capable of evoking and executing relatively well-defined programs but able to handle programs only of limited complexity.

In the next chapter, we will shift our attention to long-run considerations, and particularly to the processes in organizations that bring programs into existence and that modify them.

7

Planning and Innovation in Organizations

In the last chapter we found it useful to contrast the concept of rationality that has been employed in economics and statistics with a theory of rationality that takes account of the limits on the power, speed, and capacity of human cognitive faculties. This contrast helped us understand the mosaic of programs that constitutes the great bulk of human behavior in organizations.

At a number of points in the chapter, we found it necessary to allude to unprogrammed activity, and activity directed toward the creation of new programs, but our attention was directed toward the organizational "steady state" rather than toward change in organizations. There still remains, therefore, the task of analyzing more completely how the cognitive limits on rationality affect the processes of organizational change and program development. In the present chapter we shall try to fit this remaining piece into the picture.

7.1 The Concept of Initiation

Theories of rational choice generally have not made a distinction between continuation of an existing program of action and change in the program of action. In these theories, the chooser is simply confronted with two (or more) alternatives of action and required to select the better of the two. There is no need to designate which, if either, of these actions continues the existing program.

In such formulations there is one way, however, in which the distinction between persistence and change can be given formal representation, and can be made to influence the choice. We exclude sunk costs when computing the costs of persisting in a going program. A great deal of the inertia of "going concerns" can be explained on the basis of the sunk costs doctrine. A simple example is the decision whether to move a factory to a new location. Unless the present facilities can be sold for an amount that tends to compensate for the cost of constructing or acquiring new facilities, the new location will be severely disadvantaged in the comparison, and only rarely will a change in location prove preferable to remaining in the present location.

We may also regard the costs of discovering and developing a possible program of action as sunk costs, for these costs must be incurred if there is to be a shift to a new program of action, but not if the organization persists in its present program. Hence, even if there are no tangible sunk costs, like factory buildings or specialized equipment, there will almost always be associated with a change in program a number of sunk *costs of innovation* (7.1). Costs of innovation, whatever their origin, will tend to produce *program continuity* (7.2) [7.2:7.1].

Although tangible sunk costs often can be and sometimes are evaluated in monetary terms, it is seldom possible to make accurate estimates of the costs of innovation, and even in situations where it is possible, such estimates are seldom made. Individuals and organizations give preferred treatment to alternatives that represent continuation of present programs over those that represent change. But this preference is not derived by calculating explicitly the costs of innovation or weighing these costs. Instead, persistence comes about primarily because the individual or organization does not search for or consider alternatives to the present course of action unless that present course is in some sense "unsatisfactory." The amount of *search* (7.3) decreases as *satisfaction* (7.4) increases [7.3:7.4]. Where search for new alternatives is suppressed, program continuity is facilitated [7.2:7.3].

The importance of this proposition to participation decisions has already been shown in chapter 4. Its main consequence is that, in a theory of choice, we should distinguish between the alternative of continuing and alternatives of change, and should not treat these symmetrically as is done in most existing theories.

A theory of this kind does not attribute the persistence of behavior to any particular "resistance to change," but simply to the absence of a vigorous search for new alternatives under circumstances where the existing program is regarded as satisfactory. If a new alternative, which is superior in some or all respects to the current program, somehow presents itself to the choosing individual or organization, the theory does not predict that the program will remain unchanged; but a theory of choice without a theory of search is inadequate.

In general, we hypothesize that the *type of influence process* (7.5) involved in decision-making will be a function of the *type of choice problem* (7.6) [7.5:7.6]. When a choice problem takes the form of selecting one course of action from a set of alternatives, influence processes operate by making one alternative more attractive relative to the others. When the choice, however, is one of change versus persistence, a great part of the influence process will consist in initiation – particularly, in suggesting alternatives of action where none existed before, either (a) to solve a problem for which there was not a solution, or (b) to improve the present program even when it was accepted as satisfactory. Hence, by observing the influence processes we can distinguish pretty clearly between choice situations where the main problem is to select one out of several alternatives and choice situations where a new program is being proposed that deviates from the existing program. Most research on interpersonal influence has focused on the former situation. The results may be substantially irrelevant to the case where the alternatives are not specified in advance (March, 1955a).

One final qualification: not every change in behavior qualifies as initiation or innovation as those terms are used here. In the last chapter, an inventory and production control system was used to illustrate how, through the construction of a strategy, change could take place within the framework of a well-defined performance program. We would not regard a change in the operating level of a factory from one month to another as involving initiation or innovation.

Initiation and innovation are present when change requires the devising and evaluation of new performance programs that have not previously been a part of the organization's repertory and cannot be introduced by a simple application of programmed switching rules. The extent to which behavior in an organization can change without involving either initiation or innovation is limited only by the complexity of the strategies and switching rules that are imbedded in its performance programs. If we could describe for a particular organization what its program was, including its programmed switching rules, we would be in a position to distinguish ordinary programmed changes in behavior from changes that represent the initiation of new performance programs.

Action and inaction

We need a theory that distinguishes between persistence and change; we need also a distinction between action and inaction. Just as most theories of choice fail to distinguish between persistence and change, they also fail to distinguish between doing something and doing nothing. "Doing nothing," in such theories, is simply a particular alternative of behavior that may be chosen or rejected in exactly the same way as "doing a particular something."

Consider a system having a set of criteria to determine what constitutes a "satisfactory" situation. For an organism, these criteria may include the requirements that it not be hungry, that no danger be present, and the like. For a business concern, the demands of "satisfaction" may be a particular profit level, market share, and liquidity position. It may happen that certain of these criteria are satisfied by activities that are compatible with a wide variety of other activities. Animals, for example, require oxygen, but breathing is compatible with the simultaneous performance of a large number of other activities. Thus, an animal that is only breathing is described as "inactive." Formally, we describe an activity as "action" or "inaction" relative to a set of alternative activities. Less formally, we recognize certain activities as conspicuous cases of "inaction" in the general environment in which we live, and we need not quibble about how to classify borderline cases.

The distinction between action and inaction is clearly relevant to the everyday world of organizations as we know it. There is ordinarily little or no limit to the amount of inaction an organization can "undertake"; inaction does not absorb resources. At the same time, the distinction is more important in some situations than in others. It is more significant for organizations or individuals that satisfice than for those that optimize. For the former can reach their goals by action programs that, taken collectively, satisfy the criteria in question; they need consider action only when inaction does not achieve this, and only in the specific directions in which action relates to particular criteria. If, for example, there is no safety problem (i.e., the present safety record is accepted as satisfactory), there need be no safety action.

The significance of the action–inaction distinction also depends on characteristics of the environment. Consider a world that is mainly "empty" – in which most events are unrelated to most other events; causal connections are exceptional and not common. In a world largely empty, a theory of rational action does not have to regard each choice as affecting each component of a "utility function" – everything connected with everything else. Instead, particular action programs have few consequences except for the criteria they were undertaken to satisfy. Hence, we suggest that the greater the *use of acceptable-level decision rules* (7.7) and the less the *complexity of the environment* (7.8), the greater the *use of local changes in programs* (7.9) [7.9:7.7, 7.8]. The picture (or perhaps, nightmare) of planning as the solution of almost unimaginable numbers of simultaneous equations can be replaced by a picture of planning as the construction of a series of unrelated action programs.

"Unrelated" is perhaps too strong a term; "loosely coupled" is a more appropriate one. Even in a mostly empty world there is one important connection among action programs that must be taken into consideration in planning: that they all draw upon the resources of the organization. Action, unlike inaction, incurs opportunity costs whenever the criteria that the organization must meet are (collectively) sufficiently stiff that meeting all of them simultaneously is not a trivial matter.

A summary of the planning model

We can now summarize the essential characteristics of rational choice as we have described it, preparatory to a more detailed analysis of choice processes in organizations.

1 As in the last chapter, we assume that the main requirement of the organizational program is to *satisfy* certain requirements or criteria, these criteria being subject to gradual change over time.
2 When, in the absence of an action program, one or more criteria are not being met, we predict that an *action* program will be initiated to remedy this condition [A-7.1].
3 A change in the program of an organization – whether by adding new activities or altering existing ones – involves not just a choice process, in the traditional sense, but requires also a process of *initiation* through which new program possibilities are generated and their consequences examined [A-7.2].
4 For the most part, particular action programs are connected with particular criteria, and the world is largely empty of complicated causal interrelations. Action programs are related to each other primarily through the demands they make on the scarce *organizational resources* available for initiating and carrying on action [A-7.3].

7.2 The Process of Innovation

The innovative processes that are essential in initiating new programs in organization are closely related to the various intellective processes referred to by psychologists as "problem-solving," "productive thinking," "creative thinking," "invention," and the like. Our starting point will be to examine briefly what is known of the problem-solving process at the individual level, and then to introduce organizational considerations.

Memory and problem-solving

In virtually all human problem-solving, memory plays an enormous role. In the memory are stored both repertories of possible solutions to classes of problems that have been encountered in the past and repertories of components of problem solutions. The importance of such repertories – and their large magnitude – in difficult intellective activities like mathematical invention and chess-playing is amply documented. There can be little doubt that they are equally essential components of almost all kinds of everyday problem-solving (de Groot, 1946; Hadamard, 1945).

When problem-solving consists primarily in searching the memory in a relatively systematic fashion for solutions that are present there in nearly finished form, it is described as "reproductive." When the construction of new solutions out of more or less "raw" material is involved, the process is described as "productive." The *type of problem-solving* (7.10) used, i.e., the extent to which productive elements are present, depends on both the characteristics of the problem and on the *past experience* (7.11) of the problem solver [7.10:7.6, 7.11].

Programmed activity generally involves a great deal of problem-solving of a rather routine and reproductive sort. That is to say, only under unusual circumstances is the detail of a program so stereotyped that it is stored in the memory as a series of specific instructions. On the contrary, in most situations the execution of a program involves a considerable amount of reconstruction of the program details, but without requiring extensive and difficult searches or computations. Contrariwise, the unprogrammed activity in innovation generally requires a great deal of "productive" problem-solving.

Basic problem-solving processes

Our existing scientific knowledge of human problem-solving processes is incomplete. From what is known it is possible, however, to describe the general characteristics of these processes; and it is only these general characteristics that will be relevant for our analysis of organizational decision-making (Newell, Shaw, and Simon, 1958).

First, however complex the end products of these processes – however intricate the machine that is invented or however subtle and sophisticated the decision that is reached – the processes themselves are made up by aggregating very large numbers of elements, each element, taken by itself, being exceedingly simple. In an age of electronic computers this fact – if it is a fact – should not surprise us, for this is exactly the way in which a computer operates; it performs intricate and elaborate mathematical computations, but it performs them by executing sequences of enormous length of elementary steps, where each such step is no more complicated than adding 1 and 1 to get 2. We are not arguing that human brains are necessarily like computers, but simply that complex processes can be aggregated from simple elements (Plato, *Meno*, pp. 80–5).

Second, one large component of problem-solving consists of search processes. Search may be physical: finding a piece of correspondence in a file, or obtaining a customer by door-to-door canvassing; it may be perceptual: scanning the Patent Office Gazette to find items of relevance to a company's research activity; it may be cognitive: using associative processes to locate relevant information in the memory.

Third, another large component consists of screening processes. Items that are dredged up by search processes are examined to see whether they qualify as possible solutions to the problem at hand or possible components of such solutions. The screening of job applicants provides a simple example.

Fourth, the elementary components of the problem-solving process (the search and screening processes) are characterized by a great deal of "randomness." There is ordinarily considerable arbitrariness about the sequences in which problem-solving steps are taken, and in the order in which they are assembled. Running through the process, however, are two elements of organization that give it structure and that permit it to give rise to a highly organized product. These organizing processes are "programs" in the sense in which we have been using that term.

Two kinds of programs may be distinguished. On the one hand, although there is usually nothing inexorable in the sequence in which problem-solving steps are taken, and although many of these steps involve a great deal of search, certain broad *procedural* programs are recognizable in most problem-solving. Most of our descriptions of temporal pattern in problem-solving go back to John Dewey's analysis of the problem-solving process and to Gestalt theorizing about productive thinking. Empirical evidence generally supporting Dewey's phase hypotheses has been obtained by Bales and Strodtbeck (1951) in certain group problem-solving situations; and empirical evidence for some of the Gestalt hypotheses has been obtained, through "thinking aloud" techniques, by de Groot (1946) and others in individual problem-solving situations.

At the same time, there are *substantive* programs. By substantive programs are meant the structuring of the problem-solving process that comes about as a reflection of the structure of the problem to be solved. For example, a business policy problem of broad scope may be factored into its marketing aspects, its financial aspects, its production aspects, etc.; and at one stage in the solution process these several aspects may be dealt with separately – sequentially, or simultaneously – by different parts of the organization.

Fifth, the programs, procedural and substantive, that govern problem-solving processes have generally a hierarchical structure. From a procedural standpoint this means that the problem goes through a sequence of broad phases (e.g., "problem formulation," "search for alternatives," "evaluation of alternatives," etc.), but that each of these phases may be made up, in turn, of similar phases at a more microscopic level of detail. On the substantive side, a similar sequence of levels may be apparent: the problem is first analyzed in broad terms; each of its aspects becomes, in turn, a subproblem to be further analyzed in detail (Cyert, Simon, and Trow, 1956).

Some general hypotheses about process

We shall be concerned in the remainder of this chapter with propositions about the problem-solving and program-innovating processes as they occur in organizations. A few hypotheses are of such broad relevance that they are worth stating at the outset. Some of these have already been presented in earlier chapters; others are new.

In a search for programs of activity to achieve goals, the focus of attention will tend to move from one class of variables to another in the following general sequence [A-7.4]:

1 Those variables that are largely within the control of the problem-solving individual or organizational unit will be considered first. There will be a serious attempt to elaborate a program of activity based on the control of these variables.

2 If a satisfactory program is not discovered by these means, attention will be directed to changing other variables that are not under the direct control of the problem solvers; for example, the program will be enlarged to include activities to be performed by other, independent, organizational units, or to

include securing permission for courses of action not presently within the area of discretion of the problem solvers.

3 If a satisfactory program is still not evolved, attention will be turned to the criteria that the program must satisfy, and an effort will be made to relax these criteria so that a satisfactory program can be found.

In the search for possible courses of action, alternatives will be tested sequentially. That is to say, there will be no attempt at the first round of search to exhaust "all possible alternatives." Instead, as soon as a few possible alternatives have been found, these will be evaluated. If one proves satisfactory, when tested against the problem criteria, it will be accepted as a solution to the problem, and search will terminate. If all the alternatives discovered on the previous round of search prove unsatisfactory, this will initiate a new burst of search activity. If persistent search still fails to secure a satisfactory alternative, then the propositions listed above apply.

One higher-level procedural program that is constantly invoked in problem-solving is a search for substantive information by first instituting a higher-level search to determine the likely sources of information. That is, an important technique for obtaining information is to ask someone who has it rather than to search for it in a more painful fashion. But in order to do the former, a search may be needed to determine who has the requisite information. One important element of organization structure is a set of understandings and expectations among the participants as to what bodies of information repose where in the structure. This set of expectations and understandings is a major determinant of the use of communications channels.

Individual and group problem-solving

Up to this point, we have not troubled to distinguish between problem-solving by individuals and problem-solving in groups. Most problem-solving and decision-making in organizations involves, at one stage or another of the proceedings, the participation of a number of persons. To what extent are the individual and the group problem-solving processes the same, and to what extent are they different?

Kelley and Thibaut (Lindzey, 1954), in their assessment of the literature on problem-solving in groups, observe that "most of the analyses of the group problem-solving process appear to derive by analogy from the stages or phases believed to exist in individual problem-solving." They cite Bales' hypotheses on phases in group problem-solving as examples of this. Moreover, a number of workers have assumed implicitly a considerable similarity of the two processes when they have suggested that group situations might provide better opportunities for the study of problem-solving than individual situations. In the group situation the process requires interpersonal communication, and hence many of the steps that would otherwise take place inside the individual brain become visible to the observer. But this point of view is valid, of course, only if the processes are more or less similar.

A substantial number of experiments have been performed to detect differences between the problem-solving performance of groups and individuals respectively. Kelley and Thibaut divide the effects of the group on the problem-solving process into two main types: (1) the effects of pooling a number of independent judgments, and (2) modifications in the problem solution produced by direct social influence.

Under the first heading, the pooling of independent judgments, they examine the following factors as possible explanations for the superiority of group over individual problem-solving capacities: (a) The scattering of errors. Since not all group members make the same errors simultaneously, the majority judgment is better than the average judgment of individual members. (b) Extra influence of considered judgments. Not all proposed solutions will have equal weight with group members. Those proposals that appear to have the best basis will be the ones most likely to be accepted. Hence, again, the judgment accepted by the group will be better than the average of the group members. (c) Extra influence of confident judgments. Those members who are most likely to be correct are also most likely to be confident of their answers. Their confidence will attach extra weight to their judgments, and again this will improve the group judgment. (d) The division of labor. In handling some problems, the entire group need not deal with the whole problem, but may divide it up in some way and assign the parts to "specialists." This will almost certainly speed up the solution process and may also improve the quality of solutions.

Kelley and Thibaut examine the following kinds of "modifications produced by direct social influence." (a) The group members collectively will have available a larger number of possible solutions or contributions toward the solution than will any individual member. (b) There will be pressures upon individual group members tending to produce conformity to majority group opinion: (i) through effects on each member's confidence in his own judgment, (ii) through needs for approval. (c) The group environment will increase or decrease motivations toward effort and task completion, as compared with an isolated individual. Cooperative and competitive groups will have strongly different behaviors in this respect. (d) The requirements of communicating ideas to others will force group members to sharpen and clarify their ideas. (e) In the combination or weighting of individual solutions in a group solution there will be effects from direct social pressure to conform and from self-weighting of proposals by degree of confidence expressed and by relative interest in the problem under consideration. (f) The group environment may produce varying amounts of distraction. (g) The group environment may encourage or inhibit initiation.

Since that task has already been performed by Kelley and Thibaut, we will not examine here the available evidence about the strength and significance of these variables. However, we wish to emphasize one feature of group problem-solving that we consider important. As Thorndike (1938) has noted, abilities to evaluate the correctness of proposed solutions are not necessarily the same as abilities to devise correct solutions. In fact, we generally assume that the latter abilities are somewhat less widely shared than the former. From this, Thorndike deduced the superiority of groups over individuals in some types of problems. This adds support to the general proposition that influence theory must deal with evoking phenomena as well as the evaluative phase of decision-making.

7.3 The Occasions of Innovation

When we treat persistence and change asymmetrically, we do not need to explain why an organization continues to carry out its present program of activity, but we do need to describe the situations in which innovation and change in program will take place. To explain the occasions of innovation is to explain why a program of action that has been regarded as satisfying certain criteria no longer does so.

Determinants of the criteria of satisfaction

The notion of criteria of satisfaction is closely related to the psychological notion of "aspiration levels," and we will argue that generalizations that have been found to hold for individual aspiration levels will continue to hold in the area of organizational behavior. The most important proposition is that, over time, the aspiration level tends to adjust to the level of achievement. That is to say, the level of satisfactory performance is likely to be very close to the actually achieved level of recent performance. (See the discussion of the general model of adaptive behavior in chapter 3.)

As we have noted earlier, this generalization about the adjustment of criteria to the *status quo* needs to be qualified in several important respects. First, adjustment of criteria is a relatively slow process, and cannot be indefinitely accelerated (Gaus and Wolcott, 1940, pp. 82–4). Second, when the situation is in a "steady state" over some period of time, aspiration levels do not remain absolutely constant but tend to rise slowly. Hence, even in the absence of environmental change, there is a continuous mild pressure toward innovation and change of program. Third, although past achievement provides a primary basis for adjusting aspirations to the achievable (or that which is thought to be achievable), other bases of comparison are used as well. Individuals adjust their criteria to the achieved levels of other individuals with whom they compare themselves, and to the levels that are established as norms by relevant reference groups. Organizations adjust their criteria to the levels achieved by other organizations. In general, awareness of a definite course of action that will yield substantially better results than the present program, or awareness that some other person or organization is achieving better results – even if the exact method is not known – will lead to revision of the standards of satisfaction (Cyert and March, 1956).

These postulates have been discussed in earlier chapters with respect to their effect on individual productive behavior and turnover. From them we can also predict variations in the *rate of innovation* (7.12). The rate of innovation is likely to increase when changes in the environment make the existing organizational procedures unsatisfactory [7.12:7.4]. We would predict efforts toward innovation in a company whose share of market, total profits, or rate of return on investment had declined. We could predict which of these conditions would most likely induce innovation by determining which was attended to most carefully by the organization.

As a corollary to the first point, we would expect data in reports of operating statistics to trigger innovative effort when the data showed performance falling below present standards.

In the absence of significant environmental change, the gradual upward movement of criteria will lead to periodic demands for innovation, but to only moderately vigorous efforts.

Some innovation will result from accidental encounters with opportunities. Stated otherwise, the rate at which opportunities for more satisfactory performance are encountered, whether by accident or design, will be one of the determinants of the rate of innovation.

The concept of optimum stress

The hypotheses listed thus far attribute the parenthood of invention primarily to necessity and secondarily to opportunity. There is another common hypothesis, not derivable from these postulates, that innovation will be most rapid and vigorous when the "stress" on the organization is neither too high nor too low. By stress is meant the discrepancy between the level of aspiration and the level of achievement. According to this hypothesis, if achievement too easily exceeds aspiration, apathy results; if aspiration is very much above achievement, frustration or desperation result, with consequent stereotypy. In the first case, there is no motivation for innovation; in the second case, neurotic reactions interfere with effective innovation. Optimal "stress" results when the carrot is just a little way ahead of the donkey – when aspirations exceed achievement by a small amount.

The concept of optimal stress is central to Toynbee's theories of social progress. The same hypothesis is employed frequently in educational theory, in determining the difficulty of the successive tasks with which a learner should be confronted. It can be viewed as dealing with the same problem we noted in chapter 3: that our model of "normal" motivated behavior requires a switching rule to allow it to accommodate the neurotic behavior sometimes observed.

The institutionalization of innovation

All these hypotheses about innovation rest on the assumption that the innovative process is not itself programmed. The stimuli to innovation, in this model, are external.

The "natural" stimuli to innovation – the failure of the existing program to attain satisfactory levels of the criteria – can be supplemented by additional programmed stimuli. There are at least two ways in which this can come about or can be produced in an organization [A-7.5]. The criteria of satisfaction can themselves be stated in terms of *rates of change* (i.e., first derivatives) of performance. For example, the management of a business firm might aim at a certain annual percentage increase in sales or in profits. Then, if the existing program did not bring about such a rate of change, innovative activity would be induced in just the same way as by unfavorable environmental changes.

Second, the organization (or parts of it) can acquire criteria of satisfaction specifically stated in terms of rates of innovation. For example, if there is a formally organized research activity – a research and development department, say – the criterion that this unit might establish for itself could be a specified rate of introduction of new programs into the organization.

It should be possible to distinguish the patterns of innovation of organizations that have institutionalized the innovative process in one way or another from those that have not. For example, we would expect the rate of innovation to be less sensitive to environmental changes in the former than in the latter. On the whole, at least under conditions of a relatively stable environment, we would also expect the average rate of innovation to be higher the greater the *institutionalization of innovation* (7.13) [7.12:7.13].

The timing of innovation

One cannot really draw a sharp line between the occasions of innovation and the timing of innovation. In both cases we are concerned with the kinds of innovative changes that take place and the rates at which they occur. But when we refer to the "occasions" of innovation, we are particularly interested in determining the circumstances that initially direct the attention of the organization to the need for or the possibility of changes in the current program. When we refer to "timing," we are particularly interested in determining the pace at which the subsequent steps – following upon the initial directing of attention – are taken.

What determines the type of activity that members of an organization – and here we are particularly concerned with members at a relatively responsible level – engage in? We can cite two factors that affect the *propensity of organization members to engage in an activity* (7.14). First, the greater the explicit *time pressure* (7.15) attached to an activity, the greater the propensity to engage in it [7.14:7.15]. The stimulus of deadlines tends to direct attention to some tasks rather than others (Gaus and Wolcott, 1940, pp. 68–9). Second, the greater the *clarity of goals* (7.16) associated with an activity, the greater the propensity to engage in it [7.14:7.16]. It is easier to attach rewards and penalties, internal as well as external, to completion of tasks with clear goals than to others.

These propositions lead to a prediction that might be described as the "Gresham's Law" of planning: Daily routine drives out planning. Stated less cryptically, we predict that when an individual is faced both with highly programmed and highly unprogrammed tasks, the former tend to take precedence over the latter even in the absence of strong over-all time pressure.

How, then, does unprogrammed activity ever take place? There are two general conditions (not necessarily exclusive) for bringing it about. They represent ways of affecting either goal clarity or deadlines attached to unprogrammed activity. The first is to allocate resources to goals requiring nonprogrammed activity, and to refuse to provide substitute or alternate goals that can be reached by programmed activity. In organizations, this means to create independently budgeted "planning" units that are kept out of the stream of day-to-day operating tasks (Lanzetta and Roby, 1956).

Deadlines provide the second condition for unprogrammed activity. One of the commonest forms of deadline is not usually regarded as such: the occurrence of a "case" that has to be settled, and that cannot be settled without deciding more general issues. Thus, the process of designing a new piece of equipment may be much accelerated if its immediate acquisition becomes essential because of the breakdown of the old one. Or, a company may develop a general vacation policy because a request by a particular employee for certain vacation privileges has to be granted or refused.

There are many other ways in which deadlines get set. They are commonly set by hierarchical superiors. In other cases they are undertaken voluntarily, but become definite commitments through the reliance of other persons upon them. The process of commitment is generally sequential. An initial commitment is a commitment primarily to undertake search activity. The outcome of the initial search process becomes itself a major determinant of how rapidly and with what resources the activity will continue to be pursued. Sometimes these sequential stages in the search process become formalized, and then are especially visible. They will be discussed further in the next section, when we come to a more detailed description of the processes of program elaboration.

Where an individual or organization unit is carrying on a number of unprogrammed activities, the priorities among these and the relative rates at which they proceed tend to be determined on highly fortuitous grounds. Stimuli that direct attention to one or another of the activities may have considerable short-run influence on the allocation of resources among them. Thus, such devices as tickler files may operate in much the same way, and with almost the same effect, as deadlines.

7.4   The Elaboration of Programs

In the present section, we examine in more detail the nature of innovative activity, and particularly the processes by means of which new programs of decision and action are discovered, developed, and put into effect.

Organization resources for innovation

The "Gresham's Law" propounded in the previous section implies that if all the resources of an organization are busily employed in carrying on existing programs, the process of initiating new programs will be slow and halting at best. Frequently, when a new program is to be developed, a new organizational unit is created and charged with the task first of elaborating the new program and then carrying it on when it has been elaborated [A-7.6]. This procedure provides for a spurt of innovative, program-developing activity – a spurt that automatically diminishes as the program is elaborated and the task shifts gradually from one of planning to one of execution.

This two-phase process in the development of a new organization and a new program has often been commented upon by observers of organizations. For example, it is frequently observed that the initial stage of program elaboration is generally a period of excitement for the personnel engaged in it. They put in a great deal of overtime, and take much pride and pleasure in their work. As programmed activity begins to replace innovation, excitement wanes and feelings of anticlimax are often expressed.

Because such expectations are fairly common, it is often said that the creation of a new unit is the only way to secure innovation that is not excessively bound and hampered by tradition and precedent. Similarly, it is often claimed that the personality traits required of top executives during such an innovating phase are different from the traits required during the subsequent program-execution stage. The differences are in the obvious direction – "idea man" versus orderly bureaucrat.

A major consequence of this distinction between program elaboration and program execution is that decisions made during the former process are rarely re-examined during the latter. Selznick (1957) places great stress on the process of commitment during the program-elaboration stage, particularly as it affects, and is affected by, the power relations between the organization and its environment. More generally, we hypothesize that whatever relations are established in the initial phase will be relatively stable; hence the process of commitment is not reversible [A-7.7].

When an organization has slack money or manpower not committed to going programs, various specializations of function may arise with respect to commitment to new programs and program elaboration. In particular, there may be an "investing" function and an "entrepreneurial" function [A-7.8]. The investor is in a position to make decisions on the allocation of resources, including decisions among competing claims; the entrepreneur is the source of program suggestions. The entrepreneur–investor distinction probably has broad significance in describing specialization in decision-making generally. We may distinguish those who are influential by initiating action proposals from those who are influential by being able to implement proposals that have been made. Most analyses of authority, particularly those that stress formal authority, have considered primarily the latter function.

There may be a third function – a "broker" function [A-7.9]. Unless there are established channels for processing innovative proposals, the innovator is faced with a problem in discovering an investor who has available resources. Brokers serve to make investors visible to entrepreneurs, and to bring the innovative ideas of entrepreneurs to the attention of investors. By the manner in which he "filters" these communications, the broker can also share in the influence of entrepreneur and investor. In the next section of this chapter we will consider at what levels in the organization entrepreneurial, investment, and brokerage functions will be performed.

If investment decisions were made according to the classical theory of the firm, such considerations as these would be of little import. But when decisions are satisficing rather than optimizing decisions, *resource allocation* (7.17) to new programs will depend substantially on the *communication structure* (7.18) through which proposals are processed from entrepreneurs to investors and on the *order of presentation of alternatives* (7.19) [7.17:7.7, 7.18, 7.19]. Thus in this case, as in several others we have mentioned, organizational decisions depend at least as heavily on attention cues as on utility functions.

Sources of program ideas

In talking about the sources of program ideas, we need to draw a rough boundary around a unit that can be called the "organization." We need to do this because we wish to hypothesize that most innovations in an organization are a result of borrowing rather than invention [A-7.10]. The borrowing may take the form of more or less direct imitation or it may be accomplished by importing new persons into the organization. In either case borrowing saves an organization many of the costs associated with innovation: (a) the costs of actual invention, (b) the costs of testing, (c) the risks of error in evaluation.

To the extent that innovation does occur through borrowing, both the rate of innovation and the *type of innovation* (7.20) will be functions of exposure – thus of the communication structure of the organization [7.12, 7.20:7.18].

With respect to the rate of innovation, we predict: When the environment has changed so as to create a new problem for a number of organizations (e.g., organizations in an industry where demand has shifted) there will be a period after awareness of the problem has spread during which actual innovation will be very slow. Once an acceptable solution to the problem has been invented and introduced in one such organization, it will spread rapidly to the others in the industry (Brown, 1957; Coleman, Katz, and Menzel, 1957). Innovation will be greatly increased for a short time if a group of new persons, from a subculture not previously strongly represented in the organization, is introduced into it.

The type of innovation depends on the specific exposure of the relevant unit in the organization. Thus we would predict a difference in product innovation between companies where research men have their greatest contact with the sales department and companies where research men have contact primarily with professional colleagues in other companies. Similarly, those units in contact with a particular clientele will be the source of innovation relating to the satisfactions of the goals of that clientele (Gaus and Wolcott, 1940, pp. 52–3, 82–4). Finally, program changes innovated in units that are not in direct contact with the outside environment will largely be resource-saving in character.

Selective filtering takes place not only at the boundary of the organization but at every stage in the transmission and elaboration of program proposals. We can think of each such stage as defining a new "boundary" (with varying properties of selective and nonselective permeability) that the proposed innovation must penetrate. The selective properties of each boundary will be functions of the kinds of *expertise* represented there. Since the points in the organization where uncertainty absorption takes place are the points of greatest discretionary judgment, the selective filtering of innovative proposals will be greatest at those points.

A special class of innovations are those that change the organization's model for representing the external world. Since comparison of the model with the world and awareness of discrepancies can occur only at points of uncertainty absorption, these will be the principal points where proposals of changes in the model originate.

Where an organization becomes aware of a problem, and a proposed solution does not accompany the communication of the problem awareness, repertories of problem solutions "stored" in the memories of organization members will be the principal source of solution proposals. As awareness of the problem is communicated through the organization, solutions will be evoked from these repertories and will become attached to it. The broader the problem, the more will the solution be affected by the numbers and diversity in the people among whom it is circulated. With the increase in the number of persons who become aware of the problem (without a corresponding increase in diversity) the number of solutions will increase, but at a negatively accelerated rate.

Check lists and repertories will be used both in finding innovative solutions to problems and also in checking the feasibility of proposed innovations. As a proposed solution is circulated through the organization, particular consequences will be checked by individuals and organization units in whose specialized province they lie. The propositions of the previous paragraph apply to this feasibility testing of ideas as well as to program innovation.

From the last two paragraphs we see that a good deal of the internal communication in an organization concerning new programs is aimed at a search of the organization's (collective) memory for relevant considerations – whether in the nature of program proposals or feasibility tests. The sequential order in which feasibility tests are applied is not particularly significant (although one sequence may be more efficient than another in amending proposals early and rejecting bad proposals promptly, provided the search is thorough).

The hierarchical structure of programs

Most organizational programs, as we have seen in chapter 6, are comprised of a complex structure of interrelated decisions. We appeal again to the principle of bounded rationality – to the limits of human cognitive powers – to assert that in the discovery and elaboration of new programs, the decision-making process will proceed in stages, and at no time will it be concerned with the "whole" problem in all its complexity, but always with parts of the problem.

It has often been observed that in the search for programs this simplification is achieved by factoring the problem in a hierarchical fashion. As Barnard has described the process (1938, p. 206):

... the process of decision is one of successive approximations – constant refinement of purpose, closer and closer discriminations of fact – in which the march of time is essential. Hence those who make general decisions can only envisage conditions in general and vaguely. The approximations with which they deal are symbols covering a multitude of undisclosed details.

Means–end analysis

In the present context we are discussing nonprogrammed decision-making, specifically, the process whereby new programs of action are discovered, elaborated, and instituted. Hence, we are concerned primarily with search activities and with processes for evaluating proposals. In the elaboration of new programs, the principal technique of successive approximations is means–end analysis:

1 starting with the general goal to be achieved,
2 discovering a set of means, very generally specified, for accomplishing this goal,
3 taking each of these means, in turn, as a new subgoal and discovering a set of more detailed means for achieving it, etc. [A-7.11] (Haberstroh, 1957).

How far does this hierarchy of ends and means go in the direction of specifying detailed means? It proceeds until it reaches a level of concreteness where known, existing programs (generalized means) can be employed to carry out the remaining detail. Hence, the process connects new general purposes with an appropriate subset of the existing repertory of generalized means. When the new goal lies in a relatively novel area, this process may have to go quite far before it comes into contact with that which is already known and programmed; when the goal is of a familiar kind (e.g., a Red Cross disaster program in a particular area), only a few levels need to be constructed of the hierarchy before it can be fitted into available programmed sequences. (Metaphorically, we imagine a whole warehouse full of parts in various stages of prefabrication. The plan for the new structure must be carried to the point where it can be specified in terms of these stocked parts.)

Factorability

To carry out program elaboration by means–end analysis, two conditions must be satisfied. First, at each stage of the process, a feasibility judgment must be made: a judgment that when the time comes to specify the program in greater detail at a later stage, it will in fact be possible to discover such a detailed program. If it later turns out that this judgment was incorrect – no such program can be found – then it is necessary to return to a higher level of the means–end hierarchy and review that part of the process.

Second, each of the means, at any stage of the process, must be relatively independent of all the others. "Independence" here means two things: (a) that the means–end chain should be a genuine hierarchy, so that a given means does not affect to an important extent more than one end at the next higher level of generality; (b) that the feasibility of one of the means does not depend very much upon what other means are employed in the program. Where the conditions are violated, a means–end analysis may still be used to factor the problem into components, but additional steps will be needed in the approximation, so that the interactions among the parts of the program can be evaluated and a revised program developed that takes account of interactions.

Even when the conditions are absent that would make the end-means analysis simple and straightforward, it is still employed as the principal scheme for structuring the decision process. Where there are over-all consistency requirements, these are applied at a later stage in the process, and have only a very general influence on the initial means–end analysis.

A special case of broad practical significance is that in which the interaction among the various parts of the program can be summarized in one or a few conditions of the nature of "resource limitations." In this case, the means–end analysis may be paralleled by a sequence of allocative decisions that will guarantee the feasibility and consistency of the final detailed program.

In the simplest kinds of means–end hierarchy the relation of the specific, detailed means at the lowest level to the "payoff" or goal commonly takes one of two forms: (a) the payoff function is additive, i.e., it is a simple sum of partial payoffs attached to the individual means; (b) the payoff is all or none, and the specific means, taken collectively, constitute a set of sufficient conditions for the payoff.

Factorization and group problem-solving

Some clues as to what is involved in analysis are provided by studies of problem-solving in small groups. This sort of study contrasts the coordinative techniques available to a group of persons with those of the individual organism. These studies show generally that interpersonal communication is a more primitive and limited coordinative mechanism than are the neural processes [A-7.12]. Consequently, factorization of problems into semi-independent subparts is of more crucial importance for group than for individual problem-solving.

Modes of factorization

There is little theory about the method of performing a means–end analysis. What determines the *type of factorization* (7.21)? There grows up in any field a repertory of categories; for example, "to have a profitable company, you have to have a marketing process, a production process, and a financing process." How far does the end–means analysis reflect the intrinsic structure of the problem itself; and how far, alternatively, is it a relatively arbitrary, socially conditioned process? We have already given some attention to this question in the last section of chapter 2. We can now add to the earlier discussions some propositions that derive from our present analysis.

When payoffs are additive, the components provide a basis for factorization of the problem. Frequently, this condition is approximately met when the problem involves a sequence of actions through time. Then payoffs in each time period are generally most dependent upon contemporaneous or neighboring actions, and not on more distant actions. Generalizing this, we may say that the intrinsic causal net, and the notions of local causation on which it rests, provide the element of the factorization that may be described as "intrinsic" in the problem. The remainder must be socially conditioned.

One important social influence on factorization is the existing *organizational division of labor* (7.22) [7.21:7.22]. Existing subunits may themselves be taken as the generalized means in terms of which the problem is to be solved (e.g., the sales department, the production department, the controller's department). In this case, the factorization of the problem will parallel the specializations that are incorporated in the division of work among these organizational units. At a still broader social level, the existing occupational specializations in society may partially dictate the factorization.

We may refer at this point also to the devices, mentioned in the previous chapter, for increasing the degree of independence among program segments by standardization and by inventory-holding. Although those devices refer to the content of programs, rather than to the process of program elaboration, we see that if the former can be factored, this permits the factorization of the latter.

In general, there is an order of temporal priority implicit in the means–end hierarchy. The general goal must be split up into major subgoals before consideration can be given to goals at a lower level. Hence, the mode of subdivision has an influence on the extent to which planning can proceed simultaneously on the several aspects of the problem. The more detailed the factorization of the problem, the more simultaneous activity is possible, hence, the greater the *speed of problem-solving* (7.23) [7.23:7.21].

This indicates another respect in which individual problem-solving is to be distinguished from group problem-solving. The advantages of simultaneity in individual problem-solving are limited by the fact that the individual possesses only a single focus of attention, hence can only deal with one aspect of the problem at a time. In organizations, however, there is no limit to the number of attention centers that can be allocated to the parts of a problem. We conclude: (1) that there are important considerations other than the advantages of simultaneous processing for subdividing problems (otherwise factorization would not take place in individual problem-solving); (2) in group problem-solving it may be advantageous to introduce a greater degree of subdivision, even at some loss because of neglected interactions, in order to exploit the possibilities of simultaneous processing. This proposition parallels the corresponding proposition for programmed activities; the more rapidly changing the situation, the greater the degree of self-containment required for individual units.

7.5   Organization Level and Innovation

In the previous section, we devoted some attention to specialization of the function of innovation. In the present section we are particularly concerned with the significance of organization levels for the processes of innovation. At what levels does innovation take place, and why? Are there qualitative differences in the nature of participation in the innovation process as we move up and down the organization hierarchy? Are there differences in the types of innovation that are likely to be made at different levels?

Goal structure and organization structure

As a first step toward answering these questions, we need to examine the relation between the goal structure in an organization and the hierarchy of organizational units. A means–end analysis of the objectives of an organization and of the activities directed toward these objectives reveals something like the following: (1) We can arrange the means and ends in some kind of hierarchy. The goals at the higher levels of this hierarchy are not, however, operational (see chapter 6); i.e., there do not exist agreed-upon criteria for determining the extent to which particular activities or programs of activity contribute to these goals. (2) At lower levels of the means–end hierarchy, the goals are operational – we can measure the contribution of particular activities to these goals. (3) At some level of the hierarchy, a step or two below the highest level of operational goals, we can distinguish individual programs of action – each one contributing to some set of subgoals, and each one, in principle at least, a more or less independent set of activities that can be carried out without much reference to the other programs [A-7.13].

For example, the goal of "providing adequate municipal services" is not operational. The goal of "maintaining a low fire loss rate," however, is more or less operational; and a residential inspection program constitutes a more or less independent set of activities directed toward the (operational) subgoal of preventing fires (which is directed, in turn, toward the goal of maintaining a low fire loss rate).

Along with such a specification of a goal structure, an organization has a hierarchy of formal authority relations. We wish to relate this structure of formal authority to the hierarchy of means and ends previously described. For clarity, call the entire system we are considering the "organization"; the largest subparts, the "departments"; the subdivisions of departments, "divisions."

Consider the whole cluster of means and ends relating to the first operational goal, the cluster of means and ends relating to the second operational goal, etc. Now if we compare these clusters with the organizational units, we will discover variations among organizations with respect to the congruence between goal structure and organization structure.

Each of the clusters may represent the domain of a single department, so that each operational subgoal is the goal of a department. In this case we refer to the departments as *unitary* organizations, the organization as a whole as a *federal* organization. The divisions are *component* organizations of the unitary departments (Simon, Smithburg, and Thompson, 1950, pp. 268–72).

Each of the clusters may lie partly within the province of one or more departments, so that the organization as a whole is the smallest unit that contains an entire cluster. In this case, we refer to the organization as a whole as a *composite* organization, and the departments and divisions are *component* organizations.

There are, of course, other possibilities than the two that have been mentioned, but they are the "pure" types at the ends of the spectrum of possibilities.

Let us propose some slightly more formal definitions. An organization is *unitary* to the extent that the scope of its activity coincides with a means–end structure organized around a single operational goal. An organization is *federal* if it is composed of a number of unitary subdivisions. An organization is *composite* if the scope of its activity encompasses more than one means–end structure organized around operational goals, and if it is not composed of unitary subdivisions. Organizational units that are parts of unitary or composite organizations are referred to as *component* units.

In a hierarchy of organizational units, there will be a lowest level at which units encompass entire goal structures. The units at this level may be unitary or composite. We call this level the *level of integration*: it is the lowest level at which all activities relating to a particular operational goal can be coordinated through the formal authority mechanisms.

One particular form of composite organization deserves notice, because it is a highly prevalent form. The major subdivisions (departments) of an organization may be unitary organizations except for certain "housekeeping" activities that are split off and assigned to special departments that perform these activities for the entire organization. This kind of structure is often called line-and-auxiliary (or, less accurately, "line-and-staff") organization. The "nearly unitary" departments are called line departments, and the departments performing the common housekeeping activities are called auxiliary (or staff) departments. Examples of auxiliary departments are personnel departments, legal departments, purchasing departments, and the like.

From the standpoint of nonprogrammed decision-making, line-and-auxiliary organizations more nearly resemble federal organizations (with the departments as unitary subdivisions) than they do composite organizations. However, which they resemble most closely depends upon *how much* of the activity relating to the operational goals of each line department is separated out and assigned to the auxiliary units. The fewer the auxiliary activities (i.e., the more nearly self-contained are the line departments), the more the organization will operate as a federal structure; the more the auxiliary activities, the more the organization will operate as a composite structure.

The several operational subgoals of an organization may be independent of each other – i.e., they may compete only for organizational resources and in no other way – or they may be directly competitive.

Thus, if a company has two product divisions in rather distinct lines of business, the goals of these divisions are likely to be independent rather than competitive. On the other hand, the subgoals of sales department and production department in a business are likely to be competitive in some respects (since courses of action that reduce production costs may make the product harder to sell, whereas sales practices that would attract customers may create production difficulties).

One of the central propositions of chapters 5 and 6 on operational goals is worth repeating here: Where a choice of a course of action requires comparison of several operational goals, which are not themselves subgoals to a common operational goal, the decision-making process will be characterized by bargaining. Where the alternatives under consideration are all directed to the same operational goals, analytic decision-making processes will predominate. Hence, the prevalence of bargaining is a symptom *either* that goals are not operational or that they are not shared.

Where goals are ostensibly shared (e.g., agreement that profit maximization is the goal of the firm) but not operational, then two subcases need to be distinguished, a distinction that is significant for the character of the decision-making process. The shared goals may be held in common because they have been internalized by the members of the executive group; or they may be common organization goals that the executives accept because of the reward structure. In the former case, we would expect a good deal of ideological conflict in the bargaining process – genuine disagreement as to which means will best implement the goals. In the latter case, we would expect the bargaining to be of a more opportunistic sort, characterized by rationalizations attempting to "clothe private aims with a public interest."

Finally, we postulate that any concrete program of action will acquire a set of operational goals. They may be the goals that originally motivated the initiation of the program (if those goals were operational); or they may be goals evolved after the program was instituted (if the original goals were not operational). Once acquired, the operational goals will provide the basis for evaluation of the action program.

Specialization of innovative functions by level

At any point in the organization we would expect *sensitivity to innovations* (7.24) to be a function of *relevance of the innovation to the needs of the specific unit involved* (7.25) [7.24:7.25]. Thus, the top executive levels of an organizational unit will be particularly sensitive to needs for innovation with respect to the goals of that unit – as distinct from either particular subgoals assigned to subunits or general organizational goals. This sensitivity will be exhibited both (a) through what matters attract attention and (b) through the priority matters obtain after they have been noticed.

When the goal of a proposed innovation is inappropriate in scope (too broad or too narrow) for the particular organization level that is attending to it, it is likely to be filtered in two respects: it is less apt to receive attention or high priority than it would if it were of the "appropriate" scope; if it receives attention, the action is likely to be a referral for consideration and program elaboration to the appropriate organization level.

Suppose that a program change is proposed, or a new action program. The change may refer to one of the existing operational goals of the organization, or it may lie outside these goals and refer to a nonoperational goal of a federal unit. In the latter case, initiation involves the elaboration of a new program that falls outside the province of any of the existing unitary organizations. This is the "appropriate" and hence the characteristic type of innovative activity that will take place at top levels of a federal organization – the initiation of new programs and the definition of new operational goals that fall outside the present scope of the activities of any of the operational units.

In composite organizations, on the other hand, where the whole organization is the smallest unit that encompasses individual operational goals, we expect to find a wider range of innovative activity at the top levels. The line-and-auxiliary structure may be expected to fall between a federal structure and more extreme types of composite structure; a large part of the innovation with respect to existing operating goals can be expected to be performed at the level of the line departments rather than at the top level.

Where innovation in a federal organization (to a lesser extent, in a line-and-auxiliary organization) relates to existing operational goals, most program elaboration will take place within the unitary subdivisions of the organization; the participation of the higher levels in initiation will be confined largely to program approval. We would predict that for the various innovative functions, the relative participation of unitary subdivisions as compared with overhead levels will vary (from greatest to least) as follows: initiation, elaboration of alternatives, elaboration of consequences, evaluation, recommendation, approval.

A major significance, therefore, of the assignment of an activity or of an operational goal to a definite, recognized organizational unit is that this creates a group of employees concerned with the activity on a full-time basis – an important point of initiation for further program elaboration relating to that goal.

At the same time, in a federal or composite organization, the extent to which innovation involves levels above the unitary components depends partly on the *type of coordination* (7.26) used. Coordination by feedback will increase, and coordination by plan decrease, the *extent of involvement of top levels in innovation* (7.27) [7.27:7.26].

In line-and-auxiliary organizations, the locus and rate of innovation will depend on the degree of self-containment of the unitary line departments. In many cases, potential innovations and new programs require changes in organization structure and in existing programs of activity. In general, the proposer of an innovation will regard elements of structure and existing programs that are more than one or two steps, removed from him in the formal structure as "given" and unchangeable. Hence, the greater the *interdependence among subunits* (7.28) and the higher the dependence of line units on auxiliary units, the less vigorous will be the innovative activity of the line units [7.12:7.28]. When self-containment is low and new activities are to be elaborated, innovation will be consummated only when resources are allocated to interdependent departments as well as to the department originating the innovation.

The extent of involvement of top levels in the innovative process depends on a number of factors in addition to those we have already mentioned. In general, vigorous innovative activity will take place only in organizational units that are not assigned substantial responsibilities for programmed activity. Hence, the level at which innovation will take place depends on the levels at which there are individuals or units having planning responsibilities without heavy operating responsibilities [7.27:7.13].

In general, the pattern of attention will be less stable, the higher the organizational level. Hence the participation of high levels in particular innovative efforts will vary greatly with the number of other high-priority items on the agenda [7.27:7.15].

The attention of high levels, particularly those above the unitary organizations, will be directed principally to those proposed innovations that have significance for the maintenance of organization structure, for the survival of the organization, or for activities in more than one organization subdivision. Hence, "procedural" aspects of decisions take on increasing importance as we move upwards in the structure.

If the top levels of an organization have a program for the periodic review of the "organization character," this program will become an important stimulus to innovation at that level and lower levels [7.12:7.13].

The locus of innovation in an organization also has important consequences for the distribution of power and influence. There are two reasons for this: (1) Because of the asymmetries, noted earlier, between persistence and change, and between inaction and action, an organization's pattern of activity is as much influenced by the processes that originate proposals for activity as by the processes that evaluate proposals. (2) Because of the need for uncertainty absorption – the relatively greater ease of communicating conclusions than of communicating the evidence they are drawn from – the evaluation of proposals is much influenced by the location of the inference processes. A great deal of uncertainty absorption normally takes place near the locus where proposals originate.

That the right to initiate is a source of power is common knowledge to executives in most organizations. It probably accounts for an attitude toward delegation that is also widespread; at each administrative level in an organization, there is a favorable attitude toward centralization of decision-making up to that level, but decentralization from above down to that level.

7.6 The Planning Process

We have now set forth a number of propositions about programmed and nonprogrammed decision-making. A useful way to get a general view of the import of these propositions is to apply the theory to the discussion over the years of the process of planning – national planning and intrafirm planning. "Planning," broadly defined, is of course indistinguishable from other kinds of decision-making; hence our definition of the planning process in this discussion will be a historical one.

The discussion of planning has been carried on, in recent years, in two quite distinct contexts: (1) the "plan versus no plan" debate as to the desirable scope of central planning in a modern industrial economy; (2) discussions of the relative merits of centralization and decentralization in large industrial concerns. We begin our analysis with the former topic.

Plan or no plan: the great debate

The issue in central planning is when private enterprise, markets, and prices shall be relied upon as the central mechanisms for operating the economy, and when these mechanisms shall be supplemented or replaced by state action. Adam Smith (1937), in his famous passage on the "invisible hand," set the framework for the problem. His argument proceeded as follows:

1 The only dependable human motive is self-interest.
2 The mechanism of prices and markets is such that if an individual pursues his self-interest he is "led by an invisible hand to promote an end which was no part of his intention" – i.e., he "necessarily labours to render the annual revenue of the society as great as he can."

The first proposition raises a more or less simple question of fact. However, the second proposition has received the greater attention. This attention, until very recently, focused on two points:

1 how to define a criterion of social welfare to replace Smith's unsatisfactory "annual revenue of the society";
2 given such a criterion, to determine the exact conditions under which the pursuit of self-interest in a private enterprise economy will lead to a maximization of social welfare.

We have then to consider three questions: (1) motivation, (2a) definition of a social welfare criterion, (2b) the parallelism of self-interest with social welfare. Not all of these issues are equally germane to the present discussion, which is concerned primarily with the cognitive problem – how the information-processing capacities and limitations of humans affect planning. We will therefore dismiss the problems of motivation and goal conflict, that is to say, questions 1 and 2a, with a few comments and then proceed with the cognitive aspects that relate to question 2b.

Motivation and goal conflict

The question of whether self-interest is the only dependable human motive takes us back to the considerations of chapters 3, 4, and 5. Our current knowledge of human motivation does not suggest any simple yes-or-no answer. In any event, the motivational issue has played only a secondary role in contemporary economic analysis of planning.

The problem of defining a social welfare function also relates to the topics of chapters 3, 4, and 5. It has received a great deal of attention from welfare economists of the so-called "Paretian" variety, who have erected a structure of Thomistic subtlety on postulates of omniscient human rationality. The only implication of the theory for the planning debate is that it shows a social welfare function cannot be erected without assumptions that are stronger than the devotees of the postulational method like to make. Since our primary interest lies in planning *within* organizations, we will not concern ourselves with the problem of defining an organizational goal (which is the counterpart of the social welfare function), but will for the moment assume that such a goal exists.

The invisible hand

We are now ready to proceed with the cognitive issues that arise after we assume motivation has been taken care of and a well-defined organizational goal (or welfare function) exists.

Consider a single organization with a goal, which may simply be to maximize profit. The organization has at its disposal certain resources, and its problem is to achieve a maximum attainment of its goal subject to the limits of its resources. Clearly, if one person or group of persons possessed all the relevant information connecting possible courses of action with the utilities resulting therefrom, he or they could discover which course of action was best for the organization. (We are assuming both complete information and unlimited computing capacity.) This would constitute *central planning* in its simplest form.

As an alternative procedure, we could simulate within the organization the operation of markets and the price mechanism. We could designate various subparts of the organization, establish a separate criterion for each subpart (e.g., its "profit"), and create "markets" for all commodities that flow between parts. Then each part of the organization would purchase its inputs and sell its outputs, whether to other parts of the organization or outside the organization. We call a procedure of this kind *decentralized decision-making through prices*.

We might hope that if the criteria of the subparts of the organization were properly chosen, and *if* the markets were operated in an appropriate fashion, the same course of action would be taken as under central planning – i.e., that the invisible hand would make optimal choices with respect to the criterion of each subpart correspond to optimal choices for the organization as a whole. The fundamental theorems of welfare economics are concerned with showing the precise circumstances under which this will happen.

The "classical" theorem of welfare economics states that with perfect competition among firms (in our case, among the subparts of the organization) and in the absence of external economies or diseconomies (costs or revenues not reflected directly or through the prices in the profit and loss statements of the separate units) profit maximization by individual firms (by subparts of the organization) will maximize social welfare for the economy (maximize profit for the whole firm).

However significant to the plan-or-no-plan debate, this theorem has little relevance for decentralization through pricing within the firm; for the conditions of perfect competition are met only for those intermediate products that have a market outside the firm as well as internally. In the absence of external markets to provide a measuring stick for prices, the organization is beset internally with all the problems of monopoly and imperfect competition in general.

However, there is a more modern theorem, due to Barone, which states that the invisible hand will operate satisfactorily without perfect competition but still assuming the absence of external economies or diseconomies, provided we substitute for profit-maximizing the rule that each subpart of the organization sets marginal cost (i.e., variable cost) equal to price for each of the variables it can control. This rule will clear markets (e.g., prevent continued accumulation or disaccumulation of inventories) and will, under the given assumptions, lead to profit maximization for the firm (but not, in general, for the individual subparts) [A-7.14].

Barone's theorem does not remove the need for the assumption that external economies and diseconomies are absent. This assumption is far from trivial and creates serious difficulties in applying the price mechanism practically to decentralized decision-making within organizations. Recent studies by Koopmans and Beckman (1957) of the theory of the location of industry have brought a number of such difficulties to light.

The fundamental theorems of welfare economics – both the classical one and Barone's – assert that under certain circumstances the decentralized price mechanism will give *as good* a result as central planning; the theorems do not give us any *positive reason for preferring* the former to the latter. Adam Smith had such a reason in his motivational postulate 1. By neglecting that postulate, the more recent welfare theory has eviscerated the argument for decentralization. New arguments, to replace postulate 1, have been advanced during the past 20 years by von Mises (1944) and Hayek (1946). We turn to these next.

The principle of bounded rationality

The argument of von Mises and Hayek (we will use the latter's version) depends crucially on the limits of information available to humans and their abilities to use information in their computations. Hence it is closely related to the cognitive matters examined in the earlier sections of this and the preceding chapter. This argument for decentralization is essentially an argument that, *given realistic limits on human planning capacity* the decentralized system will work better than the centralized. The argument is well stated by Hayek:

What [those who invoke the complexity of modern civilization as an argument for central planning] generally suggest is that the increasing difficulty of obtaining a coherent picture of the complete economic process makes it indispensable that things should be co-ordinated by some central agency if social life is not to dissolve into chaos.

This argument is based on a complete misapprehension of the working of competition. Far from being appropriate only to comparatively simple conditions, it is the very complexity of the division of labor under modern conditions which makes competition the only method by which such co-ordination can adequately be brought about. There would be no difficulty about efficient control or planning were conditions so simple that a single person or board could effectively survey all the relevant facts. It is only as the factors which have to be taken into account become so numerous that it is impossible to gain a synoptic view of them, that decentralisation becomes imperative. But once decentralisation is necessary, the problem of co-ordination arises, a co-ordination which leaves the separate agencies free to adjust their activities to the facts which only they can know and yet brings about a mutual adjustment of the respective plans. As decentralisation has become necessary because nobody can consciously balance all the considerations bearing on the decisions of so many individuals, the co-ordination can clearly not be effected by "conscious control," but only by arrangements which convey to each agent the information he must possess in order effectively to adjust his decisions to those of others. And because all the details of the changes constantly affecting the conditions of demand and supply of the different commodities can never be fully known, or quickly enough be collected and disseminated, by any one center, what is required is some apparatus of registration which automatically records all the relevant effects of individual actions, and whose indications are at the same time the resultant of, and the guide for, all the individual decisions.

This is precisely what the price system does under competition, and which no other system even promises to accomplish. It enables entrepreneurs, by watching the movement of comparatively few prices, as an engineer watches the hands of a few dials, to adjust their activities to those of their fellows. . . The more complicated the whole, the more dependent we become on that division of knowledge between individuals whose separate efforts are co-ordinated by the impersonal mechanism for transmitting the relevant information known by us as the price system. (1944, pp. 48–50)

This, then, is the positive argument for the price mechanism: (1) under perfect competition and in the absence of external economies, optimal decisions can be secured under the decentralized scheme (by profit maximization in the separate subparts) as under the centralized one: (2) in fact, because the decentralized scheme makes very much smaller demands of information and computation than does the centralized scheme, these optimal decisions *can* practically be attained under the decentralized scheme, and *cannot* under the centralized one. If we relax the assumption of perfect competition, then the argument still holds, by Barone's theorem, provided we substitute the rule of equating marginal costs and prices for the rule of maximizing the profits of subparts.

When we take external economies and diseconomies into consideration, then the net advantage of decentralized over centralized decision-making, or vice versa, must be assessed by weighing the losses in the former through failure to take into account indirect consequences of actions (external economies) against the losses in the latter through inability to obtain the necessary facts and to carry through the necessary computations (bounded rationality). The question becomes a quantitative one of the relative importance of these two classes of "imperfections" in the decision-making mechanism. The question is identical, in fact, with the choice between self-containment and reduction in coordination needs that was analyzed in chapter 6. It cannot be settled once and for all from a priori considerations, but must be decided in each case by reference to the empirical facts of the world.

Decentralization without prices

Hayek applied his argument of bounded rationality to the debate on the relative merits of central planning as against a decentralized price mechanism. But this part of his argument, as we have just seen, is really about centralization and decentralization in general, and makes no *specific* reference to the price mechanism. Hence, we may take a more general point of view and consider other mechanisms of centralization or decentralization, unrelated to the market mechanism, that might provide advantageous procedures for decision-making in complex situations.

If we take the requirement of "optimization" seriously, it is unlikely that we will discover any new mechanisms that can compare advantageously with the price mechanism. Examination of the mathematical structure of the proofs of the welfare theorems shows that any parameter that turns up in an optimal decision rule will also have a simple interpretation as a "price" or marginal cost. However, we have also seen that the conditions necessary for optimization are unlikely to be met in the real world because of external economies. Hence, we may be willing to broaden our search, substitute the goal of satisficing for optimizing, and look for mechanisms that will produce "good" decisions and that might be preferred to central planning or the price mechanism under at least some real world conditions.

As a matter of fact, most of the available empirical evidence as to the suitability of prices as decision mechanisms in our economy is evidence that prices "work" (i.e., clear markets), not that they produce an optimum. How far are the conditions of perfect competition met, and those of the absence of external economies and diseconomies? The evidence, for the American economy at least, is inconclusive. Clearly, these conditions are not *completely* met, but no one has proposed a useful metric for assessing the seriousness of the deviations. Under ordinary circumstances the pricing mechanism satisfices: it clears the markets; it gives consumers a wide range of choices; and if external economies are commonly present, their presence is not intolerable.

Tests of the price mechanism: wartime planning

If we follow Hayek's argument to its logical conclusion, the advantages of the pricing mechanism over central planning should become greater the more complex the situation to which they are applied. There would seem to be no better place to test this hypothesis than in a modern economy under wartime conditions. It is an interesting fact, however, that precisely under wartime conditions the pricing mechanism is partially displaced by central planning. This paradox has not received the attention it deserves from economists interested in the theory of price mechanisms. It has received attention, however, from Ely Devons, an insightful English economist who participated in aircraft planning in his country during World War II (Devons, 1950). Nor was he unaware that there was a paradox to be explained:

It was always assumed without question in M.A.P. that this planning was necessary, and that without it aircraft production would have suffered. There were indeed skeptics who asserted that aircraft were produced in spite of, rather than because of, M.A.P.'s planning. But such critics never seriously suggested that M.A.P. should give up its attempts at planning; they thought that the methods and techniques used could be substantially improved. Because of this unquestioned acceptance of the need to plan aircraft production, rather than operate through a competitive price system, no one in M.A.P. ever tried to explain why such planning was necessary, or judged the methods and techinques that M.A.P. used, against the background of some general theory of war-time economic planning. To the officials concerned, M.A.P.'s planning activities were forced on them by the logic of events; they were not adopted because they fitted into some well-thought-out system of the best method of securing the maximum output of aircraft with the minimum use of resources. (p. 2)

Devons then goes on to answer the question he has posed – the reasons for central planning:

Planning was necessary in war-time, because the Government was acting as the sole consumer of the products of the economic system, and had to weigh up the relative importance of the production of different items in achieving the single objective of winning the war.

In theory, having taken this decision, the Government could then have proceeded to order these products, leaving the producers to compete for the raw materials, components and labour which they needed. But, inevitably, the Government's methods of financing the war were inflationary, and such competition would merely have served to raise the general level of prices.

. . . it was most unlikely that business men would have been willing to invest in capacity for the production of munitions. . . . For they had no basis on which to assess the likely length of the war. . . . The Government alone possessed this knowledge, and therefore had to assume the risks in choosing one line of investment rather than another. (pp. 3–4)

The first argument is exceedingly interesting, for one might suppose that under wartime conditions, when all of the typical difficulties of defining a social welfare function disappear in the face of the primary goal of winning the war, the government could most easily employ the price system for decentralizing its own decisions (using the Barone rule). What is implicit in Devons' reasoning is that the marginal returns of the several activities were unknown, hence the decisions on the proper scale of these activities could not be made apart from judgments as to their marginal contribution to the war effort. This does not prevent this factual judgment, made by the central planners, from taking the form of a purchase price, but it may well mean that the central planners would be unable to arrive at a decision on this purchase price without first estimating what supply it would bring forth – an estimate that decentralized pricing is supposed to make unnecessary.

In the terms used earlier in this chapter, the difficulty that the price mechanism encounters here is that the goals (of winning the war) are not completely operational – at least not sufficiently operational to permit simple estimates to be made of the marginal contribution of activities to the goals.

Devons' second argument, concerning inflation, need not detain us, for it raises questions of conflict of interest that are irrelevant to the present discussion.

Devons' third argument, concerning willingness to invest, rests again on observation that the facts needed for a decision are not simply "there," but have to in some way and by some process become known to the decision maker. It exposes an important assumption underlying the defense of pricing: that the information needed by individual decision makers to set marginal costs equal to prices is most easily accessible to those decision makers. When this assumption is not fulfilled – as it was not under wartime conditions – the argument for decentralization and the argument for the price mechanism become separate and distinct.

Decentralization in wartime planning

We can now see some of the deficiencies of the price mechanism for wartime decision-making, but we do not yet see how centralized planning can support the burdens of complexity against which Hayek warns. Devons has an answer to this also. *Wartime planning was not central planning in the sense in which we have defined that term.* It involved many elements of decentralization, but using devices other than prices for coordination.

> The urge to secure that all action fitted in with the Government's conception of the best way of fighting the war inevitably resulted in the centralization of decision. For it was only by centralization that it was possible to ensure that the actions of individuals would fit in with each

other, and would also fit into the desired general pattern. In theory, therefore, the supreme planning body . . . should have laid down in detail the 'Grand Plan' . . . In fact, however, that was not and could never have been done. For it is an inevitable feature of administration, which results from the limitation of human capacity, that the more highly centralized the decisions, the more generalized the basis on which they must be taken, and the fewer the relationships that can be taken into account. Therefore, although the Government was always trying to act on behalf of the community as a single individual pursuing a single objective, it was forced, by the difficulties of administration, to delegate decisions to separate, largely self-contained units of administration. The most difficult task in war-time planning was to decide the best way of breaking down the problem into constituent parts, and at the same time secure co-ordination between the actions of the constituent bodies.

Although it is true that all factors in the economic system are interrelated, the interrelation between a given set of variables may be either close or remote. The obvious way of breaking down the problems to be dealt with was to group together those factors where the interlocking seemed to be closest. (p. 5)

And he sums up the centralization–decentralization issue in these terms:

Every attempt at planning reveals these two problems: first, the need to split up the field to be covered so that each administrative unit can deal efficiently with its own sector; and second, the need to secure that the actions of these separate units all fit into the general plan. But the implemention of these principles always leads to a conflict. For the first requires delegation and devolution, so that plans can be manageable and realistic; and the second requries centralization, so that plans can be coordinated. (p. 14)

Implications for intrafirm planning

What light does the planning debate cast on decision-making within the individual firm? The debate was initially concerned with the choice between private enterprise and government control; the argument gradually shifted to the choice between central planning and decentralized decision-making with the price mechanism; exploration of the latter question has raised again the broader choice between centralization and decentralization. The particular part of the debate that was concerned exclusively with issues at a macroeconomic level (the choice between private enterprise and government control) has tended to be obscured over the years. As a result, most of the recent debate is fully as relevant to the problem of decision-making within the firm as it is to decision-making in the economy as a whole. Let us see what we can extract, in summary, from our analysis up to this point.

First, if self-interest is the only dependable human motive, then decentralization of decision-making in the firm must be accompanied by mechanisms that motivate the decision makers to choose courses of action that contribute to profit maximization by the firm. A device that has achieved popularity in recent years is the departmentalized chart of accounts with departmental profit and loss statements. However, there is no reason why an alternative yardstick would not serve equally well, provided that the yardstick correlates with company profit, and provided that the decision maker is motivated (by financial and other incentives) to pay attention to the yardstick.

Second, under favorable circumstances, particularly when the individual departments are sufficiently independent of each other so that large external economies or diseconomies are not present, the price mechanism may be a useful device for securing decentralized decision-making within the firm.

Third, the internal use of prices requires not only the absence of external economies, but also the availability to the decision makers of reasonable estimates or effective techniques for estimating marginal costs and returns (which implies, in turn, that goals must be operational). In the absence of such techniques, prices may not be an effective mechanism for decentralization. Hence, the movement toward decentralized decision-making within organizations cannot be limited to the internal use of prices.

Fourth, since there is no reason to suppose that *any* technique of decision-making – whether centralized or decentralized – will bring the organization into the neighborhood of a genuine "optimum," the search for decision mechanisms cannot take criteria of optimization too seriously, but must seek "workable" techniques for satisficing.

The exploration of decision-making techniques along these lines is still in a very undeveloped state. A few generalizations are available in the older management literatures. Marschak and Radner (1954; Marschak, 1955), adhering quite closely, however, to optimizing models, have explored the design of efficient decision nets in highly simplified situations; and some of their work can be related to laboratory experiments using the Bavelas network. A number of decision rules for production control and scheduling decisions in individual firms have been developed – but again with only small forays beyond the familiar terrain of optimization (Churchman, Ackoff, and Arnoff, 1957).

The dynamics of planning

Up to this point we have invoked the principle of bounded rationality as an important force making for decentralization; but we have not made any use of the distinction between programmed and unprogrammed decision-making. As long as we restrict ourselves to the classical model of choice among given alternatives, the main points on which the planning question depends are the possibility of estimating certain functions (the production function and the demand function) and of forecasting certain future data. Whether prices are effective devices for decision-making has to be determined by examining the equilibrium toward which they will lead the system, the effect on the equilibrium of errors of estimation and forecasting, and the dynamic properties induced into the system through revisions of estimates and forecasts.

For example, we could compare a decentralized planning system in a firm in which production decisions in each department were regulated by prices with a decentralized system in which these decisions were regulated by sales forecasts and feedback of inventory data. (Most actual formal inventory and production control schemes are of the latter kind.) As far as we are aware, no actual empirical comparisons of this sort have been made, unless we put Devons's assessment of alternative wartime planning methods in this category.

A comparison of alternative planning mechanisms under conditions where new programs are being elaborated is even more difficult. A particular communications and decision-making structure may have quite different consequences for the efficency of day-to-day operations than it has for the ability of the organization to handle changes in its own structure or other unprogrammed changes. Since classical planning theory applies literally only to the static case – to the comparison of equilibria – it does not provide a framework for normative propositions about planning under conditions of unprogrammed change. To the extent to which such dynamic considerations are important, therefore, the classical thoery is largely irrelevant to the issue. The propositions set forth in earlier sections of this chapter represent an alternative approach, less fully developed but ultimately perhaps more relevant.

7.7 Conclusion

In this chapter and the previous one we have examined the cognitive aspects of human behavior in organizations. The study of organizations was generally dominated in the first quarter of this century by the point of view of scientific management; in the second quarter by the interests and approaches usually labeled "human relations." In the former case, the human actors in organization were viewed primarily as "instruments" that could be described in terms of a few physiological and simple psychological properties. In the latter case, the human actors were endowed with feelings and motives, but relatively little attention was paid to their properties as adaptive, reasoning beings. Our analysis of cognition fits into the broader outline of organization theory not as a substitute for, but as a supplement to, these earlier approaches.

Because there has been less concern with cognitive than with other phenomena in organization, the treatment of the theory in the last two chapters has necessarily been more fragmentary and less systematic than the analysis in the first five chapters. In particular, empirical evidence of a reliable and persuasive kind is almost nonexistent - a complaint we have made throughout this volume, but which applies with special force to the topic of cognition. Our labors in writing these chapters will be more than repaid if they encourage others to join in the task of replacing fancy with fact in understanding the human mind and human behavior in an organizational setting.

Postscript

It would certainly be difficult, and probably superfluous, to summarize the content of a volume that is already a summary of a vast mass of theorizing and (to a far lesser extent) empirical verification of theories. We can best conclude this volume by referring back to the statement of our intent in the first chapter. We have surveyed the literature on organization theory, starting with those theories that viewed the employee as an instrument and physiological automaton, proceeding through theories that were centrally concerned with the motivational and affective aspects of human behavior, and concluding with theories that placed particular emphasis on cognitive processes.

We have seen that the areas we have surveyed are very uneven with respect to the stage that theory formulation has reached, and particularly with respect to the extent of actual testing of propositions. What evidence we have been able to gather for our propositions has mostly related to the middle chapters of the book, those dealing with motivation and attitudes. The cognitive aspects of organizational behavior are to date almost unexplored terrain.

At the same time, we have observed that the problems of testing empirically the propositions about organizational behavior that are set forth here raise a number of technical and methodological issues. Because we have discussed some of these in other places, we will not burden this volume with a detailed discussion of method beyond what has appeared in the earlier chapters. We should like, however, to cite four methodological questions that seem particularly important for research on organizational behavior.

1 The question of identification. Econometricians and others (Koopmans, 1950; Hood and Koopmans, 1953) have devoted considerable attention to the problem of testing theoretical models with empirical data. At several points we have noted that some of the models that we and others have

presented in organization theory are substantially underidentified.

2 The question of inferring the program that an organization unit uses from observation of behavior by members of the unit. A substantial amount of work has been done on the methodology of program inference (Cyert, Simon, and Trow, 1956; Newell, Shaw, and Simon, 1958).

3 The question of inferring the presence or absence, and strength, of influence relations among members of an organization. Some of the major problems involved in measuring influence have been discussed by us and by other researchers in the past few years (Simon, 1953a, March, 1955a, 1956, 1957; Dahl, 1957).

4 The question of the status of field research in general and the single case study of organizational behavior in particular in organizational research. We do not feel the area is well developed and wish we could report some new contributions. Unfortunately, we cannot. As in the case of the substantive theory, the methodology of organization theory is uneven and invites further development.

We hope that we have described with reasonable accuracy the meaning and intent of the propositions and theories that others have contributed to the literature without concealing our own judgments of the basic theories of human behavior on which they rest. We hope even more earnestly that we have pointed to a hundred opportunities for using human behavior in organizations as an empirical testing ground for some of the central generalizations and major methodological innovations of the behavioral sciences.

Bibliography

This bibliography contains all of the references cited in the text of the book. It also includes a substantial number of works that have not been cited. Despite its length, however, it is a sample of the literature rather than a comprehensive listing. For other related, but somewhat different, bibliographies see H. R Bowen, *The Business Enterprise as a Subject for Research* (Social Science Research Council, 1955); A. de Grazia, *Human Relations in Public Administration* (Public Administration Service, 1949); R. Dubin, *The World of Work* (Prentice-Hall, 1958); V. Prestridge and D. Wray, *Industrial Sociology: An Annotated Bibliography* (University of Illinois Institute of Labor and Industrial Relations, 1953).

Abruzzi, A. (1952) *Work Measurement*. New York.
The Acton Society Trust (1953) *Size and Morale*. London.
Adams, D. K. (1954) Conflict and integration. *Journal of Personality*. **22**, 548–56.
Adams, S. (1953) Status congruency as a variable in small group performance. *Social Forces*. **32**, 16–22.
—— (1954) Social climate and productivity in small military groups. *American Sociological Review*. **19**, 421–5.
Adams, W. (1953) Competition, monopoly, and countervailing power. *Quarterly Journal of Economics*. **68**, 469–92.
Albert, R. S. (1953) Comments on the scientific function of the concept of cohesiveness. *American Journal of Sociology*. **59**, 231–4.
Alchian, A. A., S. Enke, and E. T. Penrose (1953) Biological analogies in the theory of the firm: comment and rejoinder. *American Economic Review*. **43**, 600–7.
Amar, J. (1920) *The Human Motor*. London.
Anderson, C. A., J. C. Brown, and M. J. Bowman (1952) Intelligence and occupational mobility. *Journal of Political Economy*. **60**, 218–39.

Annett, J., and H. Kay (1957) Knowledge of results and "skilled performance." *Occupational Psychology.* **31**, 69–79.

Ansoff, H. I. (1957) Strategies for diversification. *Harvard Business Review.* **35**, 113–24.

Argyle, M. (1957) Social pressure in public and private situations. *Journal of Abnormal and Social Psychology.* **54**, 172–5.

Argyris, C. (1952) The Impact of Budgets on People. New York.

—— (1954) Human relations in a bank. *Harvard Business Review.* **32**, 63–72.

—— (1954) The fusion of an individual with an organization. *American Sociological Review.* **19**, 267–72.

—— (1954) *The Present State of Research in Human Relations in Industry.* New Haven.

—— (1955) Organizational leadership and participative management. *Journal of Business.* **28**, 1–7.

—— (1957) The individual and organization: some problems of mutual adjustment. *Administrative Science Quarterly.* **2**, 1–22.

Aristotle. *Politics.*

Arnold, D. G. (1951) Attitude toward authority and sociometric status as factors in productivity and job satisfaction. Unpublished Ph. D. thesis, University of California at Los Angeles.

Arrow, K. J. (1951) Alternative approaches to the theory of choice in risk-taking situations. *Econometrica.* **17**, 404–37.

Ashby, W. R. (1940) Adaptiveness and equilibrium. *Journal of Mental Science.* **86**, 478.

—— (1945) Effect of controls on stability. *Nature.* **155**, 242–3.

—— (1945) The physical origin of adaptation by trial and error. *Journal of General Psychology.* **32**, 13–25.

—— (1947) Principles of the self-organizing dynamic system. *Journal of General Psychology.* **37**, 125–8.

Babchuk, N., and W. J. Goode (1951) Work incentives in a self-determined group. *American Sociological Review.* **16**, 679–87.

Bach, G. L. (1957) *Economics.* 2nd ed. Englewood Cliffs, N. J.

Back, K. W. (1951) Influence through social communication. *Journal of Abnormal and Social Psychology.* **46**, 9–23.

Bailey, N. R. (1942) *Motion Study for the Supervisor.* New York.

Bakke, E. W. (1950) *Bonds of Organization.* New York.

——, P. M. Hauser, G. L. Palmer, C. A. Myers, D. Yoder, and C. Kerr (1954) *Labor, Mobility, and Economic Opportunity.* New York.

Baldamus, W. (1951) Type of work and motivation. *British Journal of Sociology.* **2**, 44–51.

Bales, R. F., and P. E. Slater (1957) Notes on "role differentiation in small discussion-making groups": reply to Dr. Wheeler. *Sociometry.* **20**, 152–5.

Bales, R. F., and F. L. Strodtbeck (1951) Phases in group problem-solving. *Journal of Abnormal and Social Psychology.* **46**, 485–95.

Balfour, W. C. (1953) Productivity and the worker. *British Journal of Sociology.* **4**, 257–65.

Barish, N. N. (1951) *Systems Analysis for Effective Administration.* New York.

Barker, R. G. (1942) An experimental study of the resolution of conflict by children. *Studies in Personality.* **2**, 13–34.

Barnard, C. I. (1938) *The Functions of the Executive.* Cambridge, Mass.

Barnes, R. M. (1949) *Motion and Time Study.* New York.

—— and N. A. Englert (1946) *Bibliography of Industrial Engineering and Management Literature.* Dubuque, Iowa.

Bartlett, F. C. (1948) Men, machines and productivity. *Occupational Psychology.* **22**, 190–6.

Bass, B. M. (1954) The leaderless group discussion. *Psychological Bulletin.* **51**, 465–92.

——, C. R. McGehee, W. C. Hawkins, P. C. Young, and A. S. Gebel (1953) Personality variables related to leaderless group discussion behavior. *Journal of Abnormal and Social Psychology.* **48**, 120–8.

Baumgartel, H. (1956) Leadership, motivations, and attitudes in research laboratories. *Journal of Social Issues.* **12**, 24–31.

Bavelas, A. (1948) Some problems of organizational change. *Journal of Social Issues.* **3**, 48–52.

Bayton, J. A., and H. W. Conley (1957) Deviation of success background and the effect of failure upon performance. *Journal of General Psychology.* **56**, 179–85.

Becker, H. S., and J. Carper (1956) The elements of identification with an occupation. *American Sociological Review.* **21**, 341–8.

—— (1956) The development of identification with an occupation. *American Journal of Sociology.* **61**, 289–98.

Behrend, J. (1953) Absence and labour turnover in a changing economic climate. *Occupational Psychology.* **27**, 69–79.

Bell, G. B., and H. E. Hall, Jr. (1954) The relationship between leadership and empathy. *Journal of Abnormal and Social Psychology.* **49**, 156–7.

Bellows, R. M. (1954) *Psychology of Personnel in Business and Industry.* New York.

Bendix, R. (1947) Bureaucracy: the problem and its setting. *American Sociological Review.* **12**, 493–507.

—— and S. M. Lipset, eds (1953) *Class, Status, and Power: A Reader in Social Stratification.* Glencoe, Ill.

Bennett, E. B. (1955) Discussion, decision, commitment and consensus in "group decision." *Human Relations* **8**, 251–73.

Bennis, W. G. (1956) Values and organization in a university social research group. *American Sociological Review.* **21**, 555–63.

—— and H. A. Shepard (1956) A theory of group development. *Human Relations.* **9**, 415–37.

Berelson, B. R., P. F. Lazarsfeld, and W. N. McPhee (1954) *Voting, A Study of Opinion Formation in a Presidential Campaign.* Chicago.

Berkowitz, L. (1953) Sharing leadership in small, decision-making groups. *Journal of Abnormal and Social Psychology.* **48**, 231–8.

—— (1954) Group standards, cohesiveness, and productivity. *Human Relations.* **7**, 509–14.

—— and R. M. Lundy (1957) Personality characteristics related to susceptibility to influence by peers or authority figures. *Journal of Personality.* **25**, 306–16.

Berliner, J. S. (1952) The informal organization of the Soviet firm. *Quarterly Journal of Economics.* **66**, 342–65.

Berlyne, D. E. (1954) A theory of human curiosity. *British Journal of Psychology.* **45**, 180–91.

—— (1957) Conflict and choice time. *British Journal of Psychology.* **48**, 106–18.

—— (1957) Attention to change, conditional inhibition ($_sI_R$) and stimulus satiation. *British Journal of Psychology.* **48**, 138–40.

Bernard, J. (1950) Where is the modern sociology of conflict? *American Journal of Sociology.* **56**, 11–16.

—— (1951) The conceptualization of intergroup relations. *Social Forces.* **29**, 243–51.

—— (1954) The theory of games of strategy as a modern sociology of conflict. *American Journal of Sociology.* **59**, 411–24.

Bernberg, R. E. (1952) Socio-psychological factors in industrial morale. *Journal of Social Psychology.* **36**, 73–82.

—— (1954) Personality correlates of social conformity. *Journal of Applied Psychology.* **38**, 148–9.

Bethel, L. L., F. S. Atwater, G. H. E. Smith, and A. Stackman, Jr. (1945) *Industrial Organizations and Management.* New York.

Biera, J. (1953) Changes in interpersonal perceptions following social interaction. *Journal of Abnormal and Social Psychology.* **48**, 61–6.

Bilkey, W. J. (1953) A psychological approach to consumer behavior analysis. *Journal of Marketing.* **18**, 18–25.

Bilodeau, E. A. (1954) Recent experiments on knowledge of results with psychomotor devices. *USAF Personnel Training Reserve Center Bulletin.* No. AFPTRC-TR-54-68.

Birch, H. G. (1945) The role of motivational factors in insightful problem-solving. *Journal of Comparative Psychology.* **38**, 295–317.

Black, D. (1948) On the rationale of decision-making. *Journal of Political Economy.* **56**, 23–34.

Blackett, D. W. (1928) *Factory Labor Turnover in Michigan.* University of Michigan Business Studies, Volume II.

Blake, R. R., H. Helson, and J. S. Mouton (1957) The generality of conformity behavior as a function of factual anchorage, difficulty of task and amount of social pressure. *Journal of Personality.* **25**, 294–305.

Blau, P. M. (1954) Patterns of interaction among a group of officials in a government agency. *Human Relations*. 7, 337–48.

—— (1954) Cooperation and competition in a bureaucracy. *American Journal of Sociology*. 59, 530–5.

—— (1955) *The Dynamics of Bureaucracy*. Chicago.

—— (1957) Occupational bias and mobility. *American Sociological Review*. 22, 392–9.

Bluestone, A. (1955) Major studies of workers' reasons for job change. *Monthly Labor Review*. 78, 301–6.

Blum, F. H. (1953) *Toward a Democratic Work Process*. New York.

Blum, M. C. (1949) *Industrial Psychology and Its Social Foundations*. New York.

Blumen, I., M. Kogan, and P. J. McCarthy (1955) *The Industrial Mobility of Labor as a Probability Process*. N.Y.

Bolanovich, D. J. (1948) Interest tests reduce factory turnover. *Personnel Psychology*. 1, 81–92.

Borgatta, E. F., and R. F. Bales (1953) Interaction in reconstituted groups. *Sociometry*. 16, 302–20.

Boskoff, A. (1953) Postponement of social decision in transitional society. *Social Forces*. 31, 229–34.

Boulding, K. E. (1955) Contributions of economics to the theory of conflict. *Bulletin of the Research Exchange on the Prevention of War*. 3, 51–9.

Bovard, E. W., Jr. (1951) Group structure and perception. *Journal of Abnormal and Social Psychology*. 46, 398–405.

—— (1956) Interaction and attraction to the group. *Human Relations*. 9, 481–9.

Brayfield, A. H., and W. H. Crockett (1955) Employee attitudes and employee performance. *Psychological Bulletin*. 52, 396–424.

Breed, W. (1955) Social control in the newsroom: a functional analysis. *Social Forces*. 33, 326–35.

Brehm, J., and L. Festinger (1957) Pressures toward uniformity of performance in groups. *Human Relations*. 10, 85–91.

Bressler, M., and C. F. Westoff (1954) Leadership and social change: the reactions of a selected group to industrialization and population influx. *Social Forces*. 32, 235–43.

Brinton, C. C. (1952) *The Anatomy of Revolutions*. New York.

Brissenden, P. F., and E. Frankel (1922) *Labor Turnover in Industry*. New York.

Britton, C. E. (1953) *Incentives in Industry*. Employee Relations Department, Esso Standard Oil Company: New York.

Brown, A. (1945) *Organization: A Formulation of Principle*. New York.

Brown, C. W., and E. E. Ghisselli (1953) The prediction of labor turnover by aptitude tests. *Journal of Applied Psychology*. 37, 9–12.

Brown, J. S. (1956) Union size as a function of intra-union conflict. *Human Relations*. 9, 75–89.

Brown J. S. and I. E. Farber (1951) Emotions conceptualized as intervening variables – with suggestions toward a theory of frustration. *Psychological Bulletin.* **48**, 465–95.

Brown, P. (1954) Bureaucracy in a government laboratory. *Social Forces.* **52**, 259–68.

Brown, W. B. D. (1945) Incentives within the factory. *Occupational Psychology.* **19**, 82–92.

Brown, W. H. (1953) An instrument for studying viscidity within small groups. *Educational and Psychological Measurement.* **13**, 402–17.

—— (1957) Innovation in the machine tool industry. *Quarterly Journal of Economics.* **71**, 406–25.

Browne, C. G. (1951) Study of executive leadership in business, IV: sociometric pattern. *Journal of Applied Psychology.* **35**, 34–7.

—— (1952) and B. J. Neitzel. Communication, supervision and morale. *Journal of Applied Psychology.* **36**, 86–91.

Bruner, J. S., J. J. Goodnow, and G. A. Austin (1956) *A Study of Thinking.* New York.

Buchanan, J. M. (1954) Individual choice in voting and the market. *Journal of Political Economy.* **62**, 334–43.

Bullock, R. P. (1952) *Social Factors Related to Job Satisfaction.* Ohio State University Bureau of Business Research Columbus.

—— (1953) Position, function and job satisfaction of nurses in the social system of a modern hospital. *Nursing Research.* **2**, 4–14.

Burchard, W. W. (1954) Role conflicts of military chaplains. *American Sociological Review.* **19**, 528–35.

Burgess, F. W., and H. J. Locke (1953) *The Family,* 2nd ed. New York.

Burns, T. (1954) The directions of activity and communication in a departmental executive group. *Human Relations.* **7**, 73–97.

Burtt, H. E. (1929) *Psychology and Industrial Efficiency.* New York.

Butler, W. P. (1954) Wage incentives in operation – Case Study No. 6. *Personnel Practices Bulletin* (Melbourne). **10**, 21–9.

Byrt, W. J. (1953) Some aspects of wage incentives. *Bulletin Industrial Psychology.* **9**, 3–14.

—— (1954) Human factor in wage incentives. *Personnel Practices Bulletin* (Melbourne). **10**, 16–21.

—— and B. L. Pordevirs (1955) Wage incentives in operation – Case Study No. 8. *Personnel Practices Bulletin* (Melbourne). **11**, 44–52.

Campbell, D. T., and B. B. Tyler (1957) The construct validity of work-group morale measures. *Journal of Applied Psychology.* **41**, 91–2.

Campbell, H. (1952) Group incentive payment schemes: the effects of lack of understanding and of group size. *Occupational Psychology.* **26**, 15–21.

—— (1953) Some effects of joint consultation on the status and role of the supervisor. *Occupational Psychology.* **27**, 200–6.

Canter, R. R. (1951) The use of extended control-group designs in human relations studies. *Psychological Bulletin.* **48**, 340–7.

Carlin, E. A. (1952) John R. Commons – institutional theorist. *Social Forces.* **30,** 379–87.

Carlson, E. R. (1956) Attitude change through modification of attitude structure. *Journal of Abnormal and Social Psychology.* **52,** 256–61.

Carter, L., W. Haythorn, B. Meirowitz, and J. Lanzetta (1951) The relation of categorizations and ratings in the observation of group behavior. *Human Relations.* **4,** 239–59.

—— W. Haythorn, B. Shiver, and J. Lanzetta (1951) The behavior of leaders and other group members. *Journal of Abnormal and Social Psychology.* **46,** 589–95.

Cartwright, D. (1941a) Relation of decision-time to the categories of response. *American Journal of Psychology.* **54,** 174–96.

—— (1941b) Decision-time in relation to the differentiation of the phenomenal field. *Psychological Review.* **48,** 425–42.

—— (1949) Some principles of mass persuasion. *Human Relations.* **2,** 253–67.

—— (1951) Achieving change in people: some applications of group dynamics theory. *Human Relations.* **4,** 381–92.

—— (1943) and L. Festinger. A quantitative theory of decision. *Psychological Review.* **50,** 595–621.

—— and A. Zander (1953) *Group Dynamics: Research and Theory.* Evanston, Ill.

—— J. Seeman, and D. L. Grummon (1956) Patterns of interpersonal relations. *Sociometry.* **19,** 166–77.

Cassinelli, C. W. (1953) The law of oligarchy. *American Political Science Review.* **47,** 773–84.

Cattell, R. B. (1951) New concepts for measuring leadership, in terms of group syntality. *Human Relations.* **4,** 161–84.

——, D. R. Saunders, and G. F. Stice (1953) The dimensions of syntality in small groups. *Human Relations.* **6,** 331–56.

Chane, G. W. (1942) *Motion and Time Study.* New York.

Charters, W. W., Jr. (1952) A study of role conflict among foremen in a heavy industry. Unpublished doctoral thesis, University of Michigan.

Child, I. L. (1941) Morale: a bibliographical review. *Psychological Bulletin.* **38,** 393–420.

—— and J. W. M. Whiting (1949) Determinants of level of aspiration: evidence from everyday life. *Journal of Abnormal and Social Psychology.* **44,** 303–14.

Choate, J. S. (1953) Labour turnover. *Journal of the Institute of Personnel Management.* **37,** 95–101.

Chowdry, K., and T. M. Newcomb (1952) The relative abilities of leaders and non-leaders to estimate opinions of their own groups. *Journal of Abnormal and Social Psychology.* **47,** 51–7.

Christie, L. S. (1954) Organization and information handling in task groups. *Journal of the Operations Research Society of America*. 2, 188–96.

Christie, N. Fangevoktere i Konsentrasjonsleire (Guards in concentration camps). *Nordisk Tidskrift for Kriminalvidenskap*. 1952, issue no. 4; 1953, no. 1.

Christie, R., and J. Garcia (1951) Subcultural variation in authoritarian personality. *Journal of Abnormal and Social Psychology*. 46, 457–69.

Christner, C. A., and J. K. Hemphill (1955) Leader behavior of B-29 commanders and changes in crew members' attitudes towards the crew. *Sociometry*. 18, 82–7.

Churchman, C. W., and R. L. Ackoff (1950) Purposive behavior and cybernetics. *Social Forces*. 29, 22–39.

—— and E. L. Arnoff (1957) *Introduction to Operations Research*. New York.

Clark, B. R. (1956) Organizational adaptation and precarious values: a case study. *American Sociological Review*. 21, 327–36.

Clark, L. H., ed. (1958) *Consumer Behavior*. New York.

Clark, W. (1938) *The Gantt Chart*. London.

Clarke, A. C. (1956) The use of leisure and its relation to levels of occupational prestige. *American Sociological Review*. 21, 301–7.

Cleland, S. (1955) *The Influence of Plant Size on Industrial Relations*. Princeton, N. J.

Coates, C. H., and R. J. Pellegrin (1957) Executives and supervisors: contrasting self-conceptions and conceptions of each other. *American Sociological Review*. 22, 217–20.

Coch, L., and J. R. P. French (1948) Overcoming resistance to change. *Human Relations*. 1, 512–33.

Cochran, T. C. (1951) The executive mind: the role of railroad leaders, 1845–1890. *Bulletin of the Business Historical Society*. 25, 230–41.

Cohen, A. (1947) *Time Study and Common Sense*. London.

Cohen, J. (1953) The ideas of work and play. *British Journal of Sociology*. 4, 312–22.

Cohen, M. B., and R. A. Cohen (1954) Personality as a factor in administrative decisions. *Psychiatry*. 14, 47–53.

Colberg, M. R. (1951) Priorities, allocations, and limitations. *Southern Economic Journal*. 18, 145–59.

Coleman, J., E. Katz, and H. Menzel (1957) Diffusion of an innovation among physicians. *Sociometry*. 20, 253–70.

Collins, O., M. Dalton, and D. Roy (1946) Restriction of output and social cleavage in industry. *Applied Anthropology*. 5, 1–31.

Commons, J. R. (1951) *The Economics of Collective Action*. New York: Macmillan.

Comrey, A. L., J. M. Pfiffner, and H. P. Beem. (1952) Factors influencing organizational effectiveness I: the US Forest Service. *Personnel Psychology*. 5, 307–28.

Cook, P. H., and A. J. Wyndham (1953) Patterns of eating behavior: a study of industrial workers. *Human Relations.* **6**, 141–60.

Cooper, J. B., and L. J. Michiels (1952) A study of attitudes as functions of objective knowledge. *Journal of Social Psychology.* **36**, 59–71.

Copley, F. R. (1923) *Frederick W. Taylor, Father of Scientific Management.* New York.

Corman, B. R. (1957) The effect of varying amounts and kinds of information as guidance in problem solving. *Psychological Monographs.* **71**, No. 2.

Cornell, W. B. (1936) *Organization and Management in Industry and Business.* New York.

Coser, L. (1955) *The Functions of Social Conflict.* Glencoe, Ill.

Cousins, A. N. (1951) Social equilibrium and the psychodynamic mechanism. *Social Forces.* **30**, 201–9.

Covner, B. J. (1950) Management factors affecting absenteeism. *Harvard Business Review.* **28**, 42–8.

Crockett, W. H. (1955) Emergent leadership in small, decision-making groups. *Journal of Abnormal and Social Psychology.* **51**, 378–83.

Cuber, J. F. (1952) Current research activity in social organization. *American Sociological Review.* **17**, 477–9.

Cunningham, R. M. (1956) Brand loyalty – what, where, how much? *Harvard Business Review.* **34**, 116–28.

Curle, A. (1949a) Incentives to work: an anthropological appraisal. *Human Relations.* **2**, 41–7.

—— (1949b) The sociological background to incentives. *Occupational Psychology.* **23**, 21–3.

Cyert, R. M., and J. G. March (1955) Organizational structure and pricing behavior in an oligopolistic market. *American Economic Review.* **45**, 129–39.

—— (1956) Organizational factors in the theory of oligopoly. *Quarterly Journal of Economics.* **70**, 44–64.

—— H. A. Simon, and D. B. Trow (1956) Observation of a business decision. *Journal of Business.* **29**, 237–48.

Dahl, R. A. (1947) Validity of organization theory. *Public Administration Review.* **7**, 281–3.

—— (1957) The concept of power. *Behavioral Science.* **2**, 201–15.

—— (1953) and C. E. Lindblom. *Politics, Economics, and Welfare.* New York.

Dale, E. (1952) *Planning and Developing the Organizational Structure.* New York.

Dalton, M. (1948) The industrial rate buster. *Applied Anthropology.* **7**, 5–18.

—— (1951) Informal factors in career achievement. *American Journal of Sociology.* **51**, 407–15.

—— (1955) Managing the managers. *Human Organization.* **14**, 4–10.

Darley, J. G., N. Gross and W. C. Martin (1952) Studies of group behavior: factors associated with the productivity of groups. *Journal of Applied Psychology.* **36**, 396–403.

Davidson, H. O. (1952) *Functions and Bases of Time Standards*. Columbus, Ohio.

Davies, A. F. (1952) Prestige to occupations. *British Journal of Sociology*. **3**, 134–47.

Davis, A. K. (1951) Conflict between major social systems: the Soviet-American case. *Social Forces*. **30**, 29–36.

Davis, F. J. (1954) Conceptions of official leader roles in the Air Force. *Social Forces*. **32**, 253–8.

Davis, J. (1956) Status symbols and the measurement of status perception. *Sociometry*. **19**, 154–65.

Davis, K. (1953) A method of studying communication patterns in organizations. *Personnel Psychology*. **6**, 301–12.

Davis, L. E., and P. D. Josselyn (1953) How fatigue affects productivity. *Personnel Psychology*. **30**, 54–9.

Davis, N. (1944) Some psychological effects on women workers of payment by the individual bonus method. *Occupational Psychology*. **18**, 53–62.

—— (1953) A study of the merit-rating scheme in a factory. *Occupational Psychology*. **27**, 57–68.

Davis, R. C. (1940) *Industrial Organization and Management*. New York.

—— (1954) *Factors Related to Scientific Research Performance*. Survey Research Center, University of Michigan.

Dean, L. R. (1954) Social integration, attitudes and union activity. *Industrial and Labor Relations Review*. **8**, 48–58.

—— (1954) Union activity and dual loyalty. *Industrial and Labor Relations Review*. **7**, 526–36.

Dearborn, D. C., and H. A. Simon (1958) Selective perception: a note on the departmental identifications of executives. *Sociometry*. **21**, 140–4.

Dember, W. M., and R. W. Earl (1957) Analysis of exploratory, manipulatory and curiosity behaviors. *Psychological Review*. **64**, 91–6.

Denerly, R. A. (1953) Workers' attitudes toward an establishment scheme. *Occupational Psychology*. **27**, 1–10.

Dent, J. K., and R. G. Griffith (1957) *Employee Health Services: A Study of Managerial Attitudes and Evaluations*. Survey Research Center, University of Michigan.

Derse, J. C. (1946) *Machine Operation Times for Estimators*. New York.

Detambel, M. H., and L. M. Stolurow (1957) Probability and work as determiners of multichoice behavior. *Journal of Experimental Psychology*. **53**, 73–81.

Deutsch, K. W. (1952) On communication models in the social sciences. *Public Opinion Quarterly*. **16**, 357–80.

—— (1954) Application of game theory to international politics. *Canadian Journal of Economics and Political Science*. **20**, 76–83.

Deutsch, M. (1949) An experimental study of the effects of cooperation and competition upon group process. *Human Relations*. **2**, 199–231.

Deutsch, M. (1949) A theory of cooperation and competition. *Human Relations.* 2, 129–52.

—— and H. B. Gerard (1955) A study of normative and informational social influences upon individual judgment. *Journal of Abnormal and Social Psychology.* 51, 629–36.

Deutscher, V., and I. Deutscher (1955) Cohesion in a small group. *Social Forces.* 33, 336–41.

Devons, E. (1950) *Planning in Practice.* Cambridge, England.

—— (1952) Planning by economic survey. *Economica.* 19, 237–53.

Dickinson, C. Z. (1937) *Compensating Industrial Effort.* New York.

Diebold, J. (1952) *Automation.* New York.

Dinneen, G. P. (1955) Programming pattern recognition. *Proceedings of the Western Joint Computer Conference.* Institute of Radio Engineers.

Dodd, S. C. (1953) Testing message diffusion in controlled experiments: charting the distance and time factors in the interactance hypothesis. *American Sociological Review.* 18, 410–16.

—— (1957) Conditions for motivating: comprehensive and testable models for predictive behavior. *Journal of Personality.* 25, 489–504.

Douty, H. M. (1956) Post-war wage bargaining in the United States. *Economica.* 23, 315–27.

Dreese, M., and K. E. Stromsen (1951) Factors related to the rapidity of rise of interns in the Federal service. *Public Personnel Review.* 12, 31–7.

Dreyer, A. C. (1954) Aspiration behavior as influenced by expectation and group comparison. *Human Relations.* 7, 175–90.

Drucker, P. F. (1953) The employee society. *American Journal of Sociology.* 58, 358–63.

Drury, H. B. (1915) *Scientific Management. A History and Criticism.* New York.

Dubin, R. (1949) Decision-making by management in industrial relations. *American Journal of Sociology.* 54, 292–7.

—— (1957) Power and union-management relations. *Administrative Science Quarterly.* 2, 60–81.

Duncan, O. D., and B. Duncan (1955) Residential distribution and occupational stratification. *American Journal of Sociology.* 60, 493–503.

Dunlop, J. T., and W. F. Whyte (1950) Framework for the analysis of industrial relations: two views. *Industrial and Labor Relations Review.* 3, 383–412.

Durish, L. L., and R. E. Lowry (1953) The scope and content of administrative decision: the TVA illustration. *Public Administration Review.* 13, 219–26.

Dynes, R. R., A. C. Clarke, and S. Dinitz (1956) Levels of occupational aspiration: some aspects of family experience as a variable. *American Sociological Review.* 21, 212–15.

East, V. (1955) Wage incentives in operation – Case Study No. 9. *Personnel Practices Bulletin* (Melbourne). 11, 24–32.

Eaton, J. W. (1951) Social processes of professional teamwork. *American Sociological Review.* **16**, 707-13.

Eaton, W. H. (1952) Hypotheses related to worker frustration. *Journal of Social Psychology.* **35**, 59-68.

Edwards, R. S. (1951) Industrial technologists and the social sciences. *Economica.* **18**, 379-96.

Edwards, W. (1953) Probability-preferences in gambling. *American Journal of Psychology.* **66**, 349-64.

—— (1954) The theory of decision making. *Psychological Bulletin.* **51**, 380-417.

—— (1954) Variance preferences in gambling. *American Journal of Psychology.* **67**, 441-52.

Eisenstadt, S. N. (1953) Conditions of communicative receptivity. *Public Opinion Quarterly.* **17**, 363-74.

—— (1954) Reference group behavior and social integration: an exploratory study. *American Sociological Review.* **19**, 175-85.

—— (1954) Studies in reference group behaviour. I. Reference norms and social structure. *Human Relations.* **7**, 191-216.

Ellsberg, D. (1956) Theory of the reluctant duelist. *American Economic Review.* **46**, 909-23.

Elmer, G. A. (1951) An experiment in measurement of identification with the work situation. Ph.D. thesis, Ohio State University.

Elwell, J. L., and G. C. Grundley (1938) The effect of knowledge of results on learning and performance. I: a coordinated movement of the two hands. *British Journal of Psychology.* **29**, 39-53.

Emerson, H. (1917) *The Twelve Principles of Efficiency.* New York.

Escalona, S. K. (1940) The effect of success and failure upon the level of aspiration and behavior in manic-depressive psychoses. *University of Iowa Studies in Child Welfare.* **16**, 199-307.

Fayol, H. (1930) *Industrial and General Administration.* London.

Fearing, F. (1953) Toward a psychological theory of human communication. *Journal of Personality.* **20**, 71-88.

Feely, J. K., Jr. (1951) An analysis of administrative purpose. *American Political Science Review.* **45**, 1069-80.

Feldman, H. (1937) *Problems in Labor Relations.* New York.

Fenchel, G. H., J. H. Monderer, and E. L. Hartley (1951) Subjective status and the equilibration hypothesis. *Journal of Abnormal and Social Psychology.* **46**, 476-9.

Fensterheim, H., and M. E. Tresselt (1953) The influence of value systems on the perception of people. *Journal of Abnormal and Social Psychology.* **48**, 93-8.

Festinger, L. (1943a) Studies in decision: I. Decision-time, relative frequency of judgment and subjective confidence as related to physical stimulus difference. *Journal of Experimental Psychology.* **32**, 291-306.

Festinger, L., (1943b) Studies in decision: II. *Journal of Experimental Psychology.* **32**, 411-23.

—— (1954) A theory of social comparison processes. *Human Relations.* **7**, 117-40.

——, H. B. Gerard, B. Hymovitch, H. H. Kelley, and B. Raven (1952) The influence process in the presence of extreme deviates. *Human Relations.* **5**, 327-46.

—— S. Schachter, and K. Back (1950) *Social Pressures in Informal Groups.* New York.

—— and J. Thibaut (1951) Interpersonal communication in small groups. *Journal of Abnormal and Social Psychology.* **46**, 92-9.

——, J. Torrey, and B. Willerman (1954) Self-evaluation as a function of attraction to the group. *Human Relations.* **7**, 161-74.

Fiedler, F. E. (1954) Assumed similarity measures as predictors of team effectiveness. *Journal of Abnormal and Social Psychology.* **49**, 381-8.

—— (1957) A note on leadership theory: the effect of social barriers between leaders and followers. *Sociometry.* **20**, 87-94.

Filipetti, G. (1946) *Industrial Management in Transition.* Chicago.

Fisher, S., I. Rubinstein, and R. W. Freeman (1956) Intertrial effects of immediate self-committal in a continuous social influence situation. *Journal of Abnormal and Social Psychology.* **52**, 200-7.

Fleishman, E. A. (1953) The measurement of leadership attitudes in industry. *Journal of Applied Psychology.* **37**, 153-8.

Foldes, L. (1955) The delegation of authority to spend. *Economica.* **22**, 246-60.

Follet, M. P. (1924) *Creative Experience.* New York.

Foote, N. N. (1951) Identification as the basis for a theory of motivation. *American Sociological Review,* **16**, 14-21.

—— (1953) The professionalization of labor in Detroit. *Americal Journal of Sociology.* **58**, 371-80.

Fostatt, J. M. (1955) Social structure and social participation. *American Sociological Review.* **20**, 431-8.

Fouriezos, N. T., M. L. Hutt, and H. Guetzkow (1950) Measurement of self-oriented needs in discussion groups. *Journal of Abnormal and Social Psychology.* **45**, 682-90.

Fox, J. B., and J. F. Scott (1943) *Absenteeism: Management's Problem.* Boston.

Francis, R. G., and R. C. Stone (1956) *Service and Procedure in Bureaucracy.* Minneapolis.

Frankel, S. (1955) On the design of automata and the interpretation of cerebral behavior. *Psychometrika.* **20**, 149-62.

Freeman, J. L. (1955) *The Political Process, Executive Bureau-Legislative Committee Relations.* New York.

French, E. G., and R. R. Ernst (1955) The relation between authoritarianism and acceptance of military ideology. *Journal of Personality.* **24**, 181-91.

French, J. W. (1954) The validity of some objective personality tests for a leadership criterion. *Educational Psychology Measurement.* 14, 34–49.

French, R. L. (1949) Sociometric measures in relation to individual adjustment and group performance among Naval recruits. *American Psychologist.* 4, 262.

Friedman, G. (1954) Outline for a psycho-sociology of assembly line work. *Human Organization.* 12, 15–20.

—— (1955) *Industrial Society.* Glencoe, Ill.

Friedsam, H. J. (1954) Bureaucrats as heroes. *Social Forces.* 32, 269–74.

Gadel, M. S., and P. H. Kriedt (1952) Relationships of aptitude, interest, performance and job satisfaction of IBM operators. *Personnel Psychology.* 5, 207–12.

Gage, N. L. (1953) Accuracy of social perception and effectiveness in interpersonal relations. *Journal of Personality.* 22, 128–41.

Gantt, H. L. (1910) *Work, Wages, and Profits.* New York.

Gardner, B. B. (1946) *Human Relations in Industry.* Chicago.

Gardner, G. (1956) Functional leadership and popularity in small groups. *Human Relations.* 8, 491–509.

Gaudet, F. J., and A. R. Carli (1957) Why executives fail. *Personnel Psychology.* 10, 7–21.

Gaus, J. M. (1950) Trends in the theory of public administration. *Public Administration Review,* 10, 161–8.

—— and L. O. Wolcott (1940) *Public Administration and the United States Department of Agriculture.* Chicago.

Gekoski, N. (1952) Predicting group productivity. *Personnel Psychology.* 2, 281–92.

George, F. H. (1957) Thinking and machines. *Philosophy.* 32, 168–9.

Georgopoulos, B., and A. S. Tannenbaum (1957) A study of organizational effectiveness. *American Sociological Review.* 22, 5, 534–40.

Geppinger. H. C. (1955) *DMT: Dimensional Motion Times, Development and Application.* New York.

Gerard, H. (1952) The effect of different dimensions of disagreement on the communication process in small groups. Ph.D. thesis, University of Michigan.

—— (1954) The anchorage of opinions in face-to-face groups. *Human Relations.* 7, 313–25.

—— (1957) Some effects of status, role clarity, and group goal clarity upon the individual's relations to group process. *Journal of Personality.* 25, 475–88.

Gerver, I., and J. Bensman (1954) Towards a sociology of expertness. *Social Forces.* 32, 226–35.

Getzels, J. W., and E. G. Guba (1954) Role, role conflict and effectiveness: an empirical study. *American Sociological Review.* 19, 164–75.

Ghiselli, E. E., and C. W. Brown (1955) *Personnel and Industrial Psychology.* New York.

Gibb, C. A. (1950) The sociometry of leadership in temporary groups. *Sociometry*. 13, 226–43.

—— (1951) An experimental approach to the study of leadership. *Occupational Psychology*. 25, 233–48.

Gilbert, T. F. (1956) Experiments in morale. *Journal of Social Psychology*. 43, 299–308.

Gibreth, F. B. (1909) *Bricklaying System*. Chicago.

—— (1911) *Motion Study*. New York.

—— (1912) *Primer of Scientific Management*. New York.

—— and L. M. Gilbreth. (1917) *Applied Motion Study*. New York.

—— (1919) *Fatigue Study*. 2nd ed. New York.

—— (1920) *Motion Study for the Handicapped*. London.

Gilbreth, L. M. (1914) *The Psychology of Management*. New York.

Gillespie, J. J. (1951) *Dynamic Motion and Time Study*. Brooklyn.

Ginzberg, E. (1954) Perspectives on work motivation. *Personnel*. 31, 43–9.

Giroux, C. R. (1954) Supervisors' incentives and job satisfactions. Unpublished Ph.D. dissertation, Purdue University.

Glover, J. G., and C. L. Maze (1937) *Managerial Control*. New York.

Goffman, I. W. (1957) Status consistency and preference for change in power distribution. *American Sociological Review*. 22, 275–81.

Gomberg, W. (1948) *A Trade-Union Analysis of Time Study*. Chicago.

Goodacre, D. M. (1953) Group characteristics of good and poor performance in contract units. *Sociometry*. 16, 168–79.

Goode, W. J., and I. Fowler (1949) Incentive factors in a low morale plant. *American Sociological Review*. 14, 618–24.

Gorden, R. L. (1952) Interaction between attitude and the definition of the situation in the expression of opinion. *American Sociological Review*. 17, 50–8.

Gordon, L. V. (1952) Personal factors in leadership. *Journal of Social Psychology*. 36, 245–8.

Gordon, O. J. (1955) A factor analysis of human needs and industrial morale. *Personnel Psychology*. 8, 1–18.

Gore, W. G. (1956) Administrative decision-making in federal field offices. *Public Administration Review*. 16, 281–91.

Gottheil, E. (1955) Changes in social perceptions contingent upon competing or cooperating. *Sociometry*. 18, 132–7.

Gough, H. G., H. McClosky, and P. E. Meehl (1951) A personality scale for dominance. *Journal of Abnormal and Social Psychology*. 46, 361–6.

Gouldner, A. W. (1954) *Patterns of Industrial Bureaucracy*. Glencoe, Ill.

—— (1957) Theoretical requirements of the applied social sciences. *American Sociological Review*. 22, 91–102.

Grabe, J. (1933) *New Methods of Work – New Methods of Leadership*. Moscow (cited in Viteles 1953).

Graham, D., and W. Gluckin (1954) Different kinds of rewards as industrial incentives. *Research Review, Durham*. 5, 54–6.

Granick, D. (1954) *Management of the Industrial Firm in the USSR.* New York.

Grant, J. McB., and R. L. Matthew (1957) Accounting conventions, pricing policies and the trade cycle. *Accounting Research.* 8, 145–64.

Greer, F. L., E. H. Galanter, and P. G. Nordlie (1954) Interpersonal knowledge and individual and group effectiveness. *Journal of Abnormal and Social Psychology.* 49, 411–14.

Gregson, R. A. M. (1957) Interrelation of attitudes and communications in a subdivided working group. *Occupational Psychology.* 31, 104–12.

Greystoke, J. R., G. F. Thomason, and T. J. Murphy (1952) Labour turnover surveys. *Journal of the Institute of Personnel Management.* 34, 158–65.

Grodzins, M. (1951) Public administration and the science of human relations. *Public Administration Review.* 11, 88–102.

de Groot, A. D. (1946) *Het Denken van Den Schaker.* Amsterdam.

Gross, E. (1953) Some functional consequences of primary controls in formal work organizations. *American Sociological Review.* 18, 368–73.

—— (1954) Primary functions of the small group. *American Journal of Sociology.* 60, 24–9.

—— (1956) Symbiosis and consensus as integrative factors in small groups. *American Sociological Review.* 21, 174–9.

Grossack, M. M. (1954) Some effects of cooperation and competition upon small group behavior. *Journal of Abnormal and Social Psychology.* 49, 341–8.

Grosser, D., N. Polansky, and R. Lippitt (1951) A laboratory study of behavioral contagion. *Human Relations.* 4, 115–42.

Guest, L. (1955) Brand loyalty twelve years later. *Journal of Applied Psychology.* 39, 405–9.

Guest, R. H. (1954) Work careers and aspirations of automobile workers. *American Sociological Review.* 19, 155–63.

Guetzkow, H. (1953) An exploratory empirical study of the role of conflict in decision-making conferences. *International Social Science Bulletin.* 5, 286–300.

—— (1957) and W. R. Dill. Factors in the organizational development of task-oriented groups. *Sociometry.* 20, 175–204.

——, and J. Gyr (1954) An analysis of conflict in decision-making groups. *Human Relations.* 7, 367–82.

——, and H. A. Simon (1955) The impact of certain communication nets upon organization and performance in task-oriented groups. *Management Science.* 1, 233–50.

Gulick, L. H., and L. Urwick, eds (1937) *Papers on the Science of Administration.* New York.

Gullahorn, J. T. (1956) Measuring role conflict. *American Journal of Sociology.* 61, 299–303.

Gusfield, J. R. (1957) The problem of generations in an organizational structure. *Social Forces.* 35, 323–30.

Gyr, J. (1951) Analysis of committee member behavior in four cultures, *Human Relations*. **4**, 193–202.

—— (1953) A theory of interpersonal decisions. Ph.D. thesis, University of Michigan.

Haberstroh, C. J. (1957) Processes of internal control in firms. Ph.D. Thesis, University of Minnesota.

Hacker, A. (1955) The use and abuse of Pareto in industrial sociology. *American Journal of Economics and Sociology*. **14**, 321–34.

Hadamard, J. (1945) *The Psychology of Invention in the Mathematical Field*. Princeton.

Hadden, A. A., and V. K. Genger (1954) *Handbook of Standard Time Data*. New York.

Haire, M. (1954) Industrial social psychology, in G. Lindzey, ed. *Handbook of Social Psychology*. Cambridge, Mass. 1104–23.

—— (1955) Role-perceptions in labor-management relations. *Industrial and Labor Relations Review*. **8**, 204–16.

Haldane, R. B. H. (1918) *Report of the Machinery of Government Committee*. London.

Halpin, A. W. (1954) The leadership behavior and combat performance of airplane commanders. *Journal of Abnormal and Social Psychology*. **49**, 19–22.

Handyside, J. D. (1953) Raising job satisfaction: a utilitarian approach. *Occupational Psychology*. **27**, 89–97.

Harary, F., and I. C. Ross (1954) The number of complete cycles in a communication network. *Journal of Social Psychology*. **40**, 329–32.

Harbison, F. (1956) Entrepreneurial organization as a factor in economic development. *Quarterly Journal of Economics*. **60**, 364–79.

—— and E. W. Burgess (1954) Modern management in western Europe. *American Journal of Sociology*. **60**, 15–23.

Hare, P. (1952) A study of interaction and consensus in different sized groups. *American Sociological Review*. **17**, 261–7.

Hariton, T. (1951) Conditions influencing the effects of training foremen in new human relations principles. Unpublished doctoral thesis, University of Michigan.

Harsanyi, J. C. (1956) Approaches to the bargaining problem before and after the theory of games: a critical discussion of Zeuthen's, Hicks', and Nash's theories. *Econometrica*. **24**, 144–57.

Hart, P. E., and E. H. Phelps-Brown (1957) The sizes of trade unions: a study in the laws of aggregation. *Economic Journal*. **68**, 1–15.

Hayek, F. A. (1946) *The Road to Serfdom*. London.

Hayes, S. P. (1950) Some psychological problems of economics. *Psychological Bulletin*. **47**, 289–330.

Hays, D. G., and R. R. Bush (1954) A study of group action. *American Sociological Review*. **19**, 693–701.

Haythorn, W., A. Couch, D. Haefner, P. Langham, and L. F. Carter (1956) The behavior of authoritarian and equalitarian personalities in groups. *Human Relations.* **9**, 57-74.

Hearnshaw, L. S. (1954) Attitudes to work. *Occupational Psychology.* **28**, 129-39.

Heimann, E. (1950) On economic planning. *Social Research.* **17**, 269-92.

Heinicke, C., and R. F. Bales (1953) Developmental trends in the structure of small groups. *Sociometry.* **16**, 7-38.

Heise, G. A., and G. A. Miller (1951) Problem solving by small groups using various communication nets. *Journal of Abnormal and Social Psychology.* **46**, 327-35.

Hemphill, J. K. (1950) Relations between size of the group and the behavior of 'superior' leaders. *Journal of Social Psychology.* **32**, 11-22.

Henry, J. (1954) The formal social structure of a psychiatric hospital. *Psychiatry.* **17**, 139-51.

—— (1957) Types of institutional structure. *Psychiatry.* **20**, 47-60.

Henry, W. E., and H. Guetzkow (1951) Group projection sketches for the study of small groups. *Journal of Social Psychology.* **33**, 77-102.

Heron, A. (1954) Satisfaction and satisfactoriness: complementary aspects of occupational adjustment. *Occupational Psychology.* **28**, 140-53.

Hersey, R. B. (1955) *Zest for Work - Industry Rediscovers the Individual.* New York.

—— (1925) Rests - authorized and unauthorized. *Journal of Personnel.* **4**, 37-45.

Herskovits, M. J. (1954) Motivation and culture-pattern in technological change. *International Social Science Bulletin.* **6**, 388-400.

Herson, L. J. R. (1957) China's imperial bureaucracy: its direction and control. *Public Administration Review.* **17**, 44-53.

Hewitt, D., and J. Parfit (1953) A note on working morale and size of group. *Occupational Psychology.* **27**, 38-42.

Hicks, J. R. (1932) *The Theory of Wages.* London.

High, W. S., L. L. Goldberg, and A. L. Comrey (1955) Factored dimensions of organizational behavior, II. *Educational and Psychological Measurement.* **15**, 371-82.

—— (1955) R. D. Wilson, and A. Comrey. Factors influencing organizational effectiveness VIII. *Personal Psychology.* **8**, 355-68.

Hill, A. V. (1926) *Muscular Activity.* Baltimore.

—— (1927a) *Living Machinery.* New York.

—— (1927b) *Muscular Movement in Man: The Factors Governing Speed and Recovery from Fatigue.* New York.

Hill J. M. M. (1951) A consideration of labour turnover as the resultant of a quasistationary process. *Human Relations.* **4**, 255-64.

—— and E. L. Trist (1955) Changes in accidents and other absences with length of service. *Human Relations.* **8**, 121-50.

Hilman, N. A. (1955) Conflicting social norms in a formal organization: a study of interpersonal expectations. Ph.D. dissertation, Cornell University.

Hoffman, M. L. (1957) Conformity as a disguise mechanism and a form of resistance to genuine group influence. *Journal of Personality*. 25, 412–24.

Hollander, E. P. (1954) Studies of leadership among naval aviation cadets. *Journal of Aviation Medicine*. 25, 164–70, and 200.

—— (1954) Authoritarianism and leadership choice in a military setting. *Journal of Abnormal and Social Psychology*. 49, 365–70.

—— (1954) and J. T. Bair. Attitudes toward authority-figures as correlates of motivation among naval aviation cadets. *Journal of Applied Psychology*. 38, 150–3.

Hollander, E. P., and W. B. Webb (1955) Leadership, followership, and friendship: an analysis of peer nominations. *Journal of Abnormal and Social Psychology*. 50, 163–7.

Holmes, W. G. (1938) *Applied Times and Motion Study*. New York.

Homans, G. C. (1950) *The Human Group*. New York.

—— (1953) Status among clerical workers. *Human Organization*. 12, 5–10.

—— (1954) The cash posters: a study of a group of working girls. *American Sociological Review*. 19, 724–33.

Hood, W. C., and T. C. Koopmans, eds (1953) *Studies in Econometric Method*. New York.

Hope, J., II. (1952) Industrial integration of Negroes: the upgrading process. *Human Organization*. 11, 5–14.

Hoppock, R. (1935) *Job Satisfaction*. New York.

Horwitz, M. (1954) The recall of interrupted group tasks: an experimental study of individual motivation in relation to group goals. *Human Relations* 7, 3–38.

—— and F. J. Lee (1954) Effects of decision making by group members on recall of finished and unfinished tasks. *Journal of Abnormal and Social Psychology*. 49, 201–10.

Hoselitz, B. F. (1952) Entrepreneurship and economic growth. *American Journal of Economics and Sociology*. 12, 97–110.

Hovland, C. I., I. L. Janis, and H. H. Kelley (1953) *Communication and Persuasion*. New Haven.

——, and W. Weiss (1951) The influence of source credibility on communication effectiveness. *Public Opinion Quarterly*. 15, 635–50.

Howard, J. A. (1957) *Marketing Management*. Homewood, Ill.

Hoxie, R. F. (1915) *Scientific Management and Labor*. New York.

Hull, C. L. (1952) *A Behavior System*. New Haven.

Hunt, E. E. (1924) *Scientific Management Since Taylor*. New York.

Hunt, J. McV. ed. (1944) *Personality and the Behavior Disorders*. Vol. I. New York.

Hunter, F. (1953) *Community Power Structure*. Chapel Hill, N. C.

Jackson, J. M. (1953) The effect of changing the leadership of small work groups. *Human Relations*. 6, 25–44.

Jaco, E. G., and I. Belknap (1953) Is a new family form emerging in the urban fringe? *American Sociological Review*. **18**, 551-7.

Jacobson, E. (1951) Foreman–steward participation practices and work attitudes in a unionized factory. Unpublished doctoral thesis, University of Michigan.

—— (1956) The growth of groups in a voluntary organization. *Journal of Social Issues*. **12**, 18–23.

——, W. W. Charters, Jr., and S. Lieberman (1951) The use of the role concept in the study of complex organizations. *Journal of Social Issues*. **7**, 19–27.

——, R. L. Kahn, C. F. Mann, and N. C. Morse (1951) Research in functioning organizations. *Journal of Social Issues*. **7**, 64–71.

——, and S. E. Seashore (1951) Communication practices in complex organizations. *Journal of Social Issues*. **7**, 28–40.

Jaffe, A. J., and R. O. Carleton (1954) *Occupational Mobility in the United States 1930-1960*. New York.

——, and C. D. Stewart (1951) *Manpower Resources and Utilization*. New York.

Jahoda, M. (1942) Incentives to work: a study of unemployed adults in a special situation. *Occupational Psychology*. **16**, 20–30.

James, H. E. O., and C. Tenen (1946) Grievances and their displacement. *Occupational Psychology*. **20**, 181-7.

Jaques, E. (1951) *The Changing Culture of a Factory*. London.

—— (1953) On the dynamics of social structure. *Human Relations*. **6**, 3–24.

——, A. K. Rice, and J. M. M. Hill (1951) The social and psychological impact of a change in method of wage payment. *Human Relations*. **4**, 315–40.

Jeffreys, M. (1952) Job changing under full employment. *Industrial Welfare*. **34**, 105-9.

Jenkin, N. (1957) Affective processes in perception. *Psychological Bulletin*. **54**, 100–27.

Jessor, R., and J. Readio (1957) The influence of the value of an event upon the expectancy of its occurrence. *Journal of General Psychology*. **56**, 219–28.

Jonas, H. (1953) A critique of cybernetics. *Social Research*. **20**, 172–92.

Jones, M. R. (1956) *Nebraska Symposium on Motivation*: 1956. Lincoln, Neb.

Kahn, R. L. (1956) The prediction of productivity. *Journal of Social Issues*. **12**, 41-9.

——, and D. Katz (1953) Leadership practices in relation to productivity and morale, in D. Cartwright and A. Zander, eds., *Group Dynamics: Research and Theory*. Evanston.

——, and N. C. Morse (1951) The relationship of productivity to morale. *Journal of Social Issues*. **7**, 8–17.

——, and A. S. Tannenbaum (1957) Union practices and member participation. *Personnel Psychology*. **10**, 227–92.

Kahn-Freund, O. (1954) Intergroup conflicts and their settlement. *British Journal of Sociology.* 5, 193–227.

Kaiser, R. L., and R. R. Blake (1955) Aspiration and performance in a simulated group atmosphere. *Journal of Social Psychology.* 42, 193–202.

Kalish, G. K, J. W. Milnor, J. F. Nash, and E. D. Nering (1952) Some experimental *n*-person games. RAND Research Memorandum RM-948.

Kapp, K. W. (1954) Economics and the behavioral sciences. *Kyklos.* 7, 205–25.

Katona, G. (1951) *Psychological Analysis of Economic Behavior.* New York.

—— (1953) Rational behavior and economic behavior. *Psychological Review.* 60, 307–18.

—— and J. Morgan (1952) The qualitative study of factors determining business decisions. *The Quarterly Journal of Economics.* 66, 67–90.

Katz, D. (1947) Morale and motivation in industry, in Dennis, W., ed., *Current Trends in Industrial Psychology.* Pittsburgh.

—— (1949) Employee groups: what motivates them and how they perform. *Advanced Management.* 14, 1.

——, N. Maccoby, G. Gurin, and L. G. Floor (1951) *Productivity, Supervision and Morale among Railroad Workers.* Survey Research Center, University of Michigan.

——, N. Maccoby, and N. C. Morse (1950) *Productivity, Supervision and Morale in an Office Situation.* Survey Research Center, University of Michigan.

Katz, E., P. M. Blau, M. L. Brown, and F. L. Strodtbeck (1957) Leadership stability and social change: an experiment with small groups. *Sociometry.* 20, 36–50.

Katz, J. (1951) How to resolve disagreement in "attitude." *Journal of Philosophy.* 48, 721–6.

Katz, L. (1953) A new status index derived from sociometric analysis. *Psychometrika.* 18, 39–43.

Kelley, H. H. (1950) Communication in experimentally created hierarchies. *Human Relations.* 4, 39–56.

—— (1950) The warm–cold variable in first impressions of persons. *Journal of Personality.* 18, 431–9.

—— (1955) Salience of membership and resistance to change of group-anchored attitudes. *Human Relations.* 8, 275–89.

—— and C. L. Woodruff (1956) Members' reactions to apparent group approval of a counternorm communication. *Journal of Abnormal and Social Psychology.* 52, 67–74.

Kellogg, W. M. (1931) The time of judgment in psychometric measures. *American Journal of Psychology.* 83, 65–86.

Kelly, J., and T. W. Harrell (1949) Job-satisfaction among coal miners. *Personnel Psychology.* 2, 161–70.

Kendall, P. L. (1954) *Conflict and Mood: Factors Affecting Stability of Response.* Glencoe, Ill.

Kerlinger, F. N. (1951) Decision-making in Japan. *Social Forces.* **30**, 36–41.

Kerr, W. A. (1947) Labor turnover and its correlates. *Journal of Applied Psychology.* **31**, 366–77.

——, G. J. Koppelmeier, and J. J. Sullivan (1951) Absenteeism, turnover, and morale in a metals fabricating factory. *Occupational Psychology.* **25**, 50–5.

Kidd, J. S., and D. T. Campbell (1955) Conformity to groups as a function of group success. *Journal of Abnormal and Social Psychology.* **51**, 390–3.

Killian, L. M. (1952) The significance of multiple-group membership in disaster. *American Journal of Sociology.* **57**, 309–14.

Klein, L., and J. Lansing (1955) Decisions to purchase consumer durable goods. *The Journal of Marketing.* **20**, 109–32.

Klubeck, S., and B. M. Bass (1954) Differential effects of training on persons of different leadership status. *Human Relations.* **7**, 59–72.

Koivisto, W. A. (1953) Value, theory, and fact in industrial sociology. *American Journal of Sociology.* **58**, 564–72.

Koopmans, T. C., ed. (1956) *Statistical Inference in Dynamic Economic Models.* New York.

—— and M. Beckman (1957) Assignment problems and the location of economic activities. *Econometrica.* **25**, 53–76.

Kornhauser, A., R. Dubin, and A. M. Ross (1954) *Industrial Conflict.* New York.

Kosma, A. R. (1943) *The A. B. C.'s of Motion Economy.* Newark, N. J.

Kriedt, G. (1953) Prediction of turnover among clerical workers. *Journal of Applied Psychology.* **37**, 338–40.

Kriesberg, L. (1952) The retail furrier: concepts of security and success. *American Journal of Sociology.* **57**, 478–85.

—— (1955) Occupational controls among steel distributors. *American Journal of Sociology.* **61**, 203–12.

Kriesberg, M. (1949) Cross pressures and attitudes. *Public Opinion Quarterly* **13**, 5–16.

Krulee, G. K. (1955) Company-wide incentive systems. *Journal of Business.* **28**, 37–47.

Kuehn, A. (1958) An analysis of the dynamics of consumer behavior and its implications for marketing management. Ph.D. thesis, Carnegie Institute of Technology.

Kuhn, H. W. (1955) The Hungarian method for the assignment problem. *Naval Research Logistics Quarterly.* **1**, 83–97.

—— and Tucker, A. W., eds (1953) *Contributions to the Theory of Games,* Volume II. Princeton.

Landecker, W. S. (1951) Types of integration and their measurement. *American Journal of Sociology.* **56**, 332–40.

—— (1952) Integration and group structure: an area for research. *Social Forces.* **30**, 194–400.

Landsberger, H. A. (1955) Interaction process analysis of the mediation of labor-management disputes. *Journal of Abnormal and Social Psychology*. **51**, 552–8.

—— (1955) Interaction process analysis of professional behavior: a study of labor mediators in twelve labor-management disputes. *American Sociological Review*. **20**, 566–75.

Lane, R. E. (1953) Why businessmen violate the law. *Journal of Criminal Law, Criminology and Political Science*. **44**, 151–65.

—— (1953) Businessmen and bureaucrats. *Social Forces*. **32**, 145–52.

Lanzetta, J. T., D. Haefner, P. Langham, and H. Axelrod (1954) Some effects of situational threat on group behavior. *Journal of Abnormal and Social Psychology*. **49**, 445–53.

——, and T. B. Roby (1956) Group performance as a function of work-distribution patterns and task load. *Sociometry*. **19**, 95–104.

——, G. R. Wendt, P. Langham, and D. Haefner (1956) The effects of an 'anxiety-reducing' medication on group behavior under threat. *Journal of Abnormal and Social Psychology*. **52**, 103–8.

Lanzillotti, R. F. (1957) Competitive price leadership – a critique of price leadership models. *Review of Economics and Statistics*. **39**, 55–64.

Lasswell, H. D. (1955) Current studies of the decision process: automation versus creativity. *Western Political Quarterly*. **8**, 381–99.

Laulicht, J. (1955) Role conflict, the pattern variable theory and scalogram analysis. *Social Forces*. **33**, 250–4.

Lawrence, L. C., and P. C. Smith (1955) Group decision and employee participation. *Journal of Applied Psychology*. **39**, 334–7.

Lawshe, C. H., and B. F. Nagle (1953) Productivity and attitude toward supervisor. *Journal of Applied Psychology*. **37**, 159–62.

Lazarus, R. S., J. Deese, and S. F. Osler (1952) The effects of psychological stress upon performance. *Psychological Bulletin*. **49**, 293–317.

Learner, L. (1955) A comparative study of the effects of individual and group wage incentive plans upon productivity and interpersonal relations. Unpublished Ph.D. thesis, University of Pittsburgh.

Leavitt, H. J. (1951) Effects of certain communication patterns on group performance. *Journal of Abnormal and Social Psychology*. **46**, 38–50.

—— (1955) Small groups in large organizations. *Journal of Business*. **28**, 8–17.

—— (1958) *Managerial Psychology*. Chicago.

Lesperance, J. P. (1953) *Economics and Techniques of Motion and Time Study*. Dubuque, Iowa.

Levin, H. S. (1956) *Office Work and Automation*. New York.

Lewin, K. (1935) *A Dynamic Theory of Personality*. New York.

—— (1936) *Principles of Topological Psychology*. New York.

—— (1951) *Field Theory in Social Science*. New York.

Lewis, V. B. (1952) Toward a theory of budgeting. *Public Administration Review*. **12**, 42–54.

Lichtner, W. O. (1921) *Times Study and Job Analysis.* New York.

Liddell, F. D. K. (1954) Attendance in coalmining industry. *British Journal of Sociology.* **5**, 78–86.

Lieberman, S. (1956) The effects of changes in roles on the attitudes of role occupants. *Human Relations.* **9**, 385–402.

Likert, R. (1953) Motivation: the core of management. *American Management Association Personnel Series, No. 155.*

—— (1956) Motivation and increased productivity. *Management Record.* **18**, 128–31.

—— and D. Katz (1948) Supervisory practices and organizational structure as they affect employee productivity and morale. *American Management Association Personnel Series, No 120.*

Lindzey, G., ed. (1954) *Handbook of Social Psychology.* Cambridge, Mass.

Lippitt, R., N. Polansky, and S. Rosen (1952) The dynamics of power. *Human Relations.* **51**, 37–64.

Lipset, S. M. (1950) *Agrarian Socialism.* Berkeley, Calif.

—— and F. T. Malm (1955) First jobs and career patterns. *American Journal of Economics and Sociology.* **14**, 247–61.

Livingston, R. T. (1949) *The Engineering of Organization and Management.* New York.

Louden, J. K. (1944) *Wage Incentives.* New York.

Lovell, H. G. (1952) The pressure lever in mediation. *Industrial and Labor Relations Review.* **6**, 20–30.

Lowell, E. L. (1952) Experimental studies of the motivational effect of conflict (abstract). *American Psychologist.* **7**, 253–4.

Lowry, S. M., H. B. Maynard, G. J. Stegemerten (1940) *Times and Motion Study.* New York.

Luce, R. D. (1954) A definition of stability for n-person games. *Annals of Mathematics,* **54**, 357–66.

—— (1955a) x-stability: a new equilibrium concept for n-person game theory. In *Mathematical Models of Human Behavior.* Stamford.

—— (1955b) x-stability of symmetric and of quota games. *Annals of Mathematics.* **62**, 517–27.

—— and H. Raiffa (1957) *Games and Decisions.* New York.

——, and A. A. Rogow (1956) A game theoretic analysis of congressional power distributions for a stable two-party system. *Behavioral Science.* **2**, 83–95.

Luchins, A. S., and E. H. Luchins (1957) Cooperativeness of task in relation to discovery of source of contradictory communications. *Journal of General Psychology.* **56**, 159–78.

Lytle, C. W. (1942) *Wage Incentives Methods.* Rev. ed. New York.

Maccoby, N. (1950) A quantitative comparison of certain psychological conditions related to group productivity in two widely different industrial situations. Unpublished doctoral thesis, University of Michigan.

McCormick, C. P. (1938) *Multiple Management: A Plan for Human Relations in Industry.* New York.

MacFie, A. L. (1953) Choice in psychology and as economic assumption. *Economic Journal.* **63**, 352–67.

McGlothlin, W. H. (1956) Stability of choices among uncertain alternatives. *American Journal of Psychology.* **69**, 604–15.

Machlup, F. (1955) The problem of verification in economics. *Southern Economic Journal.* **22**, 1–21.

Mack, R. W. (1954) The prestige system of an air base. *American Sociological Review.* **19**, 281–7.

—— (1954) Ecological patterns in an industrial ship. *Social Forces.* **32**, 351–6.

——, R. J. Murphy, and S. Yellin (1956) The Protestant ethic, level of aspiration, and social mobility: an empirical test. *American Sociological Review.* **21**, 295–300.

McKenzie, D. (1944) Wage incentives. *Advanced Management.* **9**, 129–35.

MacKenzie, W. J. M. (1952) Science in the study of administration. *The Manchester School of Economic and Social Studies.* **20**, 1–22.

MacMahon, A. W., J. D. Millett, and G. Ogden (1941). *The Administration of Federal Work Relief.* Chicago.

Macy, J., Jr., L. S. Christie, and R. D. Luce (1953) Coding noise in a task-oriented group. *Journal of Abnormal and Social Psychology.* **48**, 401–9.

Madge, C. (1948) Payment and incentives. *Occupational Psychology.* **22**, 39–45.

Mahoney, G. M. (1956) Unidimensional scales for the measurement of morale in an industrial situation. *Human Relations.* **9**, 3–26.

Maier, N. R. F. (1949) *Frustration.* New York.

—— (1953) An experimental test of the effect of training on discussion leadership. *Human Relations.* **6**, 161–73.

—— (1955) *Psychology in Industry.* 2nd ed. Boston.

—— (1952) and A. R. Solem. The contribution of a discussion leader to the quality of group thinking: the effective use of minority opinions. *Human Relations.* **5**, 277–88.

Mandell, M. M. (1953) The effect of organizational environment on personnel selection. *Personnel.* **30**, 13–16.

Manis, J. G., and B. N. Meltzer (1954) Attitudes of textile workers to class structure. *American Journal of Sociology.* **60**, 30–5.

Mann, F. (1951) Changing superior-subordinate relationships. *Journal of Social Issues.* **7**, 56–63.

—— and H. Baumgartel (1952) *Absences and Employee Attitudes in an Electric Power Company.* Survey Research Center, University of Michigan.

—— (1953) *The Supervisor's Concern with Costs in an Electric Power Company.* Survey Research Center, University of Michigan.

——, and J. Dent (1954) *Appraisals of Supervisors and Attitudes of Their Employees in an Electric Power Company.* Survey Research Center, University of Michigan.

Mann, F., and L. R. Hoffman (1956) Individual and organizational correlates of automation. *Journal of Social Issues*. **12**, 7–17.

March, J. G. (1954) Group norms and the active minority. *American Sociological Review*. **19**, 733–41.

—— (1955a) An introduction to the theory and measurement of influence. *American Political Science Review*. **49**, 431–51.

—— (1955b) Group autonomy and internal group control. *Social Forces*. **33**, 322–6.

—— (1956) Influence measurement in experimental and semi-experimental groups. *Sociometry*. **19**, 260–71.

—— (1957) Measurement concepts in the theory of influence. *Journal of Politics*. **19**, 202–26.

Marriot, R. (1949) Size of working group and output. *Occupational Psychology*. **23**, 47–57.

—— (1951) Socio-psychological factors in productivity. *Occupational Psychology*. **25**, 15–24.

Marron, A. J., and J. R. P. French (1945) Changing a stereotype in industry. *Journal of Social Issues*. **1**, No. 3, 33–8.

Marschak, J. (1949) The role of liquidity under complete and incomplete information. *Econometrica*. **17**, 180–2.

—— (1950) Rational behavior, uncertain prospects, and measurable utility. *Econometrica*. **18**, 111–41.

Marschak, J. (1955) Elements for a theory of teams. *Management Science*. **1**, 127–37.

—— and R. Radner (1954) The firm as a team (abstract). *Econometrica*. **22**, 523.

Marstrander, N. P. (1955) "Trivsel blant kvinnelige industriarbeidere" (Morale among female workers in industry). *Bedriftsokonomen*. **17**, 121–7.

Martin, N. H. (1956) Differential decisions in the management of an industrial plant. *Journal of Business*. **29**, 249–60.

—— and A. L. Strauss (1956) Patterns of mobility within industrial organizations. *Journal of Business*. **29**, 101–10.

Marvick, D. (1954) *Career Perspectives in a Bureaucratic Setting*. Ann Arbor.

Masuoka, J. (1940) The structure of the Japanese family in Hawaii. *American Journal of Sociology*. **46**, 168–78.

Mayberry, J. P., J. F. Nash, and M. Shubik (1953) A comparison of treatments of a duopoly situation. *Econometrica*. **21**, 141–54.

Maynard, H. B., and G. J. Stegemerten (1939) *Operation Analysis*. New York.

—— and J. L. Schwab (1948) *Methods-Time Measurement*. New York.

Mayo, E. (1924) Reverie and industrial fatigue. *Journal of Personnel Research*. **5**, 273–81.

—— and G. F. Lombard (1944) *Teamwork and Labor Turnover in the Aircraft Industry of Southern California*. Boston.

Mead, M., ed. (1953) *Cultural Patterns and Technical Change*. Paris.

Medalia, N. Z. (1955) Authoritarianism, leader acceptance and group cohesion. *Journal of Abnormal and Social Psychology.* **51**, 207–13.

—— and D. C. Miller (1955) Human relations leadership and the association of morale and efficiency in work groups. *Social Forces*, **33**, 348–52.

Meier, R. L. (1956) Automatism in the American economy. *Journal of Business.* **29**, 14–27.

Melbin, M. (1953) The action-interaction chart as a research tool. *Human Organization.* **12**, 34–5.

Mellinger, G. (1951) Status and deviancy in an automobile factory. M.A. thesis, University of Michigan.

—— (1956) Interpersonal trust as a factor in communication. *Journal of Abnormal and Social Psychology.* **52**, 304–9.

Meltzer, L. (1956) Scientific productivity in organizational settings. *Journal of Social Issues.* **12**, 32–40.

Merrick, D. V. (1920) *Time Studies as a Basis for Rule Setting.* New York.

Merton, R. K. (1936) The unanticipated consequences of purposive social action. *American Sociological Review.* **1**, 894–904.

—— (1940) Bureaucratic structure and personality. *Social Forces.* **18**, 560–8.

—— (1945) Role of the intellectual in public bureaucracy. *Social Forces.* **23**, 405–15.

—— (1947) The machine, the worker and the engineer. *Science.* **105**, 79–84.

—— (1957) *Social Theory and Social Structure.* 2nd ed. Glencoe, Ill.

——, A. P. Gray, B. Hockey, and H. H. Selvin (1952) *Reader in Bureaucracy.* Glencoe, Ill.

Messinger, S. L. (1955) Organizational transformation: a case study of a declining social movement. *American Sociological Review.* **20**, 3–10.

Meyer, H. D., and G. L. Pressel (1954) Personality test scores in the management hierarchy. *Journal of Applied Psychology.* **4**, 73–80.

Miernyx, W. H. (1955) *Inter-Industry Labor Mobility.* Boston.

Miller, C. R. (1946) *The Process of Persuasion.* New York.

Miller, D. C. (1946) The social factors of the work situation. *American Sociological Review.* **11**, 300–14.

Miller, N. E. (1951) Comments on theoretical models, illustrated by the development of conflict behavior. *Journal of Personality.* **52**, 82–100.

—— and J. Dollard (1941) *Social Learning and Imitation.* New Haven.

Mills, T. M. (1953) Power relations in three-person groups. *American Sociological Review.* **18**, 351–7.

—— (1954) The coalition pattern in three-person groups. *American Sociological Review.* **19**, 657–67.

Minnis, M. S. (1953) Cleavage in women's organizations: a reflection of the social structures of a city. *American Sociological Review.* **18**, 47–53.

Mintz, A. (1951) Non-adaptive group behavior. *Journal of Abnormal and Social Psychology.* **46**, 150–8.

Mishler, E. G. (1953) Personality characteristics and the resolution of role conflicts. *Public Opinion Quarterly.* **17**, 115–35.

—— and A. Tropp. (1956) Status and interaction in a psychiatric hospital. *Human Relations.* **9**, 187–205.

Monk, M., and T. M. Newcomb (1956) Perceived consensus within and among occupational classes. *American Sociological Review*, **21**, 71–9.

Monypenny, P. (1953) A code of ethics as a means of controlling administrative conduct. *Public Administration Review.* **13**, 184–7.

Mooney, J. D. (1947) *The Principles of Organization.* New York.

—— and A. C. Reiley (1939) *The Principles of Organization.* New York.

Moore, D. G., and R. Renck (1955) The professional employee in industry. *Journal of Business.* **28**, 58–66.

Moore, O. K., and S. B. Anderson (1954) Search behavior in individual and group problem solving. *American Sociological Review.* **19**, 702–14.

Morgensen, A. H. (1932) *Common Sense Applied to Motion and Time Study.* New York.

Morrow, R. L. (1946) *Time Study and Motion Economy.* New York.

Morse, N. C. (1953) *Satisfactions in the White-Collar Job.* Survey Research Center, University of Michigan.

—— and E. Reimer (1955) Experimental change of a major organizational variable. *Journal of Abnormal and Social Psychology.* **52**, 120–9.

—— and A. S. Tannenbaum (1951) Regulation and control in hierarchical organizations. *Journal of Social Issues.* **7**, No. 3, 41–8.

——, and R. S. Weiss (1955) The function and meaning of work and the job. *American Sociological Review.* **20**, 191–8.

Morsh, J. E., *et al.* (1953) Job satisfactions of Air Force technical school instructors – 1950 and 1953. USAF, Human Resources Research Center, Technical Report, 53–8.

Mundel, M. E. (1950) *Motion and Time Study Principles and Practice.* New York.

Muscio, B. (1920) *Lectures on Industrial Psychology.* London.

Myers, C. A., and W. R. MacLaurin (1943) *The Movement of Factory Workers.* New York.

—— and G. P. Shultz (1951) *The Dynamics of a Labor Market.* New York.

Myers, H. (1932) *Human Engineering.* New York.

—— (1944) *Simplified Time Study.* New York.

Nadler, G. (1955) *Motion and Time Study.* New York.

Nadworny, M. J. (1955) *Scientific Management and the Unions, 1900–1932.* Cambridge, Mass.

Nagle, B. F. (1954) Productivity, employee attitude and supervisor sensitivity. *Personnel Psychology.* **7**, 219–32.

Nash, J. F., Jr. (1950) The bargaining problem. *Econometrica.* **18**, 115–62.

—— (1953) Two-person co-operative games. *Econometrica.* **21**, 128–40.

Nelson, P. B., Jr. (1953) The morale of the individual soldier. *Military Review, Ft. Leavenworth.* **33**, (3), 43–7.

Nettl, J. P. (1957) A note on entrepreneurial behavior. *Review of Economic Studies.* **24**, 87–94.

Newell, A. (1955) The chess machine: an example of dealing with a complex task by adaptation. *Proceedings of the Western Joint Computer Conference.* Institute of Radio Engineers.

——, J. C. Shaw, and H. A. Simon (1958) Elements of a theory of human problem solving. *Psychological Review.* **65**, 151–66.

——, and H. A. Simon (1956) The logic theory machine: a complex information processing system. *Transactions on Information Theory.* Institute of Radio Engineers, September.

Newman, W. H. (1951) *Administrative Action.* New York.

Niebel, B. W. (1955) *Motion and Time Study.* Homewood, Ill.

Norris, T. L. (1953) Decision-making activity sequences in a hacienda community. *Human Organization.* **12**, 26–30.

Nosow, S. (1956) Labor distribution and the normative system. *Social Forces.* **35**, 25–33.

Ort, R. S. (1950) A study of role-conflicts as related to happiness in marriage. *Journal of Abnormal and Social Psychology.* **45**, 691–9.

—— (1952) A study of role-conflicts as related to class level. *Journal of Abnormal and Social Psychology.* **47**, 425–32.

Palmer, G. L. (1954) *Labor Mobility in Six Cities.* New York.

—— and A. Ratner (1949) *Industrial and Occupational Trends in National Employment.* University of Pennsylvania.

Passer, H. C. (1952) Development of large scale organization. *Journal of Economic History.* **11**, 278–395.

Patton, A. (1957) Annual report on executive compensation. *Harvard Business Review.* **35**, 125–36.

Payne, R. (1954) An approach to the study of relative prestige of formal organizations. *Social Forces.* **32**, 244–7.

Payne, R. B., and G. T. Hauty (1955) Effect of psychological feedback upon work decrement. *Journal of Experimental Psychology.* **50**, 343–51.

Pearson, N. (1945) Fayolism is the necessary complement of Taylorism. *American Political Science Review.* **39**, 68–80.

Pellegrin, R. J. (1953) The achievement of high statuses and leadership in the small group. *Social Forces.* **32**, 10–16.

Pelz, D. C. (1951) Leadership within a hierarchical organization. *Journal of Social Issues.* **7**, No. 3, 49–55.

—— (1951) The influence of the supervisor within his department as a conditioner of the way supervisory practices affect employee attitudes. Unpublished doctoral thesis, University of Michigan.

—— (1952) Influence: a key to effective leadership in the first-line supervisor. *Personnel.* **3**, 209–17.

Pelz, D. C. (1956) Some social factors related to performance in a research organization. *Administrative Science Quarterly.* 1, 310–25.

Pen, J. (1952) A general theory of bargaining. *American Economic Review.* 42, 24–42.

Pepinsky, H. B. (1954) Research on productive behavior. *Personnel Guidance Journal.* 33, 140–4.

Pepitone, A. (1950) Motivational effects in social perception. *Human Relations.* 3, 57–76.

—— (1952) Responsibility to the group and its effects on the performance of members. Ph.D. thesis, University of Michigan.

Peterson, E., and E. G. Plowman (1941) *Business Organization and Management.* Chicago.

Pfiffner, J. M. (1953) Research in organization effectiveness. *Public Personnel Review.* 14, 49–54.

—— and R. C. Wilson (1953) "Management-mindedness" in the supervisory ranks. *Personnel.* 30, 122–5.

Phelps, O. W. (1957) A structural model of the U.S. labor market. *Industrial and Labor Relations Review.* 10, 403–23.

Phillips, B. H. (1956) Effect of cohesion and intelligence on the problem solving efficiency of small face to face groups in cooperative situations. *Journal of Educational Research.* 50, 127–32.

Plato, *Meno*, from *Dialogue of Plato*, vol. 1, B. Jowett (translator), NY: Random House, 1937.

Plody, L. A. (1954) Factors related to the formal social participation of twenty-six selected rural persons with case studies. Unpublished Ph.D. dissertation, Cornell University.

Presgrave, R. (1945) *The Dynamics of Time Study.* 2nd ed. New York.

Purcell, T. V. (1953) *The Worker Speaks His Mind on Company and Union.* Cambridge, Mass.

Quandt, R. E. (1956) A probabilistic theory of consumer behavior. *Quarterly Journal of Economics.* 70, 507–36.

Raven, B. (1952) Group pressures toward selection and distortion of content in cognition and communication. Ph.D. thesis, University of Michigan.

Reynolds, L. G. (1951) *The Structure of Labor Markets.* New York.

—— and J. Shister (1949) *Job Horizons.* New York.

Ricciuti, H. N. (1955) Ratings of leadership potential at the United States Naval Academy and subsequent officer performance. *Journal of Applied Psychology.* 39, 194–9.

Rice, A. K. (1951) An examination of the boundaries of part institutions: an illustrative study of departmental turnover in industry. *Human Relations.* 4, 393–400.

—— (1955) Productivity and social organization in an Indian weaving mill, II. *Human Relations.* 8, 399–428.

——, J. M. M. Hill, and E. L. Trist. (1950) The representation of labour turnover as a social process. *Human Relations.* 3, 349–72.

Rice, A. K., and E. L. Trist (1952) Institutional and sub-institutional determinants of change in labour turnover. *Human Relations.* 5, 347–71.

Richardson, S. A. (1952) Technological change: some effects on three Canadian fishing villages. *Human Organization.* 11, No. 3, 17–27.

Richmond, A. H. (1954) Conflict and authority in industry. *Occupational Psychology.* 28, 24–33

Ridley, C. E., and H. A. Simon (1938) *Measuring Municipal Activities.* Chicago.

Riegel, J. W. (1941) *Wage Determination.* Rev. ed. Ann Arbor.

—— (1956) *Employee Interest in Company Success.* Ann Arbor.

Riley, M. W., and S. H. Flowerman (1957) Group relations as a variable in communications research. *American Sociological Review.* 16, 174–80.

——, and J. W. Riley, Jr. (1951) A sociological approach to communications research. *Public Opinion Quarterly.* 15, 445–60.

Roberts, D. R. (1956) A general theory of executive compensation based on statistically tested propositions. *Quarterly Journal of Economics.* 70, 270–95.

Robinson, H. A. (1953) Job satisfaction researches of 1952. *Personnel Guidance Journal.* 32, 22–5.

—— (1954) Job satisfaction researches of 1953. *Personnel Guidance Journal.* 33, 26–9.

—— (1955) Job satisfaction researches of 1954. *Personnel Guidance Journal.* 33, 520–33.

Roby, T. B., and J. T. Lanzetta (1956) Work group structure, communication, and group performance. *Sociometry.* 19, 105–13.

Rock, M. L., and E. N. Hay (1953) Investigation of the use of tests as a predictor of leadership and group effectiveness in a job evaluation situation. *Journal of Social Psychology.* 38, 109–19.

Roe, A. (1956) *The Psychology of Occupations.* New York.

Rogers, M. (1951) The human group: a critical review with suggestions for some alternative hypothesis. *Sociometry.* 14, 20–31.

Rose, A. M. (1951) The social psychology of desertion from combat. *American Sociological Review.* 16, 614–29.

—— (1952a) The potential contribution of sociological theory and research to economics. *Amercian Journal of Economics and Sociology.* 12, 23–33.

—— (1952b) *Union Solidarity.* Minneapolis.

—— and C. B. Rose (1954) Intergroup conflict and its mediation. *International Social Science Bulletin.* 6, 25–43.

Rosen, H., and R. A. H. Rosen (1955) *The Union Member Speaks.* New York.

—— (1957) Personality variables and role in a union business agent group. *Journal of Applied Psychology.* 41, 131–6.

Rosenberg, S., D. E. Erlick, and L. Berkowitz (1955) Some effects of varying combinations of group members on group performance measures and leadership behaviors. *Journal of Abnormal and Social Psychology.* 51, 195–206.

Rothe, H. F. (1946) Output rates among butter operators. *Journal of Applied Psychology.* **30**, 199–222; 320–37.

—— (1947) Output rates among machine operators. *Journal of Applied Psychology.* **31**, 484–9.

—— (1951) Output rates among chocolate sippers. *Journal of Applied Psychology.* **35**, 94–7.

Roy, D. F. (1952) Quota restriction and goldbricking in a machine shop. *American Journal of Sociology.* **57**, 427–42.

—— (1952) Do wage incentives reduce costs? *Industrial Labor Relations Review.* **5**, 195–208.

—— (1953) Work satisfaction and social reward in quota achievement: an analysis of piecework incentives. *American Sociological Review.* **18**, 507–14.

—— (1954) Efficiency and 'the Fix': informal intergroup relations in a piecework machine shop. *American Journal of Sociology.* **60**, 255–66.

Ruesch, J. (1953) Synopsis of the theory of human communication. *Psychiatry* **16**, 215–43.

Ryan, T. A. (1947) *Work and Effort.* New York.

Sampter, H. C. (1941) *Motion Study.* New York.

Sarbin, T., and D. S. Jones. (1955) The assessment of role-expectations in the selection of supervisory personnel. *Educational and Psychological Measurement.* **15**, 236–9.

Sayles, L. R., and G. Strauss (1953) *The Local Union.* New York.

Schachter, S. (1951) Deviation, rejection and communication. *Journal of Abnormal and Social Psychology.* **46**, 190–207.

——, N. Ellertson, D. McBride, and D. Gregory (1951) An experimental study of cohesiveness and productivity. *Human Relations.* **4**, 229–38.

Schaul, M. W. (1953) A study of the relationship between employee attitudes and productivity in a group of factory workers. Unpublished Ph.D. dissertation. Columbia University.

Schelling, T. C. (1956) An essay on bargaining. *The American Economic Review.* **46**, 281–306.

—— (1957) Bargaining, communication, and limited war. *Conflict Resolution.* **1**, 19–36.

Schneider, L., and L. Sverre (1952) Deficiency and conflict in industrial sociology. *American Journal of Economics and Sociology.* **12**, 49–61.

Schreiber, R. J. (1957) Estimates of expected value as a function of distribution parameters. *Journal of Experimental Psychology.* **53**, 218–20.

Schutt, W. H. (1943) *Time Study Engineering.* New York.

Schutz, W. C. (1955) What makes groups productive? *Human Relations.* **8**, 429–65.

Scott, J. C., Jr. (1957) Membership and participation in voluntary associations. *American Sociological Review.* **22**, 315–26.

Scott, M. G. (1942) *Analysis of Human Motions.* New York.

Scott, W. D. (1955) Financial incentives – why and how. *Personnel Practices Bulletin* (Melbourne). **11** (2), 8–18.

Scudder, R., and C. A. Anderson (1954) Migration and vertical occupational mobility. *American Sociological Review.* **19**, 329–34.

Seashore, S. E. (1954) *Group Cohesiveness in the Industrial Work Group.* Survey Research Center, University of Michigan.

Seeman, M. (1953) Role conflict and ambivalence in leadership. *American Sociological Review.* **18**, 373–80.

Selznick, P. (1943) An approach to a theory of organization. *American Sociological Review.* **8**, 47–54.

—— (1948) Foundations of the theory of organization. *American Sociological Review.* **13**, 25–35.

—— (1949) *TVA and the Grass Roots.* Berkeley.

—— (1957) *Leadership in Administration.* Evanston, Ill.

Shartle, C. L. (1950) Leadership aspects of administrative behavior. *Advanced Management.* **15**, 12–15.

Shaw, A. G. (1952) *The Purpose and Practice of Motion Study.* Manchester, N. H.

Shaw, M. E. (1954) Some effects of unequal distribution of information upon group performance in various communication nets. *Journal of Abnormal and Social Psychology.* **49**, 547–53.

—— (1954) Some effects of problem complexity upon problem solution efficiency in different communication nets. *Journal of Experimental Psychology.* **48**, 211–17.

—— (1954) Group structure and the behavior of individuals in small groups. *Journal of Psychology.* **38**, 139–49.

—— (1955) A comparison of two types of leadership in various communication nets. *Journal of Abnormal and Social Psychology.* **50**, 127–34.

—— and J. C. Gilchrist (1956) Inter-group communication and leader choice. *Journal of Social Psychology.* **43**, 133–8.

Shepard, H. A. (1956) Patterns of organization for applied research and development – superiors and subordinates in research. *Journal of Business.* **29**, 261–7.

Shepherd, C., and I. R. Weschler (1955) The relation between three interpersonal variable and communication effectiveness. *Sociometry.* **18**, 103–10.

Sheppard, H. L. (1954) Approaches of conflict in American industrial sociology. *British Journal of Sociology.* **5**, 324–41.

Sherif, M., and C. W. Sherif (1956) *An Outline of Social Psychology.* New York.

Shimmin, S. (1955) Incentives. *Occupational Psychology.* **29**, 240–4.

Shockley, W. (1955) Individual variations of productivity in research laboratories. *Science* (abstract). **122**, 879.

Shubik, M. (1953) The role of game theory in economics. *Kyklos.* **6**, 21–34.

—— (1956) A game theorist looks at the antitrust laws and the automobile industry. *Stanford Law Review.* **8**, 594–630.

Shumard, F. W. (1940) *A Primer of Time Study.* New York.

Siegel, S. (1957) Level of aspiration and decision making. *Psychological Review*. **64**, 253–62.

Simmel, G. (1904) The sociology of conflict – I. *American Journal of Sociology*. **9**, 490–525.

—— (1904) The sociology of conflict – II. *American Journal of Sociology*. **9**, 672–89.

—— (1904) The sociology of conflict – III. *American Journal of Sociology*. **9**, 798–811.

Simon, H. A. (1943) *Fiscal Aspects of Metropolitan Consolidation*. Berkeley, Calif.

—— (1947) *Administrative Behavior*. New York.

—— (1950) Modern organization theories. *Advanced Management*. **15**, 2–4.

—— (1951) A formal theory of the employment relationship. *Econometrica*. **19**, 293–305.

—— (1952–3) A comparison of organization theories. *The Review of Economic Studies*. **20**, 40–8.

—— (1952a) A formal theory of interaction in social groups. *American Sociological Review*. **17**, 202–11.

—— (1952b) Comments on the theory of organizations. *American Political Science Review*. **46**, 1130–39.

—— (1953) Notes on the observation and measurement of political power. *Journal of Politics*. **15**, 500–16.

—— (1953b) Birth of an organization: the economic cooperation administration. *Public Administration Review*. **13**, 227–36.

—— (1955) A behavioral model of rational choice. *Quarterly Journal of Economics*. **69**, 99–118.

—— (1956) Rational choice and the structure of the environment. *Psychological Review*. **63**, 129–38.

—— (1957) The compensation of executives. *Sociometry*. **20**, 32–5.

—— and H. Guetzkow (1955a) Mechanisms involved in group pressures on deviate members. *British Journal of Statistical Psychology*. **8**, 93–100.

—— (1955b) A model of short- and long-run mechanisms involved in pressures toward uniformity in groups. *Psychological Review*. **62**, 56–68.

——, G. Kozmetsky, and G. Tyndall (1954) *Centralization vs. Decentralization in Organizing the Controller's Department*. New York, The Controllership Foundation.

——, D. W. Smithburg, and V. A. Thompson (1950) *Public Administration*. New York.

Smith, A. (1937 (1776)) *The Wealth of Nations*. New York: Random House, Modern Library.

Smith, A. J., H. E. Madden, and R. Sobol (1957) Productivity and recall in cooperative and competitive discussion groups. *Journal of Psychology*. **43**, 251–60.

Smith, F. J., and W. A. Kerr (1953) Turnover factors as assessed by the exit interview. *Journal of Applied Psychology*. **37**, 352–5.

Smith, P. C. (1953) The curve of output as a criterion of boredom. *Journal of Applied Psychology*. **37**, 69–74.

Solomon, D. N. (1954) Sociological research in a military organization. *Canadian Journal of Economics and Political Science*. **20**, 531–41.

Spector, A. J. (1956) Expectations, fulfillment and morale. *Journal of Abnormal and Social Psychology*. **52**, 51–6.

Spriegel, W. R., and C. E. Myers, eds (1953) *The Writings of the Gilbreths*. Homewood, Ill.

Stagner, R. (1954) Attitude toward authority: an exploratory study. *Journal of Social Psychology*. **40**, 197–210.

——, D. R. Flebbe, and E. V. Wood (1952) Working on the railroad: a study of job satisfaction. *Personnel Psychology*. **2**, 293–306.

Stansfield, R. G. (1951) Levels of expectation in productivity. *Occupational Psychology*. **25**, 25–34.

Steiner, I. D., and J. S. Dodge (1956) Interpersonal perception and role structure as determinants of group and individual efficiency. *Human Relations*. **9**, 467–80.

Stephan, F. F. (1952) The relative rate of communication between members of small groups. *American Sociological Review*. **17**, 482–6.

—— and E. G. Mishler (1952) The distribution of participation in small groups: an exponential approximation. *American Sociological Review*. **17**, 398–608.

Stewart, D. D. (1951) The place of volunteer participation in a bureaucratic organization. *Social Forces*. **29**, 311–17.

Stockford, L. O., and K. R. Kunze (1950) Psychology and the pay check. *Personnel*. **27**, 2–15.

Stogdill, R. M., C. L. Shartle, R. J. Wherry, and W. E. Jaynes (1955) A factorial study of administrative behavior. *Personnel Psychology*. **8**, 165–80.

Stone, R. C. (1952a) Mobility factors as they affect workers' attitudes and conduct toward incentive systems. *American Sociological Review*. **17**, 58–64.

—— (1952b) Conflicting approaches to the study of worker-manager relations. *Social Forces*. **31**, 117–24.

—— (1953) Factory organization and vertical mobility. *American Sociological Review*. **18**, 28–35.

Story, M. L. (1953) Defining the administrative function. *Journal of Educational Research*. **46**, 371–4.

Stouffer, S. A. (1949) An analysis of conflicting social norms. *American Sociological Review*. **14**, 707–17.

—— and J. Toby (1951) Role conflict and personality. *American Journal of Sociology*. **56**, 395–406.

——, *et al.* (1949) *The American Soldier: Adjustment during Army Life*. Princeton.

Strauss, G. (1953) Factors in the unionization of a utilities company: a case study. *Human Organization*. **12**, 17–25.

Strauss, G. and L. R. Sayles (1952) Patterns of participation in local unions. *Industrial and Labor Relations Review*. **6**, 31–43.
—— (1953) Occupation and the selection of local union officers. *American Journal of Sociology*. **58**, 585–91.
Strodtbeck, F. L., and A. P. Hare (1954) Bibliography of small group research (1900–1953). *Sociometry*. **17**, 101–93.
Sturmthal, A., ed. (1957) *Contemporary Collective Bargaining in Seven Countries*. Ithaca.
Taft, R. (1953) The social grading of occupations in Australia. *British Journal of Sociology*. **4**, 181–7.
Talland, G. A. (1954) The assessment of group opinion by leaders and their influence on its formation. *Journal of Abnormal and Social Psychology*. **49**, 431–4.
—— (1955) Task and interaction process: some characteristics of therapeutic group discussion. *Journal of Abnormal and Social Psychology*. **50**, 105–9.
Tannenbaum, A. S. (1954) The relationship between personality and group structure. Ph.D. thesis, Syracuse University.
—— (1956) Mechanisms of control in local trade unions. *British Journal of Sociology*. **7**, 306–13.
—— (1956) The concept of organizational control. *Journal of Social Issues*. **12**, 50–60.
—— (1956) Control structure and union functions. *American Journal of Sociology*. **61**, 536–45.
—— and R. L. Kahn (1957) Organizational control structure: a general descriptive technique as applied to four local unions. *Human Relations*. **10**, 127–40.
Tannenbaum, R. (1949) The manager concept: a rational synthesis. *Journal of Business*. **22**, 225–41.
—— (1950) Managerial decision-making. *Journal of Business*. **23**, 22–9.
Tawney, R. H. (1937) *Religion and the Rise of Capitalism*. New York.
Taylor, F. W. (1907) On the art of cutting metals. *Transactions of the A.S.M.E.* **28**, 31–350.
—— (1911) *The Principles of Scientific Management*. New York.
—— (1919) *Shop Management*. New York.
—— (1947) *Scientific Management*. New York.
Tead, O. (1929) *Human Nature and Management*. New York.
Thibaut, J. (1950) An experimental study of the cohesiveness of underprivileged groups. *Human Relations*. **3**, 251–78.
—— and J. Coules (1952) The role of communication in the reduction of interpersonal hostility. *Journal of Abnormal and Social Psychology*. **47**, 770–7.
Thirlby, G. F. (1952) The economist's description of business behaviour. *Economica*. **19**, 148–67.
Thompson, C. B. (1917) *The Theory and Practice of Scientific Management*. New York.

Thorndike, E. L. (1927) The law of effect. *American Journal of Psychology*. **39**, 212-22.

—— (1938) The effect of discussion upon the correctness of group decisions when the factor of majority influence is allowed for. *Journal of Social Psychology*. **9**, 343-62.

Thorner, I. (1952) Ascetic Protestantism and the development of science and technology. *American Journal of Sociology*. **58**, 25-33.

Thrall, R. M., C. H. Coombs, and R. L. Davis (1954) *Decision Processes*. New York.

Tiffin, J., B. J. Parker, and R. W. Habereat (1947) The analysis of personnel data in relation to turnover on a factory job. *Journal of Applied Psychology*. **36**, 615-16.

Titus, H. E., and E. P. Hollander (1957) The California F scale in psychological research: 1950-1955. *Psychological Bulletin*. **54**, 47-64.

Toby, J. (1952) Some variables in role conflict analysis. *Social Force*. **30**, 323-7.

Tolman, E. C. (1932) *Purposive Behavior in Animals and Man*. Berkeley.

—— and E. Brunswick (1935) The organism and the causal texture of the environment. *Psychological Review*. **42**, 43-77.

Torrance, E. P. (1953) Methods of conducting critiques of group problem solving performance. *Journal of Applied Psychology*. **37**, 394-8.

—— (1954) The behavior of small groups under the stress conditions of "survival." *American Sociological Review*. **19**, 751-5.

—— (1955) Perception of group functioning as a predictor of group performance. *Journal of Social Psychology*. **42**, 271-82.

—— (1957) Group decision-making and disagreement. *Social Forces*. **35**, 314-18.

Trapp, E. P. (1955) Leadership and popularity as a function of behavioral predictions. *Journal of Abnormal and Social Psychology*. **51**, 452-7.

Trist, E. L., and K. W. Bamforth (1951) Some social and psychological consequences of the longwall method of coal-getting. *Human Relations*. **4**, 3-38.

Trow, D. B. (1957) Autonomy and job satisfaction in task-oriented groups. *Journal of Abnormal and Social Psychology*. **54**, 204-7.

Troxell, J. P. (1954) Elements in job satisfactions. *Personnel*. **31**, 199-205.

Truman, D. B. (1951) *The Governmental Process*. New York.

Turner, A. N. (1955) Interaction and sentiment in the foreman–worker relationship. *Human Organization*. **14**, 10-16.

—— (1957) Foreman, job, and company. *Human Relations*. **10**, 99-112.

Turner, K. H. (1947) The Navy disbursing officer as a bureaucrat. *American Sociological Review*. **12**, 342-8.

Turner, R. H. (1956) Role-taking, role standpoint, and reference-group behavior. *American Journal of Sociology*. **61**, 316-28.

Urwick, L. (1943) *The Elements of Administration*. New York.

Urwick, L. (1953) Profitably using the general staff position in business. *American Management Association General Management Series, No. 165.*

Van Zelst, R. H. (1952) Sociometrically selected work teams increases production. *Personnel Psychology.* **5**, 175–85.

—— (1951) Worker popularity and job satisfaction. *Personnel Psychology.* **4**, 405–12.

Venable, T. C. (1954) The relationship of selected factors to the social structures of a stable group. *Sociometry.* **17**, 355–7.

Vernon, H. M. (1921) *Industrial Fatigue and Efficiency.* London.

Villiers, R. (1954) *The Dynamics of Industrial Management.* New York.

Viteles, M. S. (1932) *Industrial Psychology.* New York.

—— (1934) *The Science of Work.* New York.

—— (1953) *Motivation and Morale in Industry.* New York.

—— (1955) Motivation and morale – whose responsibility? *Personnel Practices Bulletin* (Melbourne). **11** (1), 27–42.

Vollmer, H. M. and J. A. Kinney (1955) Age, education and job satisfaction. *Personnel.* **32**, 38–43.

Von Mises, L. (1944) *Bureaucracy.* New Haven.

Von Neumann, J. (1928) Zur Theorie der Gesellschaftsspiele. *Mathematische Annalen.* **100**, 295–320.

—— (1937) Über ein ökonomisches Gleichungssystem und eine Verallgemeinerung des Brouwerschen Fixpunktsatzes. *Ergebnisse eines Mathematik Kolloquiums.* **8**, 73–83.

—— and O. Morgenstern (1944) *Theory of Games and Economic Behavior.* Princeton.

Wallin, P. (1950) Cultural contradictions and sex roles: a repeat study. *American Sociological Review.* **15**, 288–93.

Walter, J. E. (1957) Dividend policy and the process of choice. Unpublished ms.

Warren, R. L. (1949) Social disorganization and the inter-relationship of cultural roles. *American Sociological Review.* **14**, 83–7.

Warriner, C. K. (1955) Leadership in the small group. *American Journal of Sociology* (abstract). **60**, 361–9.

Watson, W. F. (1935) *Machines and Man.* London.

Weber, M. (1930) *The Protestant Ethic and the Spirit of Capitalism.* Parsons, trans. New York.

—— (1946) *From Max Weber: Essays in Sociology.* Gerth and Mills, trans. Oxford.

—— (1947) *The Theory of Social and Economic Organization.* Henderson and Parsons, trans. Oxford.

Wechsler, D. (1952) *The Range of Human Capacities.* Baltimore.

Weiss, E. C. (1957) Relation of personnel statistics to organizational structure. *Personnel Psychology.* **10**, 27–42.

Weiss, R. S. (1956) A structure-function approach to organization. *Journal of Social Issues.* **12**, 61–7.

Weiss, R. S. and E. Jacobson (1955) A method for the analysis of the structure of complex organizations. *American Sociological Review.* 20, 661–8.

Weitz, J. (1952) A neglected concept in the study of job satisfaction. *Personnel Psychology.* 5, 201–5.

Weschler, I. R., M. Kahane, and R. Tannenbaum (1952) Job satisfaction productivity and morale: a case study. *Occupational Psychology.* 26, 1–14.

Whitehead, T. N. (1938) Social motives in economic activities. *Occupational Psychology.* 12, 271–90.

Whitin, T. M. (1954) On the span of central direction. *Naval Research Logistics Quarterly.* 1, 25–35.

Whorf, B. L. (1956) *Language, Thought, and Reality.* New York.

Whyte, W. F. (1947) *Human Problems of the Restaurant Industry.* New York.

—— (1948) Incentives for productivity: the Bundy Lubing Company case. *Applied Anthropology.* 71, 1–16.

—— (1952) Economic incentives and human relations. *Harvard Business Review.* 30, 73–80.

—— (1953) Interviewing for organizational research. *Human Organization.* 12, 15–22.

—— *et al.* (1955) *Money and Motivation.* New York.

Wickert, F. R. (1951) Turnover and employees' feelings of ego-involvement in the day-to-day operations of a company. *Personnel Psychology.* 4, 185–97.

Wickham, O. P. (1952) Labour turnover as a dynamic process. *Bulletin of Industrial Psychology and Personnel Practices.* 8, 3–12.

Wiles, P. J. D. (1951) Notes on the efficiency of labour. *Oxford Economic Papers*, n.s. 3, 158–80.

Willerman, B. (1949) Group identification in industry. Unpublished doctoral thesis, Massachusetts Institute of Technology.

—— and L. Swanson (1953) Group prestige in voluntary organizations: a study of college sororities. *Human Relations.* 6, 57–77.

Williams, J. (1955) The incentive in bonus payment schemes. *Bulletin British Psychological Society* (abstract). 27, 9.

Wilson, J. R. (1952) Maximization and business behavior. *The Economic Record.* 28, 29–39.

Wispe, L. G., and K. E. Lloyd (1955) Some situational and psychological determinants of the desire for structured interpersonal relations. *Journal of Abnormal and Social Psychology.* 51, 57–60.

Wolman, B. (1956) Leadership and group dynamics. *Journal of Social Psychology.* 43, 11–25.

Worthy, J. C. (1950a) Factors influencing employee morale. *Harvard Business Review.* 29, 61–73.

—— (1950b) Organizational structure and employee morale. *American Sociological Review.* 15, 169–79.

Wotton, G. (1955) Wage incentives in operation – Case Study No. 7. *Personnel Practices Bulletin.* 11, 19–27.

Woytinsky, W. S. (1942) *Three Aspects of Labor Dynamics.* Washington, D. C.

Wrape, H. E. (1952) Tightening work standards. *Harvard Business Review.* **30**, 64–74.

Wright, Q. (1951) The nature of conflict. *Western Political Quarterly.* **4**, 193–209.

Wyatt, S. (1934) *Incentives in Repetitive Work*, (cited in Viteles 1953).

—— (1953) A study of output in two similar factories. *British Journal of Psychology.* **44**, 5–17.

Yoder, D. (1948) *Demands for Labor: Opportunities for Research.* New York.

Yost, E. (1949) *Frank and Lillian Gilbreth.* New Brunswick, N. J.

Young, H. (1954) The role of the extended family in a disaster. *Human Relations.* **7**, 383–91.

Yuker, H. E. (1955) Group atmosphere and memory. *Journal of Abnormal and Social Psychology.* **51**, 17–23.

Zajonc, R. (1954) Cognitive structure and cognitive turning. Ph.D. thesis, University of Michigan.

Zaleznik, A. (1956) *Worker Satisfaction and Development: A Case Study of Work and Social Behavior in a Factory Group.* Harvard University, Division of Research, Graduate School of Business Administration. Boston.

Zeleney, L. D. (1939) Sociometry of morale. *American Sociological Review.* **4**, 799–808.

Zentner, H. (1955) Primary group affiliation and institutional group morale. *Social Science Research.* **40**, 31–4.

Zeuthen, F. (1930) *Problems of Monopoly and Economic Welfare.* London.

Ziller, R. C. (1957) Group size: a determinant of the quality and stability of group decisions. *Sociometry.* **20**, 165–73.

Numerical Index to Variables

3.1 Control, demand for
3.2 Reliability of behavior, emphasis on
3.3 Relationships, personalized
3.4 Goals, internalization of organization rules
3.5 Decision-making, use of categorization as a technique
3.6 Search for alternatives
3.7 Rigidity of behavior
3.8 Goals, extent to which goals are perceived as shared among members of group
3.9 Defensiveness, propensity of organization members to defend each other against outside pressures
3.10 Defensibility of individual action
3.11 Clients, difficulty with
3.12 Authority, use of trappings of
3.13 Defensibility of individual action, felt need for
3.14 Authority, delegation of
3.15 Training in specialized competences
3.16 Goals, difference between organizational goals and achievement
3.17 Interests, bifurcation of
3.18 Costs of changing personnel
3.19 Conflict among organizational subunits
3.20 Decisions, content of
3.21 Goals, internalization of organizational goals by participants
3.22 Subunit ideologies, elaboration of
3.23 Goals, internalization of subgoals by participants
3.24 Goals, operationality of organizational
3.25 Rules, use of general and impersonal
3.26 Power relations within group, visibility of
3.27 Equality norms, extent to which held
3.28 Supervisory role, legitimacy of
3.29 Tension, level of interpersonal
3.30 Standards, knowledge about minimum acceptable behavior

Index

This is a subject index both to the variables that are formally designated (and numbered) and to the concepts and topics that appear in the less formalized parts of the text. Following the name of each of the formally designated variables is its number (in parenthesis), and reference to the page on which it is introduced, followed by references to the other pages where it is discussed. References in *italics* refer to inclusions in figures. Thus, 'Alternatives, subjective unacceptability of' is variable (5.4), introduced on page 135, discussed on pages 136 and 140 and included in figures on pages 137 and 141.